BANISHED CITIZENS

BANISHED CITIZENS

A History of the Mexican American Women Who Endured Repatriation

MARLA A. RAMÍREZ

HARVARD UNIVERSITY PRESS
Cambridge, Massachusetts
London, England
2025

EU GPSR Authorized Representative

LOGOS EUROPE, 9 rue Nicolas Poussin,

17000, La Rochelle France

Email: Contact@logoseurope.eu

Publication of this book has been supported through the generous provisions of the Maurice and Lula Bradley Smith Memorial Fund.

Library of Congress Cataloging-in-Publication Data

Names: Ramírez, Marla Andrea, author

Title: Banished citizens : a history of the Mexican American women who
  endured repatriation / Marla A. Ramírez.

Description: Cambridge, Massachusetts : Harvard University Press, 2025. |
  Includes bibliographical references and index.

Identifiers: LCCN 2025003712 (print) | LCCN 2025003713 (ebook) |
  ISBN 9780674295940 cloth | ISBN 9780674301993 epub |
  ISBN 9780674302013 pdf

Subjects: LCSH: Mexican American women—History—20th century |
  Mexican Americans—Legal status, laws, etc.—History—20th century |
  Deportation—United States—History—20th century | Mexican American
  families—Genealogy | Repatriation—United States—History—21st century |
  Mexican Americans—Reparations—History—21st century | Citizenship—
  United States—History—20th century

Classification: LCC E184.M5 R32916 2025 (print) | LCC E184.M5 (ebook) |
  DDC 305.9/0691408968720730904—dc23/eng/20250422

LC record available at https://lccn.loc.gov/2025003712

LC ebook record available at https://lccn.loc.gov/2025003713

For the participating families in this study and the thousands of banished Mexican Americans and their descendants whose stories are yet to be documented in writing.

For *el amor de mi vida*, José, whose love and support gave me both the courage and the luxury of time to write this book.

For my parents, María de Lourdes and Leonardo Javier, who fought against all odds to allow their five daughters to achieve their dreams.

CONTENTS

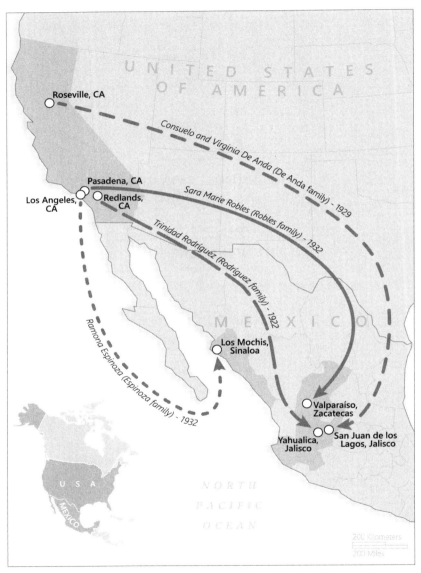

Map 1 Locations where each family was banished from the United States and relocated to in Mexico.

Map 2 Locations where each family was living in Mexico and where they resettled in the United States.

BANISHED CITIZENS

INTRODUCTION

On the sunny afternoon of February 26, 2012, over the sounds of music, laughter, and conversation, the fragrance of corn tortillas and chicken mole wafted through La Placita Olvera in Los Angeles, California. Adjacent to La Placita, at the LA Plaza de Cultura y Artes, ethnic Mexican families gathered to accept a formal apology from the California State Legislature and Los Angeles County Board of Supervisors.[1] The state and city governments were formally acknowledging their participation in the coerced removals of Mexican Americans during the Great Depression. State officials also unveiled a commemorative plaque to mark this dark chapter in US history when, eight decades earlier, California officials had expelled hundreds of thousands of ethnic Mexicans from the state as part of a mass removal scheme to reduce relief expenses and ease unemployment.[2]

One of these mass removal raids took place on August 17, 1931. That day, as 1,300 ethnic Mexicans converged at the Southern Pacific Railroad freight yard for their removal across the US-Mexico border, more than four thousand others, relatives and friends, came to bid them farewell. Women, standing alongside their children and husbands, held "little bundles in their hands" packed with only their essential belongings.[3] They had to leave everything else behind. On the perimeter of

the crowded railyard that day, "a cordon of police and immigration officials with full bellies and guns bulging from their sides" surrounded the
ethnic Mexican families.[4] US-citizen women and children of Mexican
descent were cast as not only economic dependents of their Mexican
immigrant husbands or fathers but also foreigners based on their Mexican-
ness. Amid anti-Mexican hysteria, US authorities ignored and discursively revoked Mexican Americans' US citizenship during the rushed and
heavily policed removals that often ranged in the thousands (Figs. I.1 and
I.2).[5] Exclusionary immigration policies linked gender, ethnicity, and class
status to ideas of moral character and economic responsibility that were
grounded in the outdated coverture legal doctrine. Reclassifying Mexican
American women and children as Mexicans who were economically
dependent on Mexican immigrant husbands and fathers, US officials

Figure I.1 An example of the mass removals includes this group of 1,400 ethnic
Mexican women, children, and men who were expelled on three Southern Pacific
trains, Central Station, Los Angeles, January 12, 1932.

Figure I.2 Transnational efforts removed ethnic Mexican women and children from the United States along with their husbands or fathers on four trains, Central Station, Los Angeles, March 8, 1932.

systematically targeted them for removal to facilitate the wholesale exclusion of mixed-status Mexican families from the country.[6]

Railroad companies acted as co-conspirators. They furnished special trains and coaches to transport mixed-status Mexican families from Los Angeles, California, to El Paso, Texas, and from there the banished families were mainly relocated to the Mexican states of Jalisco, Michoacán, Guanajuato, Aguascalientes, and Zacatecas.[7] The expulsions increased rapidly, leading to the removal of between 60,000 and 75,000 ethnic Mexicans by early 1931. But Rex Thomson—the assistant superintendent of charities in Los Angeles who was in charge of organizing the repatriation drives—soon realized that the "average indigent Mexican, whose family generally numbers five or more, is hesitant about going home."[8] While the head of the household enlisted for repatriation might have been a Mexican citizen, his wife and children were often US citizens unwilling to leave their native country. Thus, officials targeted women and children as a tactic to remove entire mixed-status ethnic Mexican families. Authorities predicted that if they removed only the Mexican immigrant head of household, then he would be more likely to return to the United States to reunite with his family, whereas if they expelled the entire mixed-status family, the return migration rates would decrease, effectively rendering the removals permanent.[9] In addition, raids in public spaces intimidated even those ethnic Mexicans who were not enlisted for removal into leaving the United States out of fear, especially when they were destitute after having lost their jobs. For instance, on February 26, 1931, eighty-one years before the formal apology at LA Plaza de Cultura y Artes, more than thirty immigration agents, municipal detectives, and local plainclothes police officers surrounded the plaza, blockading roughly four hundred people and pressing them to show immigration documents. Thirty people were arrested after interrogations that lasted over an hour, during which immigration officers demanded that each detainee declare their name, age, time of residence in the United States, place of entry, and employment status. Out of the thirty people arrested, seventeen—eleven Mexicans, five Chinese, and one Japanese—were incarcerated and faced possible deportation.[10] Though US officials planned and carried out these immigration raids as a scare tactic to drive out of the country Mexican American women and children, along with destitute male Mexican heads of households, the raids became wide-reaching dragnets that caused terror in the communities affected. Anyone trapped in a raid— regardless of legal status, ethnic and racial background, or length of residence—was interrogated and could potentially be removed.

These organized raids were just one tool of many that US government officials used to conduct mass removals of ethnic Mexicans during the Great Depression. Notably, officials modeled them after Mexican repatriations carried out in the economic recession that had followed World War I. During the war, US officials and employers had heavily recruited Mexican immigrants to fill labor shortages with promises of paid round-trip transportation. The economic crisis that followed, however, left many employers unable and others unwilling to cover return-transportation expenses. The stranded workers requested assistance through their Mexican consulates. From 1921 to 1923, the Mexican government covered the transportation costs for deserted Mexican citizens to return to their homeland. Anti-Mexican sentiment in the United States after World War I also contributed to a shift in the relocation process, which began with voluntary repatriation efforts and eventually transformed into removal initiatives that targeted even those ethnic Mexicans who had been residing long-term in the United States and their US-citizen children.[11] A decade later, during the Great Depression, local, state, and federal authorities collaborated to replicate similar repatriation efforts, targeting ethnic Mexicans for removal as a way to allegedly alleviate labor shortages and reduce relief expenses during the crisis. This time, however, ethnic Mexicans did not voluntarily initiate or request these relocations; instead, these "repatriations" were organized through intimidation tactics.[12]

The banishment efforts during the Great Depression, which were more aggressive than those of the early 1920s, largely ignored the legal status of those removed. During the 1930s, when ethnic Mexicans enlisted on relief rolls to receive food assistance amid the economic crisis, they often found themselves classified as "likely to become public charges" (LPC). The LPC label rendered immigrants deportable under a statute of the 1917 Immigration Act, but only if their presence in the country amounted to less than three years, a prerequisite for removal that was often ignored. Other drastic strategies were implemented, including one that Los Angeles relief officials called the "'Starve the Mexicans Out' policy." Billed as a "cure for the depression," the "choice was 'voluntary' repatriation or get off relief."[13]

Employers in Los Angeles, too, responded to the economic crises during the interwar period by coordinating mass layoffs. Ethnic Mexicans, who were considered to be temporary and foreign workers, were terminated first; once unemployed, they were more likely to request

relief assistance, which in turn led to their removal. The LPC classification was informed by racialized, classed, and gendered stereotypes
about ethnic Mexicans, and it was applied in ways that ignored US
citizenship and legal status. Its implementation meant that Mexican
Americans, legally admitted Mexican immigrants, and unauthorized
Mexican immigrants alike were registered on so-called repatriation
lists and relocated to Mexico.[14] This approach to removing ethnic
Mexicans shows clearly how racialization could limit the political
rights guaranteed by US citizenship.

The immigration raids that spanned the interwar period from 1921 to
1944, combined with denied relief and employment opportunities, led
to the expulsion of approximately one million Mexicans, a startling
60 percent of whom were US citizens of Mexican descent.[15] The 2012
ceremony at LA Plaza de Cultura y Artes brought returned banished US
citizens and their kin together for formal apologies and to commemorate their experiences with a remembrance plaque at this historically
noteworthy location. This book was born out of the oral histories that
some of the banished survivors at that ceremony, other banished people,
and their families generously shared with me in individual and transgenerational oral history interviews. Their life histories document banishment experiences that are distinct in their particular circumstances,
yet collectively document the shared trauma and other serious prolonged
consequences endured by three generations—and so trace one of the key
genealogies of Mexican racial formation in the United States. All ethnic
Mexicans in the United States—citizens and unauthorized immigrants
alike—were cast as economic scapegoats allegedly dependent on social
services and unable to assimilate. These representations thus cemented
the social perception of Mexican illegality in the United States and justified the dispossession of ethnic Mexicans' legal rights. And because
banishment interrupted Mexican Americans' ability to pass on their US
citizenship to their descendants, those children and grandchildren were
robbed of transgenerational wealth, blocked from gaining upward mobility, and cut off from acquiring political power in the United States.

Banishment, then, was not simply an event of the past; rather, it continues to affect the descendants of those removed three generations later, who have in many cases spent lifetimes attempting to reclaim their US citizenship and sense of belonging, in an ongoing, multigenerational process of resistance. As we will see from the lived experiences of banished US-citizen survivors, their children, and their grandchildren on both sides of the US-Mexico border, the displacement of banished US citizens of Mexican descent has kept them from being able to fully belong to either country. They and their descendants have been caught between two worlds.

REPATRIATION AS BANISHMENT

The mass banishment of Mexican American citizens highlights a particular process in the making of the racial state. Specifically, it captures a conjuncture during which the United States mobilized notions of race and citizenship to redefine itself as a white settler nation. To access the rights and privileges guaranteed by US citizenship, a person had to first prove their whiteness.[16] Thus, US citizens of Mexican descent were largely unable to access citizenship rights, despite their legal status. The experiences of banished women and their families across three generations demonstrates the limits that this racialization imposed on US citizenship.

For these reasons, I do not refer to the so-called *repatriation* of US citizens of Mexican descent. Instead, I invoke the term *banishment* to characterize these events for precisely what they were: coerced, forced removals of US citizens in mixed-status families. Repatriation and deportation have been used interchangeably in the literature on the mass expulsions of ethnic Mexicans during the Great Depression, but the distinctions between them are critical. *Deportation* denotes the expulsion of a noncitizen person to their native country through a legal process. This category is limited to immigrants removed under formal processes.

Repatriation represents the return of a noncitizen immigrant to their homeland (*patria*) as a voluntary process, coordinated by local authorities and supported by the federal government. Thus, ethnic Mexicans who were forced to leave despite their US citizenship cannot be accurately understood as repatriates. *Banishment,* the term I use to characterize the removal of Mexican Americans, refers to the *coerced,* state-sanctioned expulsion of US citizens to their erroneously designated "home country," usually their ethnic country of origin, with the support of governmental authorities on both sides of the US-Mexico border. Unlike repatriation, which ostensibly emphasizes the "voluntary return" process, banishment also accounts for the prolonged consequences of racialization and exclusion across multiple generations, since at its core, banishment was not simply about removing working-class Mexican immigrants deemed likely to become public charges. Instead, through state-sanctioned means, it intended to permanently excise and exclude a significant sector of the rapidly growing Mexican American population, particularly Mexican American women and children, from the US national polity.

While multiple countries, including the United States, have used banishment as a legal measure to punish citizens by sending them away to another state or country, the removals of Mexican Americans were never legally classified as banishment by US officials in policymaking or law. I decided to use the term banishment, however, in conversations with the participating families in this study. When narrators I interviewed described their removal, they used the Spanish phrase *nos echaron,* which translates to "they kicked us out" or "they threw us out." The word banishment captures that same presumption of disposability and emphasizes the one-sidedness and injustice of the process that the verb *echar* encapsulates. The immigration discourses that marked Mexican immigrants and Mexican Americans as removable without requiring formal legal changes in immigration and naturalization law invoked these ideas of disposability. The "throwing out" of US citizens of Mexican descent not only constitutes a racialized exclusion, but also gestures toward the physical and emotional violence that banished people endured. Banishment meant that direct descendants of US citizens would later experience the afterlives of being "thrown out." In other words, the anti-Mexican eugenicist discourses during the interwar period helped to impose what I call *transgenerational illegality:* the imposition, through judicial and discursive means, of a presumptive unauthorized status that upended the lives of many Mexican American women and children of that period—a status later inherited by their descendants.

Both the Mexican and US federal governments supported local authorities in their banishment efforts, and mobilized the language of repatriation to obscure the injustice of the process. The Mexican government used this term to exalt the patriotic sentiment of the expelled and their loyalty to Mexico, framing displaced ethnic Mexicans as national assets instead of the undesirable liabilities they were portrayed as in the United States. Hoping to bolster their nation-building agenda in the wake of the Mexican Revolution of 1910, Mexican officials saw the newly expelled ethnic Mexicans as ideal and timely candidates to carry out Mexico's land reform and modernization initiatives. Expelled ethnic Mexicans were expected, as part of their "patriotic" duty, to help modernize agricultural production with technologies and methods learned during their tenure in the United States.[17] On the other side of the border, US officials adopted *repatriation* to describe the removal raids. In doing so, they effectively misrepresented these removals as "voluntary" and bypassed the due process, equal protection, and Fourth and Fourteenth Amendment rights of the expelled.[18] Administratively classifying the removals as repatriation also saved the US government thousands of dollars in formal deportation proceedings and expedited the removal of immigrants and US citizens alike. Banishment was thus a strategic, transnational political tool.

A century later, banished Mexican Americans and their descendants continue to suffer the generational legacies of banishment. Historians have documented how the restrictive immigration policies enacted at the turn of the twentieth century have denied access to US citizenship, increasing the number of unauthorized Mexican immigrants.[19] In *Impossible Subjects,* Mae Ngai establishes that the period between 1924 and 1965, which gave way to the national origins quota system, became the most comprehensive immigration restriction period in US history. Specifically, Ngai argues that the Immigration Act of 1924 "remapped the nation" and produced a new category of immigrant: the "illegal alien . . . subject barred from citizenship and without rights."[20] While the Immigration Act of 1924 produced unauthorized immigrants, I contend that the LPC clause in the Immigration Act of 1917 and the legacies of coverture contributed to the illegalization of Mexican Americans. Restrictive immigration policies and increased Mexican xenophobia facilitated mass exclusion, with prolonged transgenerational repercussions. In particular, while immigration restriction laws gave way to Mexican removals, officials at all levels of government used their administrative discretion to effectively banish thousands of Mexican Americans. To the extent that it imposed illegality on its targets, banishment has had crucial economic, political, and legal consequences for multiple generations. These actions created new mixed-status families, sometimes resulting in direct descendants of banished US citizens remaining undocumented and unable to claim US citizenship. Even those with access to derivative citizenship continue to be perceived socially as foreigners with limited economic and political power. Nevertheless, undeterred by all the challenges, banished women fought tirelessly to reclaim their US citizenship and reestablish themselves and their nuclear families in their native country. Today, their descendants continue to confront and resist the impact of these injustices—and are breaking the silence to ensure that this history is not forgotten.

In exploring these complex processes, I draw from the contributions of historians who have uncovered many aspects of the Mexican repatriation campaigns.[21] Historians on both sides of the US-Mexico border, including Francisco E. Balderrama, Raymond Rodríguez, Abraham Hoffman, and Fernando Saúl Alanís Enciso, have written about repatriation by focusing on the removal of Mexican immigrants that resulted in the displacement of US citizens as an unintended consequence. I expand this historiography by examining the mass removals as an organized transnational effort that not only targeted Mexicans generally but also strategically banished Mexican American women and children to make the expulsions permanent.

TARGETING WOMEN AND CHILDREN
FOR BANISHMENT

During the interwar period, Mexican women and children were systematically at greater risk of removal, given their perceived economic dependency on men. Naturalization and deportation laws mirrored the doctrine of coverture in that it connected gender, but also ethnicity and class status, to new understandings of the importance of personal independence, moral character, and family responsibility as qualifiers for US citizenship.[22] This strategy was not new; on the contrary, women have long been excluded by immigration policies. After 1868, following the ratification of the Fourteenth Amendment, increased gender exclusions banned immigrant women deemed as undesirable. In fact, only seven years later, the 1875 Page Act, intended to exclude Chinese by prohibiting criminals, contract laborers, and "Mongolian prostitutes" from immigrating, primarily banned Chinese women who were perceived as being recruited for "immoral purposes."[23] A few years later, the Immigration Act of 1882 imposed a head tax. It also contained a clause to exclude entry to the United States of "undesirable classes," including destitute persons, which primarily targeted unaccompanied women, single mothers, and single women. This clause was incorporated in the Immigration Act of 1917 and most subsequent immigration bills.[24] The exclusion of women has been used to limit birthright citizenship rights by preventing the establishment of heterosexual family units that could result in US-citizen children of unwanted racial backgrounds. Excluding women also encouraged men of color in heterosexual relationships to return to their native countries for family reunification, preventing their long-term settlement and intermarriage. The state-sanctioned exclusion of working-class women of color limited the formation of families that were entirely nonwhite. Because Mexican women were not initially included in these gender immigration restrictions, ethnic Mexican families were allowed to establish roots in the United States. Nonetheless, following a long-established tradition of exclusion, government officials began targeting working-class ethnic Mexican women and children in their banishment efforts.

Immigration and Naturalization Service (INS) repatriation records show that if the head of the household was a Mexican male national classified as LPC, then nuclear and extended family units were expelled, including US citizens not in violation of the 1917 Immigration Act.[25] For instance, if a Mexican immigrant man married a US citizen and they had independent US-citizen adult children who married US citizens, who in turn had their own US-citizen children, the entire extended family was removed, even when everyone was a US citizen except for the Mexican immigrant man listed as "head of the household."[26] The records list only the nationality of "repatriates," not their legal status, which makes it impossible to track the potential expulsion of Mexicans who were naturalized US citizens or had been legally admitted. The children, wives, grandchildren, and children-in-law of Mexican heads of household, however, were often listed as having US nationality. As such, these documents indicate that the majority of those removed were US citizens (Table I.I). The question of Mexican American women and children's rights independent of their husbands or fathers was debated frequently in the US Congress during the early twentieth century. In 1936, Senator Everett Dirksen challenged the right of US citizens in mixed-status families to receive relief under the Works Progress Administration (WPA). Dirksen argued, "If an alien has a family consisting of an American wife and American children, what are you going to do about him? [If] you strike his name from the relief rolls, you have left a wife and her children, who are American citizens . . . hungry." But, Dirksen warned, if "the wife can apply for relief, then . . . you will have the spectacle of having stricken an alien from the rolls whose wife goes on in his place to get the same kind of relief, so that he will be eating the bitter bread of charity along with his family."[27] The WPA debates depicted how women and children came to be understood as economic dependents of the head of household, consistent with the outdated principle of coverture, which through marriage tied wife and husband into one legal identity. Coverture, which was a part of US law from colonial times to the 1880s, was best described by the English jurist William Blackstone: "By marriage, the husband and wife are one person in law: that is, the very being or legal existence of the woman is suspended during the marriage."[28] Coverture and LPC claims were used together to strategically expel Mexican American women and children. When a Mexican immigrant husband or father was on relief, unemployed, or deceased, the wife, widow, and children were automatically categorized as a "public charge," even if they were US citizens and self-reliant. And since US-citizen women and children of Mexican descent could not legally be deported, for their banishment a relic of coverture doctrine was used instead; minors were not seen as persons under the law, and married women's legal rights were subsumed by those of their husbands. Mexican American women and children thus experienced the application and enforcement of these policies in ways that challenged the nature of their jus soli—birthright—citizenship, a defining characteristic of the United States established by the Fourteenth Amendment.

As part of orchestrating the raids to remove Mexican immigrants, then, US officials broadened existing interpretations of immigration law, invoked outdated policies governing the rights of married women, and relied on administrative discretion to banish US citizens— particularly working-class Mexican American women and children. Their banishment disrupted the family nucleus of many ethnic Mexican households, facilitating the forced relocation of immediate and extended family units across legal statuses. Officials also adopted this approach to mass removals to prevent return migration and reduce the economic and political rights of the growing Mexican American population. As part of this strategy, relief and employment systems in the United States positioned men as wage earners and women as economic

NAME	GENDER	AGE	NATIONALITY (NOT LEGAL STATUS)	RELATIONSHIP TO REMOVED HEAD OF HOUSEHOLD
PEDRO CRUZ	MALE	79 YEARS	MEXICO	SELF (HEAD OF FAMILY)
Isabel Martinez	Female	—	United States	Wife
José Cruz	Male	19 years	United States	Son
Manuel Cruz	Male	17 years	United States	Son
Eusebio Cruz	Male	15 years	United States	Son
Isabel Cruz	Male	8 years	United States	Son
Julian Cruz	Male	32 years	United States	Son
María Soto	Female	35 years	United States	Daughter-in-law
Julia Cruz	Female	18 years	United States	Granddaughter
José Cruz	Male	16 years	United States	Grandson
Mauro Cruz	Male	14 years	United States	Grandson
Juana Cruz	Female	13 years	United States	Granddaughter
Horacio Cruz	Male	10 years	United States	Grandson
Felix Cruz	Male	3 years	United States	Grandson
Camilo Cruz	Male	3 years	United States	Grandson
Julian Cruz	Male	1 year	United States	Grandson
Francisco Cruz	Male	26 years	United States	Son
Guadalupe Salinas	Female	—	United States	Daughter-in-law
Francisco Cruz	Male	10 years	United States	Grandson
Juan Cruz	Male	6 years	United States	Grandson
Guadalupe Cruz	Female	4 years	United States	Granddaughter
Trinidad Cruz	Female	21 years	United States	Daughter
Alfredo Salinas	Male	22 years	United States	Son-in-law
Alfredo Salinas	Male	2 years	United States	Grandson
REFUGIO LOPEZ	MALE	49 YEARS	MEXICO	SELF (HEAD OF FAMILY)
Josefa Perez	Female	48 years	Mexico	Wife
Ramón Lopez	Male	30 years	Mexico	Son
Hilaria Lopez	Male	30 years	Mexico	Son
Macario Lopez	Male	25 years	United States	Son

Felipe Lopez	Male	24 years	United States	Son
Inocencia Alonzo	Female	24 years	Mexico	Daughter-in-law
Rebeca Cepeda	Female	18 years	United States	Daughter-in-law
Tomasa Zamora	Female	23 years	United States	Daughter-in-law
Manuel Lopez	Male	6 years	United States	Grandson
Cresenciano Lopez	Male	5 years	United States	Grandson
Petra Lopez	Female	1½ years	United States	Granddaughter
Amelia Lopez	Female	2 months	United States	Granddaughter
Luz Lopez	Female	1 year	United States	Granddaughter
Juanita Lopez	Female	1 month	United States	Granddaughter
Elena Lopez	Female	2 years	United States	Granddaughter
Andrea Lopez	Female	1 year	United States	Granddaughter
MANUEL DAVILA	**MALE**	**40 YEARS**	**MEXICO**	**SELF (HEAD OF FAMILY)**
Refugia Ysassi	Female	35 years	United States	Wife
Maria Davila	Female	11 years	United States	Daughter
Luz Elida Davila	Female	10 years	United States	Daughter
Refugia Davila	Female	9 years	United States	Daughter
Manuel Davila	Male	7 years	United States	Son
Natividad Davila	Male	6 years	United States	Son
Alfonso Davila	Male	1½ years	United States	Son

Table I.1 Author's sample assemblage from Repatriated Alien Records, May 1939 to October 1940, US Department of Labor, INS. National Archives and Records Administration, Washington, DC.

dependents, which increased the dependency logic of coverture. Men have historically received privileges based on their labor, including salaries, unemployment assistance, and retirement pensions.[29] Women, however, have usually obtained discretionary compensation based on their relation to men as daughters and wives.[30] The provisions of the welfare-state infrastructure in the United States assumed that men were the breadwinners while women held roles as wives and mothers.[31] Women's dependency on wage-earning fathers or husbands was tied to the social construction of domestic labor as their responsibility—one that did not entitle them to salary, unemployment, or retirement benefits. Even when women and children earned wages, their earnings were considered contributions to family-earned income that merely supplemented the salary of male heads of household.[32]

Mexican women were punished for their apparent double threat— that is, their likelihood to become public charges on the one hand and their reproductive power on the other. The idea that they would be public charges resulted from sexist social and labor practices that relegated women to unpaid domestic labor and positioned them as dependent on men, while the concern about their reproductive power stemmed from a fear of Mexican women's potential to reproduce US-citizen children with political rights, an outcome that could threaten power dynamics in the country. Against the backdrop of gendered, racialized, and classed presumptions about Mexican women's high fertility rates and economic dependency on men, Mexican American women and children became prime targets for removal.

A HISTORY OF REMOVAL IN THE UNITED STATES

While banishment drives during the 1930s were modeled after the repatriation efforts of the 1920s, the history of Mexican repatriation can be traced back to the 1800s. It is estimated that approximately 31,000 to 53,000 Mexicans were repatriated from the United States during the mid-nineteenth century.[33] On August 19, 1848, the same year the Treaty of Guadalupe Hidalgo was enacted, Mexican President José Joaquín de Herrera implemented a repatriation decree, to be carried out by Mexican consulates in the United States. The decree promised land, money, and transportation to Mexicans interested in repatriating south of the newly demarcated national border.[34] After Mexico ceded most of the current southwestern United States in the aftermath of the Mexican American War (1848), approximately 80,000 to 115,000 Mexicans found themselves on the US side of the new border line. Mexican relocation during the nineteenth century was designed as a voluntary movement of Mexican nationals who found themselves in a new country because of war. The treaty allowed Mexicans to either remain in the United States with claims to US citizenship, which later proved elusive, or to voluntarily repatriate.[35] During the nineteenth century, Mexicans could opt to remain in the United States or return voluntarily to their *patria,* Mexico.

Those who decided to remain in the United States were the basis of a growing Mexican American population, and Mexican immigrants who arrived over the following seven decades joined and expanded the ethnic Mexican community. In the early twentieth century, Mexican workers were heavily recruited to the United States for nation-building, only to be disposed of when they were no longer needed. While exclusion laws prevented Chinese, Japanese, and Filipinos from entering the United States during the late nineteenth and early twentieth centuries, ethnic Mexicans were expelled en masse during the interwar period through two major removal efforts. The first took place during the 1918 recession, and the second during the 1930s. During World War I, the political loyalty of ethnic Mexicans was called into question. Then, during the postwar economic recession, ethnic Mexicans were categorized as unassimilable. The combination of these factors resulted in ethnic Mexicans being denied labor and public assistance.

When the US stock market collapsed in October 1929, it caused a chain of events that affected millions of people across gender, class, racial, and ethnic lines. Unemployment reached an all-time high. In 1930, six million individuals lost their jobs; in 1932, that number nearly doubled. The following year, roughly one-third of the US workforce (fifteen million people) was unemployed.[36] In less than four years, the banking system faced an economic collapse. Thousands of people lost their life savings when close to five thousand banks dissolved. A precarious banking system, deceptive financial predictions, industrial overproduction, and diminishing international commerce were leading causes of the Great Depression.[37] Yet legislators, nativists, the media, relief representatives, social workers, and the public scapegoated immigrants for the ills of the nation.[38] Ethnic Mexicans, in particular, were again blamed for "usurping American jobs" and labeled as "unworthy burdens on local relief rolls."[39]

Removal raids originally intended to expel all unauthorized immigrants across racial and ethnic groups, but soon ethnic Mexicans became the main target for mass expulsion. Texas Congressman Martin Dies sponsored a half-dozen deportation bills, one of which called for the expulsion of all six million unauthorized immigrants living in the United States.[40] Such efforts initially sought to expel Asians, Germans, Italians, Russians, Spaniards, members of diasporic Black populations, and those in Latina/Latino immigrant groups who were deemed public charges. In some cases, Puerto Ricans were also targeted, despite their newly granted American citizenship.[41] After a cost-benefit analysis, however, immigration restrictionists decided that focusing mainly on the expulsion of ethnic Mexicans would be the best approach given the proximity of the two countries. Nativists argued that Mexican removals would yield the most employment vacancies, as well as maximum savings on relief and public-health funds. Los Angeles County estimated that there were "ten thousand Mexican alien relief cases . . . averaging $200,000 a month, or $2.4 million a year," concluding that "the cost of transporting an entire family would be quickly repaid by their disappearance from the relief load."[42] Officials mobilized this logic to expel working-class mixed-status Mexican families from Los Angeles to New York.[43]

California, however, played an especially critical role in the development of the first mass "repatriation" plan. California officials scapegoated Mexicans—the largest immigrant community in the state—and targeted them for removal as a solution to the economic downturn. Their removals overlooked the contributions of ethnic Mexicans who had helped to transform California agriculture and build industry through their labor on the railroads. In the late 1920s, California Governor C. C. Young commissioned a fact-finding committee to investigate the number of Mexicans living in the state. It found that in 1900,

90.3 percent of the Mexican population in the United States lived in Texas, Arizona, and California. More importantly, the Mexican population in California had surged when ethnic Mexicans arrived there from Texas and Arizona in search of better labor opportunities. The report noted that from 1900 to 1920, the Mexican population in Texas and Arizona had declined by 16.9 percent and 1 percent, respectively, while during the same period, California had experienced a 10.4 percent increase in its Mexican population.[44] Labor demands and recruitment heavily influenced this sizable ethnic Mexican migration to California.

As California became an important agricultural region in the United States, Mexicans became a key source of exploitable—and, eventually, disposable—labor. After the federal Reclamation Act of 1902 provided private entrepreneurs with public funds to bring water to California's Imperial Valley, turning the arid region into 120,000 acres of exhaustive crop farms, large-scale farmers in Southern California soon began recruiting Mexican workers in record numbers. This hiring trend spread northward into California's San Joaquin Valley, where Mexicans accounted for the largest single ethnic group among farmworkers in the state. Los Angeles County became another important locale in the state for Mexican communities. Mexican workers were heavily recruited by not only farmers in the county, but also railroad companies in Los Angeles that needed their labor to construct and maintain railroad tracks. Intense labor recruitment, migration, and natural population growth all contributed to the rapid expansion of urban and rural areas throughout California. For example, between 1900 and 1920, the population of the City of Los Angeles grew at an unprecedented rate, nearly quadrupling from 319,000 to 1.24 million.[45] By 1929, Los Angeles had become home to the largest concentration of Mexican nationals outside of Mexico City, even before accounting for US citizens of Mexican descent living in the city.[46]

Los Angeles became a testing ground for Mexican American banishment at the height of the Great Depression. Los Angeles County responded quickly to the call from President Herbert Hoover's Emergency Committee for Employment (PECE) to organize relief programs at the state and local levels and to create employment opportunities in the private sector. By December 1930, two committees had been formed—one for the City of Los Angeles and a second one for Los Angeles County. Charles P. Visel, the director for the city committee, went beyond his outlined duties to find additional ways to reduce unemployment and save public funds—including the proposal of a large-scale plan to remove ethnic Mexicans from Los Angeles. He argued that such an initiative would save thousands of dollars in relief aid and open up jobs for "real" Americans.[47]

Los Angeles County General Hospital also expressed interest in decreasing expenses during the Depression, and it began a campaign to transport as many ethnic Mexicans as possible to Mexico. While terminally ill patients were included in these efforts, the main objective was to remove "cripples, lepers, elderly individuals afflicted by the ravages of old age, and those suffering from tuberculosis."[48] In the early 1930s, the Los Angeles County Department of Charities initiated the "Transportation / Deportation Section," a division charged with identifying and deporting those Mexicans who were benefiting from county-subsidized medical assistance.[49] The Department of Charities justified the removal of hospital patients by classifying medical services as charity; in fact, it did not file medical and charity cases separately.[50]

Because the Mexican repatriation plan originated in Los Angeles, I focus on how banishment unfolded in the state of California, examining the specific conditions and tactics that enabled mass removals. Within months, other cities and counties in California—and states across the nation—replicated these tactics to target ethnic Mexicans, regardless of their legal status, time of residence, employment status, or health. In California, local and state officials initiated the use of the LPC classification to mark all working-class ethnic Mexicans as deportable—marking a shift in how Mexicans were racialized. The 1848

Treaty of Guadalupe Hidalgo, as well as an array of US census classifications and legal precedents, had officially classified Mexicans as racially white in the United States.[51] During the interwar period, however, ethnic Mexicans began to be racialized as nonwhite foreigners regardless of their legal status. In time, the removal efforts in California informed exclusionary tactics that officials used across the nation—and those actions, in turn, later shaped the strategies implemented in California. For instance, the LPC classification and outdated coverture doctrine used for removals in California were rapidly replicated in states across the country as early as 1931, while mass layoffs implemented in other states were later also conducted in California. During this period, too, the Colorado Mexican Welfare Committee reported an increase in xenophobic "White Trade Only" and "No Mexican Trade Wanted" signs displayed in windows of local businesses.[52] Mass ethnic Mexican layoffs began in the late 1920s in places like Colorado, but they became the norm throughout the country during the Depression.

Through the stories of families banished from California from 1921 to 1944, I aim to illuminate the broader contours of this period and the lasting repercussions of banishment for thousands of displaced people. I hope also to underscore how crucial it is that we continue listening to the voices of banished mixed-status Mexican families from across the nation. Their experiences will resonate in many ways with those related in this book, but every family's story is different. We must continue to bring as many voices as possible into reconstructing this history in order to build the fullest picture of how banishment harmed, and continues to harm, families in both the United States and Mexico.

BANISHMENT TACTICS

In the years leading up to and shortly following the Depression, from 1921 to 1944, officials recorded three main categories of removal: formal deportations, voluntary departures, and repatriation.[53] Although barishments of US citizens took place throughout these years, these removals were regularly miscategorized as voluntary departures or repatriation. Categorization itself thus became a tactic in service of validating the removal of long-term immigrants and US citizens alike. The labels "voluntary departure" and "repatriation" obscured the injustice of the process by masking the mass removals as benevolent.

Deportation accounted for the smallest number of removals, even when there was a significant number of unauthorized immigrants in the United States at the time. But, as Robert N. McLean clarified in *The Survey*—an American magazine that covered social and political issues—"insufficient funds at the disposal of the immigration service" made it "impossible to deport" Mexicans by the thousands.[54] Even with the call for a Mexican immigration quota, formal deportations remained low. Instead immigration searches capitalized on scare tactics, as evident in the 1931 La Placita Olvera and Southern Pacific Railroad removal raids. According to the Department of Labor, deportations for the entire country for the fiscal year ending on June 30, 1932—at the height of the removal efforts—amounted to 15,804, with Mexicans accounting for about half, totaling 7,116.[55] After repeatedly denying the orchestrated campaign to expel ethnic Mexicans, immigration authorities "asserted [that] the few raids on the Los Angeles Mexican center and arrests of aliens had caused an unfounded widespread fear among the foreign populace."[56] The Associated Press reported that by June 1931, only four months after the raid in La Placita Olvera, between 50,000 and 75,000 Mexicans had been coerced into leaving Southern California.[57]

The second and much larger group, "voluntary departures," consisted of people who were allegedly prone to deportation based on LPC charges, but were coerced into leaving the United States without undergoing formal removal, as a way of expediting the process and avoiding the expenses of formal deportation. People in this group were usually told to leave of their own accord or risk deportation, unemployment, and receiving no relief. In the absence of employment opportunities and relief assistance, entire mixed-status ethnic Mexican families were left without an option for subsistence in the United States and were effectively forced to leave. For the 1932 fiscal year, the US Department of Labor reported 10,775 so-called voluntary departures.[58] But the department's records were inconsistent and clearly incomplete, because the Mexican Migration Service reported a much greater number for the same fiscal year: 132,469 Mexicans.[59]

During the early 1930s there was "a marked acceleration in petitions for citizenship."[60] But, as McLean contended, the Mexican immigrant head of household in the United States "has always known that if he became a citizen he would still be a Mexican in the eyes of everybody except his own consul, whose help and protection he would immediately lose."[61] Thus, some Mexican immigrants saw no benefit in naturalizing their legal status, while others did not bother because they adhered to the idea of the Mexican Dream and had planned to eventually return to Mexico. Furthermore, during the Great Depression, US citizenship was not a guarantee against removal for ethnic Mexicans. The news media widely advertised that "the United States government is sending certain aliens home free of charge under a law providing for government payment of passage of any alien residing here not more than three years who has become a public charge."[62] The LPC provision of the 1917 Immigration Act became an important tool for removing ethnic Mexicans across all four groups.

The third category of removal was labeled "repatriation" and comprised Mexican immigrants who had been pushed into poverty when they were denied employment and relief. Under these circumstances, they were classified as LPC and enlisted for removal. The fourth and last group was composed of US citizens—that is, Mexican Americans—whose removal was labeled as repatriation or a voluntary departure but was really about banishing citizens with ties to the removed male head of the household—often a destitute husband or father. Mexican parents were forced to "choose between the homeland and the adopted country," explained McLean, which often meant deciding "between the homeland and their children, who have never known anything but this country and who refuse to leave."[63] Banishments were regularly miscategorized as repatriations or voluntary departures.

From the 1880s to 1930s, race was the constant factor that determined the citizenship status—and related rights—of women in the United States. Immigration officials and social workers often understood Mexican American women to be foreigners and dependent on their husband's citizenship status. But in fact, during the Great Depression, the citizenship status of Mexican American women did not depend on the legal status of their Mexican immigrant husbands. The Cable Act of 1922 had established the right of American women to retain their citizenship when they married an immigrant eligible for US citizenship, even if he did not opt to become a citizen.[64] As McLean concluded regarding the INS's use of the LPC provision, "The laws are the same; the interpretation is different. The immigration official is detective, judge, jury and prosecuting attorney."[65] It was already possible to remove an immigrant "liable to become a public charge," McLean asserted, but the difference is that "*any* common laborer is now liable to become a public charge."[66] Immigration officers and social workers alike used their discretionary authority to decide whom to remove, including US citizens. Thus, Mexican American children and women were often removed against their will and without regard to their citizenship rights, as the stories in this book illustrate.

Mexican immigrant women, by contrast, were often deceived by county and immigration officials, who persuaded them to accept removal offers by promising that they could return to the United States within a year, once the economic crisis had stabilized. These types of so-called voluntary departures—facilitated by the false promise of return—sidestepped formal deportation proceedings for immigrants, and so waived a potential felony charge for returning to the United States. But this encouraged incentive was deceptive because the same officials used the Department of Charity stamp to mark the visas of those being removed. When expelled Mexican women attempted to legally return, the stamped visas would alert US immigration authorities that they had received county relief, which made them inadmissible on LPC grounds.[67] On the other side of the border, the Mexican government also had a policy of discouraging banished people from returning to the United States. After investing funds in their transportation, and providing land and other assistance in Mexico, Mexican officials strongly advocated against returned migration.

Visa applications were largely denied throughout the 1930s. This forced some repatriates to return as unauthorized immigrants, whose legal status put them at risk of felony charges on LPC grounds if they became destitute—charges that would, in turn, make them permanently ineligible for status adjustment.[68] As the families in this study have shared, banished Mexican Americans were also denied reentry at the US-Mexico border, mainly during the 1930s, even if they had records of their US citizenship. Delayed returns among banished Mexican American women resulted in legal barriers to obtaining derivative citizenship for their Mexican-born children and husbands. Thus, the organized transnational efforts to remove ethnic Mexicans from the United States and actively delay their return produced generations of unauthorized immigrants, even when they had direct claims to US citizenship.

The tactics that immigration officers and relief workers used resulted in the expulsion of ethnic Mexicans with diverse legal statuses who had long-term residence in the United States. The immigration raids were regularly conducted without warrants, using procedures that violated basic human rights. People were sometimes arrested without the right to contact anyone or to receive visitors while they waited for the next removal train.[69] In a January 1930 closed session, Bureau of Immigration officials testified about US Border Patrol operations. Henry Hull, the commissioner general of immigration, explained that patrolling legally occurred not only at the border line but also anywhere within one hundred miles of the border. House committee members voiced concern that the Border Patrol, which was not a criminal law enforcement agency and thus had no statutory authority to execute search warrants, was operating well into the interior of the country. Hull stressed that "wherever [officers] find an alien, they stop him" and "take him to unit headquarters."[70] In all of these documents, the question remains: how did officers differentiate between unauthorized immigrants and US citizens? Since regulations to prevent what we now refer to as racial profiling were never established, the Border Patrol relied on their own racial presumptions about Mexicans. Immigration officers applied laws, including the LPC clause, in "humiliating and uncivil ways with the character of criminal pursuit," often exceeding the constraints of civil law enforcement.[71] For instance, in El Paso, Texas, immigration officials conducted a series of raids in public schools resulting in the removal of five hundred children, many of whom were US citizens.[72] A US Children's Bureau official explained that such indiscriminate policies pushed banished US-citizen children into extreme poverty. Reporting that "some were dying just a few hundred feet across our border," the bureau official emphasized that any witness to these conditions "would agree that the United Sates should take care of her citizens."[73] Problematic removal tactics were so common that sympathetic immigration officials, human rights advocates, and the media pressured President Hoover to intervene. In 1929, Hoover established the National Commission on Law Observance and Enforcement, commonly known as the Wickersham Commission. The commission was appointed to survey the criminal justice system and INS, to make recommendations on policies, and to expose abuses of power. A 1932 report by the Wickersham Commission sounded the alarm on the tactics that immigration officials were using to target ethnic Mexicans: "The apprehension and examination of supposed aliens" was found to be "characterized by methods" deemed "unconstitutional, tyrannic, and oppressive."[74]

The commission also provided a series of recommendations to US Secretary of Labor N. William Doak and the Border Patrol that were meant to protect the rights of immigrants. These recommendations included one guideline that "all deportees should have access to counsel" regardless of their economic status, and another that recommended using "immigration discretion to prevent deportations that would 'result in unnecessary hardship.'"[75] Doak rejected the commission's recommendations and the criticism of his actions as secretary of labor, calling those who opposed his removal methods "un-American" and "unpatriotic." Far from reprimanding Doak, the Border Patrol, and relief representatives, the Hoover administration supported nativist policies. This support continued under the Roosevelt administration, during which time Congress passed a resolution to further limit the rights of non-US-citizens: lawful residents would, like unauthorized immigrants, be excluded from relief jobs and financial support under the New Deal.[76] Congressional action cemented the idea that all Mexicans, regardless of legal status, should be denied equal rights. Human rights law scholar Daniel Kanstroom argues that "the mass deportation of a particular ethnic or racial group would seem to be among the most 'un-American' phenomena imaginable."[77] The approach to mass ethnic Mexican removals, Abraham Hoffman further asserts, "could be well called an ethnic cleansing" that deprived Mexicans and Mexican Americans "rights guaranteed them by the Constitution."[78] While the purpose of the mass removals might not have been a full ethnic cleansing, they created a class of people without access to US citizenship who became understood as a temporary and disposable workforce.

THE CHRONOLOGY OF BANISHMENT

Shamed in public discourse at the national level, deprived of social benefits, and fired first, many ethnic Mexicans often had no choice but to accept removal offers. US federal immigration officers, relief representatives, social workers, and Mexican consulates in the United States participated in the mass removals during the twenty-three-year span from 1921 to 1944. Social workers offered "repatriation" as the only aid available for destitute ethnic Mexicans who asked for relief assistance. Officials also carried out immigration raids in private homes, job sectors, and public spaces like plazas and dance halls across the country. The number of banished people rapidly increased, in part due to the special group rates offered by the Southern Pacific Railroad and Mexican National Railroad companies. While the US government covered the expenses to transport ethnic Mexicans from their place of residence to the US-Mexico border, the Mexican government subsidized transportation from the border to the interior of Mexico, especially during the second half of the 1930s.[79] The discounted rates for train travel were reserved for groups of two hundred people or more. This resulted in stronger efforts by US relief workers, the Board of Supervisors, immigration officers, and Mexican consulates to secure large groups of people to place on each departing train to maximize the savings. The relief offices of Los Angeles County began arranging for mass banishment by the trainloads, "in groups that vary from approximately 1,000 to 2,000 people every two months."[80] The railroad infrastructure that spanned the United States and extended to different locales in Mexico further facilitated the mass removals. Ironically, the railroad system used for this mass ethnic displacement had been largely constructed and maintained by ethnic Mexicans, Chinese, Japanese, and other immigrant workers.[81]

In addition to trains, other common means of transportation for the removals included buses, trucks, cars, and ships. Notably, one account reported that an airplane was used at a time when commercial aviation was in its infancy.[82] The different types of transportation and large number of removals underscore the sense of urgency to "get rid of Mexicans," regardless of their legal status and by any means necessary.[83] From the early 1900s to the early 1940s, the "Mexican problem" surged every winter, only to be replaced every spring by an "acute labor shortage problem"—a vicious seasonal cycle that relegated working-class ethnic Mexicans to their roles as a disposable work force.[84] It is estimated that during the interwar period approximately one million people were removed—60 percent of whom were US citizens coerced into banishment. As historians have demonstrated, however, the mass removals of this period did not take place all at once. Instead, they occurred in discrete episodes. In the first period, from 1921 to 1923, roughly 100,000 people of Mexican descent, including US citizen and non-citizens, either left or were removed. During this period, the Mexican government organized and sponsored the repatriation initiative after US employers refused to cover the return trip for seasonal Mexican laborers. On February 16, 1921, Mexican President Álvaro Obregón responded to the situation by assigning 250,000 pesos to the Ministry of Foreign Affairs, which then established the Mexican Department of Repatriation to help destitute and unemployed Mexicans return to Mexico. He also offered land grants, which were located mainly in the Mexican northern border states, in order to populate and govern the northern regions of the republic.[85] Though these removals to Mexico began as a voluntary process, the anti-Mexican sentiment after the war meant that some ethnic Mexicans did not leave of their own accord. Others were removed because of their labor organizing, which had become an economic nuisance for US growers.[86] While entire Mexican families were recruited to the United States during the early 1920s under the first Bracero Program, simultaneously entire mixed-status ethnic Mexican families were banished.[87] This contradiction underlines the recurrent dyad of US dependency on Mexican labor and the political insistence on Mexican exclusion. Together, they formed a discursive, cyclical regime of race, labor, and exclusion that inscribed and re-inscribed meanings of "illegality" onto all ethnic Mexicans, regardless of their legal status.

During the second period of removals, from 1929 to 1933, US President Herbert Hoover's administration carried out much larger deportation drives, overseeing the removal of some 400,000 ethnic Mexicans—four times the number of people removed in the first period. Informed by the aggressive deportation approach of Secretary of Labor Doak, the Hoover administration strongly supported mass

deportation raids at the federal level, which in turn spurred local banishment drives by relief workers, employers, and local governments—
as well as by Mexican consulates with the support of immigration and
police officers. The removals in this period were usually disguised as
voluntary departures or repatriations, but often happened through co-
ercion. Mexican presidents Obregón and Plutarco Elías Calles also
supported the relocation efforts.[88] Under both the Obregón and the
Calles administrations' land-reform initiatives, land was secured in the
border regions and well into the interior of Mexico. As Mexico fell into
the throes of the Depression, however, and as new Mexican arrivals
from the United States greatly exceeded numbers of arrivals during
the post–World War I period, the Mexican government drastically
scaled back its support for banished families.[89]

The third period spanned 1933 to 1938. In 1933, the aggressive federal
deportation campaign ceased to be a priority under the new administration of Franklin D. Roosevelt, but his policies continued to reinforce
removals at the local level. As a result, the system of removals remained
in effect and unopposed throughout the 1930s. Roosevelt's Works Progress Administration and other New Deal programs excluded non-
citizens. This exclusion, coupled with the increased nativist views during
the Depression, meant that both Mexicans and Mexican Americans
were often denied New Deal benefits.[90] Thus, ethnic Mexicans remained unable to secure employment and relief benefits under the
Roosevelt administration. Consequently, from 1933 to 1938, local US
county and city governments as well as Mexican consulates continued
to sponsor ethnic Mexican removals. This period accounted for the expulsion of at least 500,000 people, a figure that scholars argue may be
too low.[91] President Lázaro Cárdenas renewed the allocation of land for
banished people during the third period of removals from 1934 to 1938.
He viewed the new arrivals as strong candidates for his agrarian reform
efforts because of the farming skills and experience they had acquired
in the United States.[92] But when Cárdenas's agrarian reform came under
pressure starting in the mid-1930s and support quickly dissipated, he

changed course and prioritized Mexican men who had never left the country.[93] Banished families in Mexico came to be portrayed as opportunistic nationals who had escaped Mexico during the Revolution and economic recession that followed. These views pressured governmental officials to reserve resources and land for Mexican citizens who had resided in the country for a longer time.

In the fourth period of removals, from 1938 to 1944, Mexican representatives at all levels of government worked to attract ethnic Mexicans with special labor skills by painting a rosy picture of return. The Mexican government viewed skilled workers as key to improving the economy, which had been decimated by the Great Depression.[94] In addition to providing paid passage, Mexican consulates returned to the strategy of promoting farmland. In 1939, the Ministry of Foreign Affairs sent Undersecretary Ramón Beteta to the United States to promote the virtues of repatriation. Beteta offered potential repatriates a choice between "twenty irrigated acres or fifty non-irrigated acres of land which was said to be in Tamaulipas, Sinaloa, or Baja California."[95] Beteta, Mexican American labor activist Ernesto Galarza, and Andrés Landa y Piña, chief immigration officer in Mexico, warned that an unplanned mass repatriation would amount to the "indiscriminate dumping of human beings below the border."[96] Nonetheless, an optimistic President Cárdenas proceeded with the "repatriation" plans. On April 14, 1939, Mexican and US officials convened at a Department of State conference to discuss Cárdenas's proposal. In that meeting, Rafael Fuentes, counselor of the Mexican embassy, reported that Beteta had already begun "to lay the groundwork for this movement, and that it was hoped eventually to effect the repatriation of approximately 100,000 Mexican citizens, which would of course include dependent members."[97] While land had also been promised during the previous removal episodes, it was more heavily advertised: mixed-status Mexican families were told that with the farming skills they had acquired in the United States, the allocated land could provide them a comfortable life in Mexico.[98] Fewer ethnic Mexicans were coerced to accept this offer

compared to the second and third periods, however, because they had
become aware of the desperate conditions endured by banished families during the first three periods.[99] Nonetheless, the removal efforts
continued. Incomplete records for so-called repatriation cases during
the period May 1939 to October 1940, particularly July 1939, list 3,031
removals, which included 1,153 Mexican citizens and 1,879 US-citizen
women and children.[100] Some mixed-status Mexican families hoped
that the promised land grants would help them achieve economic
independence. But priority for land titles was given to repatriates with
farming experience, households headed by men, and those with funds
to invest in tools.[101] Women-led households and single women were excluded from the benefits of agrarian reform.

Starting in the early 1930s, well-known supporters of the relocation
efforts, such as artists Frida Kahlo and Diego Rivera, helped to
popularize the "Mexican Dream" by urging the Mexican government
to offer farmland and other incentives for their return to Mexico.[102] The
core ideological promise of the Mexican Dream held that working-class
Mexicans could enjoy economic independence in their homeland,
Mexico, if they first spent a few years in the United States laboring hard
and saving money for their return. Like the American Dream, the Mexican Dream often proved elusive because of legal, economic, racial,
gendered, and ethnic barriers. Instead of the Mexican Dream and all that
it promised, banished families encountered extreme poverty that prevented them from using any of the skills they had gained in the United
States because they were unable to invest in needed farming tools and
other machinery.[103] Many banished families, too, were forced to start
over from scratch after having been coerced to leave their belongings
and properties behind in the United States. The romanticized belief that
Mexico's economy and industrialization would advance thanks to the
banished families' contributions quickly dissipated. By the late 1930s,
even Frida Kahlo and Diego Rivera stopped supporting the program
when they learned of the problems with the removal process and consequences of relocation.[104]

Mexico's economy, already dependent on that of its northern neighbor, was not prepared to provide for the thousands of newly arrived Mexican nationals and their US-citizen family members. Once in Mexico, banished ethnic Mexicans "learned the hard way that Mexico was also in a depression and that the newspaper reports were exaggerated."[105] As early as January 1932, the Mexican government reported the tragic conditions that banished families were experiencing: "Thousands of Mexicans were seen . . . picking food waste from trucks filled with fruits and vegetables. These items were used to make soup that they would consume for several weeks; even infants were subjected to such a diet."[106] The humanitarian crisis pushed organizations to fundraise to assist banished families. The General Consul of Mexico in the United States asked prominent Mexican members of social clubs for donations to create the Beneficencia Mexicana, an organization that provided food, health services, and financial assistance to displaced families in need. The General Consul of Mexico reported that this charitable institution had a "budget of $8,400.00 . . . from the collaboration of diverse recreational clubs, including sports organizations as well as Mexican societies in Los Angeles."[107] While the aid coming from these Mexican mutual-aid societies in the United States proved crucial for displaced Mexicans, it dried up quickly as the economic depression wore on. As a result, banished families in Mexico were left to fend for themselves. Banished ethnic Mexicans had to fight for survival, inclusion, civil rights, and political power on both sides of the US-Mexico border after both governments' direct actions displaced and disempowered them.

As the family histories in this book reveal, the ill-planned process of mass banishment violated the civil and human rights of ethnic Mexicans on both sides of the US-Mexico border. The Rodríguez, De Anda, Robles, and Espinoza families are representative of the ethnic Mexicans targeted for banishment in the first and second periods of removal. But their stories also include—and are informed by—the changes that took place on both sides of the border in later decades. Members of all the participating families attempted to return to the

United States during the later three periods of removals, but given the ongoing politics of banishment, their returns proved unsuccessful. In this way, the policies established during the third and fourth periods of removal continued to impact families banished during the first two periods.

Banishment drives finally ended in 1944, after the Bracero Program became an orchestrated enterprise to recruit cheap labor that could be easily dismissed at the end of each labor season.[108] At the height of the Bracero Program, banishments and the so-called repatriations were replaced by formal mass deportations under Operation Wetback.[109] This period marked a turning point during which US officials ceased framing removal as a voluntary process, and the language of "repatriation" dissipated. In its place, the then-established Mexican-illegality language was used for the emerging state apparatus that focused solely on deportations. Additionally, under Operation Wetback, the Mexican state no longer provided social support to returnees. But regardless of the general intention within each period of banishment, exclusionary racial politics undergirded them all and did not differentiate between the legal status, length of residence, and employment status of banished people. Instead, their ethnic Mexican identity, working-class status, and gender were the main indicators for removal.

CONSTRUCTING A GENDERED BANISHMENT ARCHIVE

The fluidity of migration, incomplete record-keeping, and an aging generation of banished women complicate the ability of researchers to recover and restore these erased histories. Officials often documented—and mischaracterized—the removal of Mexican Americans as repatriation or deportation, but there is no record of their return and resettlement in the United States. This documentary lacuna has complicated the recuperation of the history of Mexican American women who challenged their banishment by resettling in the United States. Immigration records represent the return of banished women simply as entries by US citizens. Immigration officers had no reason to interrogate entering US citizens about their prior histories of banishment. Banished women could have resettled anywhere in the United States. Additionally, banishment started nearly a century ago, meaning that survivors were at least in their late eighties when I initiated data collection.[110] Many banished people have died, taking with them valuable historical knowledge. Their passing is a loss for their loved ones as well as for the archive. Without a material archival record of banishment, this history will be erased once the memories of banished people have faded away.[111] I conducted banishment oral histories to understand and contribute to the longevity of these important historical memories.

The narrators interviewed for this book include banished women who eventually relocated to the United States; their children who came to their parents' country of birth, some as unauthorized immigrants; and their grandchildren, most of whom were born in the United States. To allow for personal interpretations and family-based accounts, I interviewed each family member separately and the entire family collectively, which opened the way for a variety of insights and richly textured points of view. Only three generations were interviewed, because stories get lost when a descendant is far removed from the historical moment.[112] As a bridge between the past and the present, oral history was an important methodological tool for recording the transgenerational experiences of the banished women in this book. As historian Vicki L. Ruiz affirms, this methodology centers the practice of "speaking history," which has the power to connect generations.[113] Many ethnic groups use oral traditions—the verbal sharing of historical or cultural knowledge across generations—and it is a practice rooted in native customs. Oral traditions kept the memories of banishment alive and allowed me to document them through oral history interviews. At its core, oral history allows us to explore how "the past becomes memory" and "memory becomes history."[114]

With all of its imperfections, inconsistency, and impermanence, memory—a relationship between material facts and personal subjectivity—allows oral historians to examine how and why people remember.[115] The methodology of oral history requires narrators and historians to serve in the roles of the "rememberer and the teller," respectively, in order to undertake "the task of remembering and the responsibility of telling."[116] Oral historians have the opportunity to ask narrators about their silences, their contradictions, and their processes of remembering, which is impossible to do with written sources. Institutional archives also provided essential evidence for this study, allowing me to corroborate and contextualize the memories of the oral history narrators I interviewed. The sources I located in institutional archives offer plenty of evidence about "repatriated" Mexican men, but only traces of the dark yet significant historical chapter of the mass banishment of working-class Mexican American women and children. Oral historian Horacio N. Roque Ramírez correctly emphasized this limitation in archival data: "To try to find the records and memories" of historically marginalized communities "is simply a leap of faith bound to encounter historical absence. . . . I instead spent time walking, talking, waiting, and making and returning calls to the living archives of desire around me."[117] As such, oral history permits historians to transcribe oral accounts into written ones to preserve and examine the histories of historically marginalized communities whose stories were never intended to be part of the official record. The intervention of oral history allows for everyday people—walking and breathing archives— to speak against the silences created in institutional repositories.

The banished women and their families whose voices are centered in this book also created private collections of personal, printed records that document their history of exclusion.[118] Families who have experienced distressing events often refuse to forget traumatic incidents, even when it hurts to remember. Survivors of tragic historical events tend to engage in a "praxis against forgetting" by becoming historians in their own right.[119] In addition to oral histories, the private collections of participating families were crucial to recovering the history of banishment and resettlement over the course of the twentieth century. To my surprise, every participating family had a self-designated family historian who had conserved a private collection. Often, in trying to make sense of their family's memories of removal, the family historian had documented their relatives' stories in a private collection of photographs, letters, identity records, newspaper stories, census data, memorabilia, and other documents. When I began my research, I did not expect to find narrators who had created personal collections, and they were not my point of entry into each participating family. Their oral histories and donated personal documents, however, contributed immensely to the project. Institutional sources, both in Spanish and English—comprising archival records, demographic statistics, and legal histories, stored at local and national archives on both sides of the US-Mexico border—are also used here to contextualize the oral histories and to reconstruct and understand the exclusionary immigration strategies of the interwar period at the national and transnational levels. Taken together, printed and oral records in institutional repositories and private collections provide nuanced evidence of the injustices that banished families endured and the resilience of banished women in reclaiming their US citizenship. The blurriness between official and personal papers in private collections mirrors the blurriness of borders, which can at times merely be a line on the dirt, but at a different historical moment become a concrete wall dividing families indefinitely. As such, for these banished families remembering their past represents a political act of resistance.

The recollections safeguarded by survivors banished during the interwar period confront efforts by state authorities to expel a Mexican American generation in order to stop its progress, growth, and power. The memories of life in their native country encouraged some banished Mexican American women to establish claims to their US citizenship and relocate back in the United States with their Mexican-born children and husbands. But while the Mexican American matriarchs of the families in this book eventually reclaimed their US citizenship, some of their children and grandchildren are still fighting to access derivative citizenship. This transgenerational illegality—the ways in which later generations inherited the meanings of "illegality" cast on their families through their removal—constitutes a direct, substantial, prolonged consequence of banishment.

TRANSGENERATIONAL AND TRANSNATIONAL NEGOTIATIONS OF BELONGING

The four phases of removal outlined earlier are crucial to understanding the transgenerational stories of the families in the book. While *Banished Citizens* documents the history of families banished during the first two periods of removals, their stories extend temporally across all four periods. These families endured the impacts of policies established during the later phases, too. To capture this complex and nuanced history, I have organized the chapters in *Banished Citizens* by family, theme, and banishment year but discuss their experiences across all four periods. Given the transnational and transgenerational nature of these family histories, the chronology of return and resettlement in the United States for banished women and their children is nonlinear. *Banished Citizens* takes into account the delays that each family faced in their processes to reclaim US citizenship and gain access to derivative citizenship. The non-linearity of return gestures toward not only the transgenerational, prolonged consequences of banishment but also the limits of US citizenship for these banished Mexican American women.

In each chapter, I analyze each family's story to elaborate on the concepts of transgenerational illegality and impermanent legality. I use *transgenerational illegality* to refer to the juridical and discursive imposition of a presumptive undocumented status on Mexican American women and their descendants on both sides of the US-Mexico borderlands. I use the related but distinct term *impermanent legality* to refer to how Mexican American women's access to US citizenship and legal status in the United States has been rendered impermanent and always already conditional—conditional on their ethnicity, class status, age, and gender. This impermanence replaced these banished Mexican American women's legal rights to derivative US citizenship with a presumptive illegality that was imposed on their descendants.

Chapter 1 draws from the transgenerational oral histories of the Rodríguez family and their private collection to recount how racialized debates about the "Mexican problem," the LPC clause, and immigration quotas were used to target ethnic Mexican women and remove entire mixed-status families. While banishment delayed derivative US citizenship for some families, it made it an impossibility for others. Trinidad Rodríguez's banishment to Mexico precluded her own children and grandchildren from claiming US citizenship. Rodríguez attempted to return to her native country multiple times and finally, though only briefly, succeeded in 1969. It took Rodríguez forty-seven years to reclaim her US citizenship. Her goal was to open immigration petitions for her two Mexican-born children and husband. But when she was unable to save enough money for the legal expenses, Rodríguez returned to Mexico, where she died unexpectedly. Unfortunately, simple clerical mistakes on her death certificate and other identity documents have caused legal delays for subsequent generations' immigration petitions. The Rodríguez family is just one of many who have been unable to gain derivative citizenship. Their story underscores the ways in which a person's legal status and the conditions of their removal are produced historically, socially, and politically. Marked as outsiders, some direct descendants of banished Mexican American women have been denied the legal and social privileges afforded to the children of US citizens in their mothers' and grandmothers' native country.

The perception of ethnic Mexicans as outsiders on both sides of the US-Mexico borderlands is further examined in Chapter 2, which focuses on the De Andas, a banished mixed-status family. Chapter 2 draws from the oral histories of three generations of the De Anda family, their personal collections, and institutional sources from Mexican and US assimilation campaigns. I contend that Mexicans, regardless of legal status, could never fulfill the unrealistic expectations of "Americanization" or "Mexicanization" because their ethnicity and citizenship would always outweigh their cultural behavior. Americanization programs targeted ethnic Mexican women living in the United States to ensure the cultural and language assimilation of immigrants and US-citizen children in mixed-status families. Mexican mothers were viewed as key players in the eradication of the so-called Mexican problem by helping Americanize their children and husbands. Some families, including the De Andas, followed Americanization teachings to prove their loyalty to the United States and avoid removal. Those efforts often proved futile, however, when Americanization campaigns were replaced by mass removal raids. After their banishment to Mexico, many families encountered Mexicanization pressures and were similarly shamed for their un-Mexican-ness. It took the De Andas twenty-one years to resettle back in their native country, the United States. Caught in this contradiction and their own cultural liminality, Mexican Americans were not extended protections by either nation, leaving them vulnerable to banishment and the attendant loss of place, upward mobility, and transgenerational wealth.

In Chapter 3, I examine how US officials built on the "Mexican problem" debate to fabricate a racialized, gendered narrative about the "Mexican American problem" that centered on children and their mothers. This story was, in turn, reinforced by Mexican governmental representatives who cast banished Mexican American women and their children as removable Mexicans, discursively erasing their US citizenship. In this chapter, the individual and collective memories of the Robles family reveal the ingenious tactics that banished survivors used to contest the migratory restrictions that women's families and larger structural immigration policies placed on them. Historically, men in heterosexual marriages have emigrated first and then sent for their family members. Some banished women, however, had the advantage of legal capital that allowed them to enter the United States and open immigration petitions for their families. This legal strategy gave way to transnational gender formations that banished women used to negotiate their movement across national borders. Mexican American women's departure from the nucleus of their homes in Mexico also resulted in transnational family formations. Children stayed behind in Mexico with their fathers or relatives, while returning banished mothers opened immigration petitions for them in the United States. For Sara Marie Robles and her family, the process of returning to the United States took more than three decades. In this chapter, we will see how banished women adhered to gendered expectations as daughters and wives while finding creative ways to contest their restrictions, return to their native country, and manage transnational families.

Central to Chapter 4 are the transgenerational oral histories and private collections of the family of Ramona Espinoza, a US citizen banished along with her mother, Felicitas Castro, and her three siblings because they were deemed likely to become a public charge. The Espinoza family was displaced to a colonization project in Mexicali, Baja California, Mexico, during the agrarian reform. Far from the promises of *campesino* empowerment, however, they encountered extreme poverty and hunger. Then, when the United States urgently needed workers during World War II—because the 1935 Filipino Repatriation Act in combination with the mass ethnic Mexican banishment drives had reduced supplies of farmworkers—the government turned to displaced ethnic Mexicans living in border towns for their temporary, disposable wartime labor. This was the case for Ramona Espinoza, who was recruited from Mexicali, Mexico, for short-term labor contracts, which took her back to the United States, but not for permanent resettlement. While ethnic Mexican banishment drives were not legislated at the federal level, the practice informed the federal 1935 law that repatriated Filipino nationals during the Depression, all of which illustrates how different ethnic groups were racialized during the Depression through mass exclusions. Ramona Espinoza's story and that of her family help us understand the complexities of employment racialization processes and abuses that entangled these banished Mexican Americans in what I call impermanent legality—a situation in which one's legal status was linked to the oscillating desirability of Mexican labor in the United States at various historical conjunctures.

As participating families' stories reveal, banishment has injured Mexican American households and their descendants in complex, nuanced, and uneven ways that merit redress by the US and Mexican governments. Chapter 5 provides recommendations for reparations that come directly from banished women, their children, and their grandchildren. Legislation addressing the banishment of Mexican Americans has been proposed in California, Illinois, Michigan, and Washington, DC. However, formal Apology Acts were not approved by the US Congress or Michigan, making California the only state that has formally apologized for banishing Mexican Americans. Illinois and California also implemented this history into their curricula. To address inaction at the federal level, the participating families in this study made concrete redress recommendations, which are examined in this chapter.

The legacies of banishment have affected not only direct descendants of Mexican Americans removed during the interwar period, but also other ethnic and racial groups who have been cast as "undesirable" at different historical conjunctures. As I explain in the Epilogue, US and Mexican officials replicated policies and practices of banishment against Filipino nationals in the United States and Chinese Mexicans in Mexico only a few years later. Many of the fear tactics and scapegoating used for mass banishments during the interwar period have been recycled in mass deportation plans under the second term of President Donald J. Trump, which threaten to upend entire communities. Once again mixed-status families, immigrants, and their allies are organizing to fight for the right to remain in the United States.

CHAPTER ONE

THE RODRÍGUEZ FAMILY

Transgenerational Illegality

Jesús Molina never met his paternal grandmother, Trinidad Rodríguez. He knows her only through family stories, legal documents, and a few cherished mementos. One of the only pictures he has of her is the passport-sized photograph still attached with four rusty staples to a 1969 background check that Trinidad used in one of her final attempts to reclaim her US citizenship (Fig. 1.1). The picture depicts Trinidad looking directly at the camera with her hair pulled back in a ponytail and wearing a button-up blouse. She probably selected her formal outfit very deliberately given the importance of this moment, and the viewer can almost feel the heaviness of Trinadad's banishment in her pensive facial expression. The official stamp of the Yahualica police department at the bottom of the image reminds the family of Trinidad's resilience and determination to reclaim her US citizenship and return to her native California. Legal records and the family's memories document Trinidad Rodríguez's 1917 birth in Redlands, California, and her early childhood in the United States. Her US citizenship was never in doubt. But at the age of five, Trinidad— along with her US-citizen maternal half-sister and her Mexican stepfather—was banished to Mexico during the first period of removals that took place from 1921 to 1923.

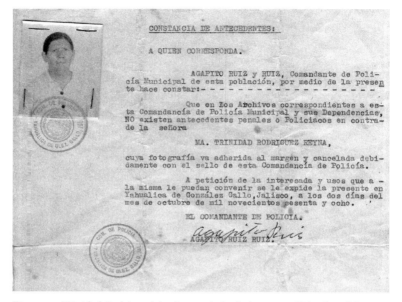

Figure 1.1 Trinidad Rodríguez's background-check document, Yahualica, Jalisco, Mexico, October 2, 1968.

During the economic recession that followed World War I, the same US employers who had heavily recruited Mexicans to fill wartime labor shortages suddenly no longer needed them. By then, some Mexicans, like Trinidad's family, had already established deep roots and had US-citizen children. Nonetheless, following the legacies of coverture doctrine, US-citizen minors and women were expected to follow the removed male head of household out of the country. Unable to return for many years, Trinidad resigned herself to a life in Jalisco, Mexico, where she found limited opportunities. But, like other banished women, Trinidad fought tirelessly to reestablish herself in her native country, and after numerous attempts, finally returned to the United States almost five decades after her banishment. By that time, Trinidad was a fifty-two-year-old married woman with two Mexican-born children. Sadly, she died shortly after successfully reclaiming her US citizenship, and before she was able to open immigration petitions for her nuclear family. Thus, Jesús Molina entered his grandmother's native country as an unauthorized immigrant, and his father, Refugio Molina, visits the United States on a tourist visa. Trinidad's banishment made her an immigrant in her own country and robbed her children and grandchildren of the right to derivative citizenship. These imbricated layers of legality and illegality that run through several generations of the Rodríguez family underscore how immigration law, racialized discourses, and banishment profoundly shaped their trajectory.

Trinidad was a second-generation Mexican American woman born to a US-citizen mother. Despite her roots in the United States, banishment interrupted the US citizenship to which her subsequent generations had a right (Fig. 1.2). As Jesús explains, "My grandma was sent to Mexico in 1922 when she was five years old. Her mother, my great grandma, died when she was four and her father died before that."[1] After being suddenly orphaned at four, Trinidad "lived with her stepfather and half-sister in California until they were kicked out because of the [economic] crisis, but she was a US citizen."[2] As Jesús puts it, "I am a US citizen, but not recognized as one."[3] Regardless of his claims to US citizenship through Trinidad, at the time of this interview Jesús continued to be classified as an unauthorized immigrant in his paternal grandmother's native country. And Jesús's father, Refugio Molina, the son of a US citizen, has been relegated to the temporary legal status afforded by his tourist visa. In the long term, Trinidad's removal meant that her own descendants—born in Mexico but eventually relocated to the United States—would be unable to claim US citizenship. Instead, as Mexican immigrants, they would be marked by a socially constructed and state-imposed notion of illegality, and thus continue to be classified as unauthorized and deportable.

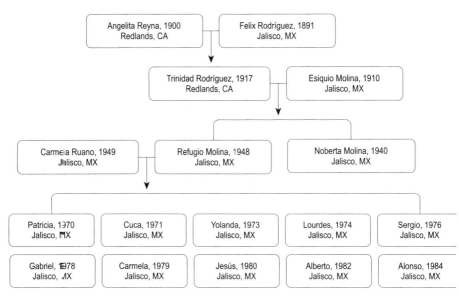

Figure 1.2 Trinidad Rodríguez's family tree. Graphic by author based on data provided by the Rodríguez family.

Despite the use of the term *illegal* and its derivatives, I contest the US-based implication that Mexicans' unauthorized status is innate. Immigration scholars' theorization of illegality demonstrates that nothing about unauthorized immigrants' position within and outside the law is natural.[4] Constructions of illegality are not limited to the deportation and inadmissibility of unauthorized immigrants, as the historiography has established. Instead, the illegality imposed on banished Mexican Americans—through specific historical, political, and social circumstances—labeled marginalized groups as removable and bypassed their actual legal status in the country. Their descendants then inherited this imposed illegality.

As Jesús's story indicates, Trinidad's banishment reverberated through three family generations. So, too, did the racialized, state-sanctioned imposition of illegality. US officials expelled Trinidad from her country of birth because, as an orphan, the state perceived her as a public charge. It did not help that Trinidad's caretaker, her stepfather, was destitute. Refugio Molina, Trinidad's son, shared that after her banishment, his mother settled in Yahualica, Jalisco, Mexico, because "her stepfather's family members lived there."[5] Prior to the banishment, all her kin lived in Redlands, California, and the greater San Bernardino County area. Tragically, after her banishment, Trinidad lost all contact with her family in the United States and never saw them again.

Trinidad's removal at a young age situates her and her family's experience within the larger historical context of banishment. Trinidad made multiple attempts to return to the United States, beginning in the 1930s when she was a teenager, until the late 1960s, when she finally—though only briefly—succeeded in returning to her native country. Her story is filled with disappointments. But in 1969, the year she finally returned to the United States, a decision in the case *In re Juan Becerra-Torres* opened the possibility for Trinidad's children to claim derivative citizenship. In her last resettlement attempt, Trinidad had planned to send her son and his family to settle her claim. Her goal was to open immigration petitions to bring her two Mexican-born children and husband to the United States. But Trinidad never realized her dream. When she was unable to save enough money for the legal expenses, Trinidad returned to Mexico, where she unexpectedly died. Unfortunately, banishment and simple clerical mistakes on her death certificate and other identity documents have caused legal delays for subsequent generations' immigration petitions. Ultimately, however, Trinidad's complicated and fraught story of forced removal and attempts to return to the United States were not without success, for they remain central to the lives, hopes, and dreams of three generations of family members.

The Rodríguez family's story is just one example of how the transgenerational illegality imposed on banished Mexican American women and their descendants has been historically, socially, and politically produced. In many ways, the multigenerational oral histories in this chapter contest the official record, allowing for a rewriting of the past. As the Rodríguez family's lived experiences demonstrate, mass removals during the post–World War I recession were not simply an attempt to reduce unemployment and stabilize the economy. Instead, they were meant to disempower a growing Mexican American population by removing Mexican immigrants and Mexican Americans, thereby obstructing their children's access to derivative and birthright citizenship. During the Great Depression this disempowerment continued through new rounds of coerced removals. Banishment created a class of people without full access to US citizenship: descendants of banished US citizens of Mexican origin who are now unauthorized immigrants, temporary immigrants, and second-class citizens treated as disposable laborers. Despite Trinidad's lifelong insistence on returning to the United States to adjust her children's legal status, her children and grandchildren are still fighting for full legal integration into their mother and grandmother's native country. Marked as outsiders, the subsequent three generations of the Rodríguez family have been denied the legal and social privileges accorded to US citizens. These repeated exclusions and the prolonged consequences of their banishment are emblematic of how transgenerational illegality affects descendants of US citizens today.

ESTABLISHING US CITIZENSHIP AND ILLEGALITY

US citizenship has been constructed over time as a privilege delineated along racial, classed, and gendered lines.[6] The United States grants citizenship through birthright and naturalization, both of which include different limitations. Only fourteen years after the founding of the nation, the 1790 Naturalization Act established the "white free person" prerequisite for US citizenship, which barred Blacks, Native Americans, and nonwhite immigrants from naturalization rights.[7] At that time, the 1790 law required physical presence for two years prior to naturalization. In 1802, this residency requirement was extended to five years.[8] That prolonged residence prerequisite delayed prospective new citizens from attaining full political power.[9] Naturalization did not broadly expand access to nationality rights. Birthright citizenship attained through jus soli was a right reserved for free white people born within the jurisdiction of the United States, a privilege gradually extended to other racial groups. Birthright citizenship also accessed through jus sanguinis, as outlined in the 1790 derivative citizenship statute, originally granted US citizenship to children born abroad to a US-citizen father. In 1934, an amendment finally provided women the right to pass US citizenship to their children.[10] In addition to race, class status became a metric for admissibility with the Immigration Act of 1882. The 1882 law mandated that an immigrant who was "unable to take care of himself or herself without becoming a public charge" was inadmissible to the United States.[11] The same metric, "likely to become a public charge," or LPC, was also applied to deportation law when Congress enacted the Immigration Act of 1891, which called for the "deportation of any alien who becomes a public charge within one year after his arrival in the United States."[12] The Immigration Acts of 1903, 1907, and 1917 extended to two, three, and then five years, respectively, the time of residence under which deportation was authorized on LPC grounds.[13] Immigration laws also dictated women's and children's lack of political autonomy. Consistent with coverture doctrine, women and children have historically derived citizenship rights from their husbands and fathers. The Naturalization Act of 1855 established that a woman who married a US-citizen husband became a citizen, but women could not confer their US citizenship to an immigrant husband. Moreover, this 1855 law confirmed derivative citizenship rights to US-citizen fathers, but not mothers.[14] This law reinforced the dependent-citizenship logic, in which "the citizenship of a wife and child followed the male head of the household."[15]

Mexicans, unlike other nonwhite groups, gained access to US citizenship through the 1848 Peace Treaty of Guadalupe Hidalgo that, in ending the Mexican-American War, granted collective US citizenship and inferred legal whiteness to Mexicans in the annexed territories.[16] This legal right, however, was highly contested in courts when applications for naturalization were denied for Mexicans who did not pass the whiteness test because of their indigenous roots.[17] Twenty years later, the Naturalization Treaty of 1868, also known as the Bancroft Treaty, established that Mexicans were eligible for US citizenship even if they were part of the "Indian race," allowing them to bypass the whiteness benchmark.[18] That same year, the Fourteenth Amendment conferred access to US citizenship to anyone born within the country's jurisdiction. Drafted to address the citizenship rights of formerly enslaved Black people, this amendment also benefited Mexicans but continued to exclude Native Americans. Legal debates about racial limitations under the Fourteenth Amendment continued for decades. In 1897, two court cases settled racial questions for US citizenship accessed through naturalization and birthright. In the case *In re Rodriguez* (1897), US District Judge for the Western Texas District, Thomas S. Maxey, ruled that the absence of a legal statute specifically naming Mexicans as excludable for US citizenship made them eligible for naturalization even if they were not racially white. And the Supreme Court held in *United States v. Wong Kim Ark* (1897) that a child born in the United States acquired birthright citizenship under the Fourteenth Amendment regardless of their race or national origin.[19] Therefore, multiple generations of Mexican immigrants and Mexican Americans enjoyed access to naturalization and birthright citizenship, given their long presence in the United States.

Nonetheless, in the early twentieth century, the exclusionary nature of US citizenship informed banishment policies that targeted Mexican

American women and children and later denied derivative citizenship to their descendants. In 1917, Trinidad was born in the rural town of Redlands, California, to Angelita Rodríguez, who was also born in California. Both Trinidad and her mother obtained birthright US citizenship through the Fourteenth Amendment as well as legal precedents established during the second half of the nineteenth century. Trinidad's banishment, despite her being a second-generation US citizen, epitomizes the early re-racialization of Mexicans that gave way to the banishment drives of the 1920s, during the first and less-known period of mass removals. Repatriation and banishment in the 1920s were a result of the economic recession of that period, as well as restrictive new federal immigration laws. The economic crises after World War I and during the Great Depression intensified the racialization of Mexican Americans as scapegoats, resulting in their banishment, even though their US citizenship was never legally changed. As the experiences of banished families will show, the mass removals of ethnic Mexicans from the United States eventually reached their peak in the 1930s but continued until 1944. Understood in their longer historical context, banishment is an episode in a longer continuum of racial, gender, and class exclusion that dates back to 1848, when Mexicans were legally defined as white but never fully integrated into the national polity.

Following the annexation of territories after the Mexican-American War, the Mexican population in those territories increased rapidly because of the 1910 Revolution in Mexico, the advent of US economic opportunities during the 1920s, and substantial labor recruitment by American railroad, farming, mining, meat-packing, factories, and steel industries.[20] At the turn of the twentieth century, Chinese and Japanese workers were excluded from these industries, which left many jobs open; Mexican labor was recruited to fill these gaps.[21] During World War I, as Chapter 2 will detail, Mexicans were recruited through the first Bracero Program to fill vacancies in those previous industries as well as in construction and maintenance.[22] Beginning with the recession of 1918, Mexicans became a central focus of social workers, in part because the population was rapidly increasing. The number of Mexicans residing in California increased tenfold between 1900 and 1920.[23] At the national level, Mexican immigration to the United States increased from 221,915 in 1910 to 486,418 in 1920, adding to an already well-established ethnic Mexican population.[24]

The population increase generated by the labor recruitments augmented the ethnic Mexican presence beyond traditional locales. The first Bracero Program contributed to the settlement of Mexicans across the United States. They were recruited to California, Texas, New Mexico, Arizona, Colorado, Michigan, Nebraska, Ohio, Utah, Idaho, Minnesota, and Montana, where they worked in agriculture, mining, and construction. Mexicans were also hired for mining in the US Southwest and western Colorado, and to work with cattle in Nevada and Wyoming. In addition, Mexicans could be found working on the railroads throughout the Southwest, as well as in Illinois, Kansas, and Nebraska. But labor demands were not limited to rural areas. The Mexican population also increased in urban centers, including in California, Illinois, Wisconsin, Indiana, and Missouri.[25] Unlike the Chinese, Filipino, and early Japanese immigrants who predominantly immigrated as single males, Mexicans usually immigrated as heterosexual family units because their families were not excluded by naturalization and immigration laws.[26] Mexican women, both immigrants and US citizens, also became an important part of the labor sector in the same geographical regions as their male counterparts during the 1920s and 1930s. Ethnic Mexican women could be found working in agriculture, canneries, the domestic service sector, packing houses, and manufacturing and mechanical industries.[27] In the absence of Mexican gendered exclusions, from the early 1910s to early 1930s, the United States also experienced a rapid growth in the number of second-generation Mexican Americans. The US Census enumerated 224,276 ethnic Mexicans in 1910, a figure that nearly tripled by 1920, to 651,596.[28]

As the ethnic Mexican population in the United States increased, so did calls for their exclusion. The economic recession that followed

World War I animated racist nativist demands for stricter immigration policies. As historian Matt Garcia has convincingly demonstrated, US dependence on ethnic Mexican labor meant that they would become a target of eugenicists and anti-immigrant propaganda.[29] In the 1920s, Mexicans were increasingly labeled a "social problem," a "biological problem," and a "race problem." These labels were popularized by restrictionist immigration proposals that gave way to the concept of the "Mexican problem," a punitive social discourse that labeled ethnic Mexicans as a social, biological, and economic burden. The Immigration Acts of 1917, 1921, and 1924 placed quotas on immigration from southern and eastern Europe, the Far East, Africa, and the Middle East. These restrictions provoked eugenicists to ask why these bills "did nothing about the 'hordes' of 'Mexican Indians' that contributed to a 'mixed-race problem' throughout the Southwest and industrial belt of the Midwest."[30] Thus the "Mexican problem" soon became the "Mexican American problem," which broadened the targets of exclusion from Mexican immigrants to their Mexican American children and wives.

Restrictions on Mexican immigration also increased after World War I. The 1917 Immigration Act regulated Mexican immigration for the first time. Immigrants were required to pass a literacy test, undergo a medical examination, pay an eight-dollar head tax, and get through an interrogation regarding their likelihood of becoming a public charge.[31] Although an exemption was granted until 1921, after this point, those unable to meet the new immigration requirements would be marked with a new state-imposed illegality—even as many Mexicans continued to casually cross the political divide and enter the United States. The 1924 Immigration Act further shifted the legal understanding of Mexicans, labeling them "illegal aliens" when before they had been legally "white."[32] While the 1924 Immigration Act did not restrict Mexican immigration and naturalization based on race, it implemented a visa requirement, effectively criminalizing those who traversed the border without one. Mexicans had been able to cross into and out of the United States without much scrutiny due to labor demands throughout the late nineteenth and early twentieth centuries. The racialization of Mexicans under the 1917 and 1924 laws, paired with the confusing terms of the new and often changing immigration acts, did not halt Mexican immigration. But these laws did succeed in illegalizing—in the minds of Americans—all Mexicans, who became understood as "outsiders" regardless of their legal status, length of residence, and generation.

Though the nativists' anti-Mexican propaganda failed to place a quota on Mexican immigration, it did generate broad support for banishment. In June of 1920, the *New York Herald* reported: "Leo Russell, head of the US deportation office, said that in January there would be a massive expulsion of Japanese, Chinese and Mexicans, who were illegally in the United States."[33] Given the geographic proximity between Mexico and the United States, it soon became more cost effective to remove peoples of Mexican origin, rather than of Asian origin, who were already inadmissible and deportable through the Chinese Exclusion Acts and the 1907–1908 Gentlemen's Agreement between the United States and Japan. Congressional debates that cited "biological" and "social" problems as primary concerns against Mexican immigration peaked around World War I, when eugenics "had reached the dimensions of a fad."[34] Eugenicist Harry H. Laughlin, a Washington, DC official with the Carnegie Institution, claimed during his testimony before the INS House Committee that immigration of Mexican "colored races" was the "sixth major racial problem in American history," comparable to the "historical mistakes" that included "the introduction of negro slaves" and "oriental migration."[35] The "biological problem" referred to Mexican's indigenous lineage and "social problem" to their alleged indigence and dependency on public services.[36] These anti-Mexican eugenics discourses of the 1920s meant that ethnic Mexicans, regardless of legal status, were understood to be removable, and the Immigration Act of 1917 became the legal justification for their expulsion.

Local civic leaders spoke out against the racial targeting of ethnic Mexicans for banishment. One such figure was Cleofas Calleros, a naturalized Mexican immigrant himself and a social worker and immigration expert affiliated with the Catholic Church. In 1934, Calleros—then working in his role as the Mexican border representative with the National Catholic Welfare Conference in El Paso, Texas—denounced the mass removals during the 1920s and 1930s, noting that many of the ethnic Mexicans being racialized as "foreigners" could trace their family roots in El Paso and the southwestern states back as early as 1680: "The question of American citizens . . . applies mostly to West Texas, especially around El Paso and some western [states] where some of these [Mexican origin] people can trace their ancestry back to the year 1680. There are many counties that question the American citizenship of these people even though they have been there for generations. In some counties the Mexicans have been told that, even though they were born in Texas they are not American citizens because their parents were not born in the United States or did not take out citizenship papers."[37] The case of West Texas was not an exception; instead, this discursive, racialized interrogation of the US citizenship of ethnic Mexicans—even when their families had been in those places for generations—became the rule in states with significant Mexican populations. Many ethnic Mexicans, even those in families that had been in the United States for many generations, suddenly found their US citizenship called into question as their ethnic identity became linked to racialized ideas of illegality and undesirability. Indeed, in Trinidad's case, an ethnic Mexican family in California with established generations of US citizens was marked as foreign and unworthy of legal rights. Banished peoples' ethnic background outweighed their US citizenship and deep-seated residence that, in some cases, spanned multiple generations. In many ways, banishment strengthened the US racial, ethnic, and class hierarchies during the interwar period.

The legal and public rhetoric, which portrayed the citizenship of ethnic Mexican US citizens as somehow less legitimate, created a hierarchy for "valued" citizens based on social whiteness, gender, and class status. US immigration discourse ascribed distinct meanings of racial, gender, and classed categories to working-class Mexican American children and women in ways that intensified their likelihood for removal. From this standpoint, immigration officials concluded—without any official ruling and relying on abolished coverture language—that US-citizen children belonged with their mothers, US-citizen wives belonged to their husbands, and Mexican immigrant men did not belong in the United States. When officials projected these assumptions of "not belonging" and "un-American"—linking them to notions of legality and illegality—onto entire mixed-status families of ethnic Mexican women, men, and children, the state-sanctioned exclusion of several generations at once foreshadowed how the legacies of banishment would also be experienced across generations. Future generations of ethnic Mexicans, who would inherit the notions of illegality that made their family's banishment possible, would have to negotiate with these modes of transgenerational illegality in their own ways.

Some officials questioned the ethics and constitutionality of expelling Mexican Americans, though with little success. For example, in 1931, Arthur G. Arnoll—general manager of the Los Angeles Chamber of Commerce—critiqued the racial politics of the mass removals in a communication to George P. Clements, manager of the Los Angeles Chamber of Commerce's Agricultural Department. He openly acknowledged that Mexicans were being racially targeted without any substantive consideration of legality: "The Mexicans [have become] a target. The slogan has gone out over the city and is being adhered to—'Employ no Mexican while a white man is unemployed; get the Mexican back into Mexico regardless by what means.' All these without taking into consideration the legality of the Mexican's status of being here. It is a question of pigment, not a question of citizenship or right."[38] Even Arnoll realized that once Mexicans had been socially constructed as a threat to the economic stability of the country, banishment became a socially justified solution to the "Mexican problem." Public and media discourses worked in tandem with immigration policies of the time, with each reinforcing the other.[39]

TRINIDAD RODRÍGUEZ'S BANISHMENT

Like most banished people, Trinidad Rodríguez and her family faced removal in 1922 based on their ethnicity and indigent status. The family first came to the attention of the authorities when Trinidad's stepfather registered for relief. He was not alone. Rather, he was among thousands of Californians to ask for relief during the post–World War I economic recession. But although in the 1920s ethnic Mexicans constituted approximately 25 percent of all residents who received public assistance in the city of Los Angeles, that percentage would drastically decrease as the economic recession intensified. Historian George J. Sánchez found that during the 1930s, in the midst of the Great Depression, Los Angeles public officials were pressured to give preference in relief allocations to unemployed white US citizens, essentially displacing Mexicans and Mexican Americans who were also in need.[40] Despite the fact that Mexicans on relief rolls were entitled to the social benefits they received, they were often denied food relief, decried as economic burdens, and targeted for removal simply for asking for aid at a time when most of the nation was afflicted by economic instability. The xenophobic zeal with which government officials carried out removals dismissed not only the US citizenship of banished women and children in mixed-status families, but also the significant contributions of ethnic Mexicans to their local and national economies (as later chapters demonstrate). Keenly aware of banishment initiatives, many destitute ethnic Mexicans turned to requesting state aid only as a last resort. The act of requesting relief almost always resulted in their removal. The LPC provision of the Immigration Act of 1917 established a legal justification for banishment by citing such deportable offenses as vagrancy, inability to pay medical bills, or application for public assistance.[41] To legally justify mass removals, including the banishment of US citizens, US immigration officials cited section 23 of the Immigration Act of 1917, which not only stressed the targeting of immigrants who became destitute and asked for public assistance, but also called for the removal of any such person "at any time within three years after entry," though only if the person is "desirous of being so removed."[42] Trinidad's stepfather was forced to request assistance after Trinidad's mother died and he was left to care for two small children on a limited income. Even though he was a Mexican immigrant, he qualified for public assistance due to his long-term residence in the United States, and his dependents (his daughter and stepdaughter) were US citizens entitled to relief benefits as well. Additionally, he was not "desirous of being removed." Despite his legal right to request assistance in the form of food and remain in the United States, he and his children were denied public relief and were instead enlisted for so-called repatriation. With no other choice, he departed the United States with Trinidad and her half-sister in tow, settling in his native Yahualica, Jalisco, Mexico, where his relatives lived. After the humiliating experience of forced removal, Trinidad's stepfather never again set foot in or even attempted to return to the United States. Trinidad, though, would make returning to the United States a central priority in her life.

In 1925, only three years after Trinidad's banishment, Mexican consuls actively organized *sociedades mutualistas,* or "mutual aid societies," so that the sick, unemployed, and destitute could obtain charity without having to risk automatic removal.[43] By 1900, Mexicans had established mutual aid societies throughout the country, including California, but the efforts intensified during the interwar period. The increase of these alternative relief sources to avoid banishment highlights how dire the situation was for mixed-status Mexican families. National religious organizations like the National Catholic Welfare Conference (which eventually became the US Conference of Catholic Bishops), established in 1919 by US bishops to provide private aid and defend immigrants' rights, were also helpful, but sometimes they were influenced by larger social assumptions and susceptible to the same information and racialized representations of ethnic Mexicans.[44]

In the absence of detailed governmental documents that can explain the reasons for banishment, some present-day families have had to come to their own conclusions about their ancestor's exclusions, often through stories shared across generations. According to several family members, Trinidad's banishment resulted from her orphaned status or alleged likelihood to become a public charge, despite her birthright as a US citizen. As Trinidad's grandson Jesús reasoned, "Both of my grandmother's parents died when she was only four years old. Her stepfather raised her and her half-sister. . . . They did not want people who were asking for [the] government's help. My grandma's stepfather must have asked for welfare for her two daughters after my great grandma died, but the government did not like that at the time and was sending all Mexicans out of the country."[45] Jesús's explanation points to the family's understanding of the race- and class-based exclusions in the years leading up to the Great Depression, which prevailed during the great economic crisis and into the early 1940s. These little-known stories, though seemingly insignificant, are crucial in helping us further understand the race- and class-based exclusions during the interwar period—and they help to fill a gap in our nation's history. Legal documents often lack the insights on race and class consciousness that the descendants of banished US citizens, like Jesús, can provide.

Banishment meant that while Trinidad's stepfather had blood relatives in Mexico to call on for support, her kin remained in the United States, effectively disconnecting Trinidad from her blood family. Trinidad's son Refugio explained the significance of her removal from the family: "They were family members, but her sister, well, she was her half-sister, and he was her stepfather. Thus, they gave her the Mercado last name, since her stepfather and half-sister's last name was Mercado. She had family, but really through their side of the family."[46] In a foreign land, and at the young age of five, Trinidad was forced to adopt a new national, cultural, and familial identity in Mexico. She had to adapt quickly to Mexican culture and traditions. More importantly, she had to adopt a new familial identity by claiming her stepfather's last name and renouncing, or at least hiding, her own. According to the stories she shared with her daughter-in-law Carmela Ruano, Trinidad resented the newly imposed identity and always regretted losing

contact with her blood relatives in the United States. As Carmela recalled, Trinidad "used to talk with me and said, 'Well, I think I have
aunts or cousins. But I am not sure because my people are not from here,
none of them are.'"[47] Trinidad's desire to reconnect with "her people"
suggests a desperate feeling of alienation and the need to belong to blood
kin. Trinidad's invocation of the term *mi gente* (my people) refers to her
blood relatives in the United States, not her adoptive family in Mexico.
While she was unsure if she even had an extended family, she knew that
she had some family members in the United States and held dear to the
idea of "my people," "my family"—a connection that she did not seem
to share with her stepfather's family in Mexico.

Despite Trinidad's hardships, she was fortunate to have had a stepfather who was willing to support her in Mexico, since many orphaned
children like her ended up in Mexican orphanages following banishment.[48] In their book on Mexican repatriation, *Decade of Betrayal,*
historians Francisco E. Balderrama and Raymond Rodríguez describe
such orphaned children as "homeless waifs without a country."[49] As
destitute orphans of Mexican descent living in the United States,
these children were triply disadvantaged: they had no money, no parents, and no country that wanted them. Once orphaned, Mexican
American children became part of a racist social construction that
called them a burden to the nation-state and rendered them disposable.
Their US citizenship was replaced with an impermanent legality; that
is, their legal right to reside in the United States suddenly became conditional. For US-citizen children and women, their legal rights were
contingent on their perceived economic independence. US-citizen
children had to have parental economic support, and US-citizen women
were expected to have marital support; otherwise, their legality became
impermanent. In 1930, for instance, Los Angeles County officials insisted on relocating orphaned US-citizen children to "La Casa del Niño"
in Mexico City, a process that in some cases took up to two years.[50] The
city's insistence on removing these children reveals the scope of banishment. Not even the vulnerability of minors, whose age guarantees

them state protections, prevented Mexican American children from being caught in the crosshairs of anti-Mexican exclusion and banishment. On the contrary, US public officials actively sought out orphaned Mexican American children for removal.

Notably, in Globe, Arizona, the Public Welfare Department searched orphanages for Mexican children—whether they were citizens or not—to initiate their removal. Orphaned children unable to provide for themselves became a public charge and were identified as a burden to the state. In a time of economic depression, when the United States was seeking to cut expenses by all means possible, orphaned ethnic Mexican children became another group targeted for removal.[51] Among the Mexican children in Globe who were banished and then placed into Mexican orphanages were Salvador Ramírez, Alicia Alfonso, and Melita Landeros.[52] Such children encountered an extremely difficult life in Mexico. Their conditions of poverty and limited opportunities forced them to work, especially once they reached the age of seven. In 1906, Mexican law defined an orphan or "abandoned child" as a minor who "by his age is incapable of providing for his own subsistence, or a child under the age of seven."[53] Thus, orphaned seven-year-old children were deemed adults who could provide for themselves, relieving the state of any responsibility. Civil law in Mexico at the time did not allow formal adoption, which prevented many orphans from securing a family and means of survival. Nevertheless, public orphanages engaged in two types of informal adoption: one for family formation and the other for labor-force participation.[54] Seven-year-old children unable to secure a family faced either discharge from the orphanage into the streets or employment as servants for well-to-do families. While the United States treated orphaned children as removable liabilities and then banished them, the Mexican government forced them into self-sufficiency. Thus, orphan children experienced multiple displacements, first when they were banished from the United States and then again when they were removed from Mexican orphanages at the age of seven. Due to state power, orphaned children were vulnerable citizens on both sides of the US-Mexico border and on both sides of banishment.

DENIED RESETTLEMENT ATTEMPTS

Trinidad's separation from her family at a young age cultivated an immense desire in her to reconnect with her blood relatives and native country. Within eleven years of her banishment, Trinidad attempted to return to the United States. Against her stepfather's wishes, the determined sixteen-year-old bravely made the solo journey north in 1933, traveling 1,551 miles by train to the US-Mexico border. But she had no documentation to prove her verbal claim of US citizenship, and immigration officers did not believe her, so she had to turn back. That unsuccessful attempt did not discourage her. Trinidad tried unsuccessfully to cross again just one year later, in 1934.

Trinidad's thwarted return attempts in 1933 and 1934 marked a moment during the Great Depression when many US policymakers supported closing the US-Mexico border to all migrants, and immigration officials used their discretion to restrict entry to working-class ethnic Mexican women. While Trinidad was banished in 1922 during the first period of removals, her resettlement attempts were directly affected and delayed by policies implemented during the second and third periods, when removals of ethnic Mexicans were still under way, and immigration officers still had significant jurisdiction and leeway in applying immigration law. Jesús explained: "She [Trinidad] tried to come back in 1933 and 1934, but during those years the border was closed to Mexicans. Even though she was a Californian, she was unable to return to her country because of the crisis."[55] Policymaker debates reflected the rampant anti-Mexican sentiment of this moment. In 1933, US Representative Thomas L. Blanton of Texas, a staunch segregationist, introduced House Resolution 109 (HR 109), an immigration bill that promised to close the border to all migrants, including banished returnees, for a period of ten years, starting on April 1, 1933.[56] Though the House Committee on Immigration and Naturalization voted down the bill, Blanton's anti-immigrant stance reflects the polemical views of some US policymakers.[57] Notably, at the US-Mexico border, immigration officers had wide discretion on who to admit. Using their own presumptions about race, class, and gender, they often denied entry to women on LPC grounds, especially when women traveled alone or as single mothers.

A return to the United States was delayed for both Mexican American women and men based on their class status, which immigration officers deciphered through their physical appearance. For instance, Crescencio Hernández was banished in 1932 to Ciudad Juárez, Mexico; like Trinidad, he had no other option than to return to his native country as an immigrant. As his nephew Refugio Hernández recounted, Crescencio "was born in San Jose, California. He was an American, but the authorities would not let him cross the border because he used to dress as a pachuco."[58] After an immigration officer turned him back at the border, despite "having his US birth certificate," he decided to change out of his pachuco suit, and "crossed under the Santa Fe immigration bridge to avoid difficulties with [immigration] authorities. Even when he was from here, the United States."[59] In Trinidad's case, given 1930s fashion and her desire to make a positive impression on the immigration officer, she probably wore a mid-calf-length dress, stockings, and low heels, and styled her hair with waves held in place with bobby pins on the right side of her face, as captured in her photograph taken circa 1935 when she returned to Yahualica from the border (Fig. 1.3). Nonetheless, unable to reproduce a copy of her birth certificate, the immigration officer erroneously informed her that she had lost US citizenship. The immigration officer could have directed Trinidad to the US consulate in Mexico to secure another copy. Instead, through misinformation, the immigration officer revoked Trinidad's US citizenship discursively, rendering her actual legal status useless. In questioning

Figure 1.3 Portrait of Trinidad Rodríguez, Yahualica, Jalisco, Mexico, circa 1935.

and even denying her citizenship, the immigration official's incorrect statement was just one of many moments when Trinidad's legality was made conditional and thus impermanent. As Vicki L. Ruiz notes, in the early 1930s, gender played a part in the experiences of many ethnic Mexicans at the border.[60] Indeed, immigration officers policed the bodies of returning Mexican American women and men and used their discretionary power based on gendered, racial, and classed assumptions that rendered young single men and unaccompanied women inadmissible.

Trinidad's longing and sense of loss of home and family motivated her to continue attempting to return, even when her efforts were unsuccessful. Carmela, Trinidad's daughter-in-law, recounted the pain of separation her mother-in-law felt, a pain that Trinidad shared with her just days after they first met: "She told me that she had no relatives here [in Mexico], nobody, because she is from [the United States]. She used to talk to me when we were doing our household chores and she said that she wanted to go, 'to see what happened to my people, with my family members.' Like someone has uncles, or cousins, and I don't know what else, and her, nothing. She said, 'I have no one! . . . I would have really liked to have known my people.'"[61] Trinidad experienced a complete sense of loss and isolation from not having any blood relatives in Mexico. While her half-sister was a blood relative in the sense that they had the same biological mother, Trinidad's stepfather's family in Mexico treated her half-sister as one of their own, while she was seen as "a free-loader."[62] In Trinidad's view, banishment completely stripped her of her ties to her homeland and of *every single* blood relative, essentially wiping out her family. Trinidad also felt abandoned because no one from her family ever contacted her after the banishment. Without any family connections in Mexico, except that of her stepfather and sister, she always felt an urgent need to return to the United States.

Banished Mexican Americans' ability to return drastically diminished as time wore on. In his report "The Mexican Problem," Calleros recounted, "Several hundred families are now living in Juárez who have found their way back to the border with the intention of re-immigrating into the United States [after their repatriation]. Very few are fortunate in gaining re-admission. Of course, those who have resided in Mexico less than six months, and who paid their own way, have a better chance to return."[63] Border immigration authorities made it virtually impossible for ethnic Mexicans to return to the United States. When they did, it was often many years after their expulsion. Part of the reason was bureaucratic. In many cases, people had left their birth certificates behind in their homes when they were banished. In other cases, immigration officers confiscated their legal documents upon their removal from the United States. Still others had their documents stamped by their local relief agencies, marking them as recipients of relief assistance and thus inadmissible under LPC charges.

Even if a banished citizen's documents were in good order, US officials established restrictive entry conditions at the US-Mexico border that allowed only a very limited number of people to gain readmission. Moreover, returnees who stayed in Mexico for longer than six months were less likely to be readmitted because they were seen as long-term residents of Mexico. This prejudice affected many banished people, who understood that the anti-Mexican hostility in the United States limited their opportunities and so did not even attempt to return immediately following their forced removals. All the other families whose experiences are described in this book were able to take their birth certificates or baptismal records with them when they were banished, because officials coordinated the 1930s removals around train departure schedules. The predictability of a set departure date and time of banishment allowed families to gather their important documents before their banishment.

If Trinidad had retained a copy of her birth certificate, she could have proven her citizenship to immigration officials and would have had a better chance of being able to return to the United States. Many years earlier, however, immigration officers had taken it away from her to prevent this from happening. The confiscation of personal documents by immigration officers became standard practice in US-Mexico border towns, as INS Commissioner George L. Coleman highlighted in a 1933 report on conditions at the US-Mexico border: "The Mexican Consul at Los Angeles felt that many were not leaving voluntarily but did not blame that to [sic] the Immigration Service. He did say, however, that he had been informed that the papers and documents of those being repatriated were taken away from them at the border, some of which might be of value for their returning at some future date, legally. He questioned the right of the immigration officers to seize such documents and felt it unfair. That this was being done was confirmed by our San Diego Office."[64] Immigration officers bent the rules by taking people's legal documents when they banished them, leaving Mexican Americans in a state-imposed legal limbo. Nonetheless, some women found creative workarounds. The inability to return without a birth certificate and the desperation to reunite with family across the border pushed some banished people, like Trinidad, to fabricate identities as temporary visitors to the United States. Tourist visas allowed migrants to stay up to six months in the United States, which could have given some people enough time to secure copies of their US birth certificates and reclaim their citizenship. This is what Trinidad was eventually able to do, using this legal strategy as her way of fighting back, of rejecting her banishment.

AN IMMIGRANT IN HER OWN LAND

During the mass banishments, relief representatives across the nation promoted repatriation by assuring mixed-status Mexican families that they could return to the United States once economic stability had returned. But Coleman notes in his 1933 US Immigration Service report that this was untrue and most banished people were unable to return: "The Secretary of the Chamber of Commerce of Brownsville stated that they believed the Border Patrol method of getting Mexicans to return to Mexico in order that they could return to the United States legally was an unfair representation, since 99 percent of them were unable to come back."[65] This was certainly true for Trinidad. It was not until 1969—when she strategically and temporarily gave up her claim to US citizenship and settled for a visitor tourist visa, so that she could enter the United States and secure a copy of her birth certificate—that Trinidad was able to affirm her US citizenship and so, in theory, pass on that citizenship to her children. Trinidad's strategy to enter the United States in this way captures some of the legal ironies of the transgenerational illegality that the Rodríguez family inherited.

Trinidad returned to the United States at a time when anti-Mexican
hysteria was on the rise. Historically in the United States, attitudes
toward immigration integration versus immigration exclusion have been
determined largely by national economic conditions. For instance,
during the mid-1960s, the United States experienced rapid economic
growth and low unemployment and inflation levels. Not surprisingly,
during this period, it was widely believed that immigrants could be integrated into the country.[66] By 1969, however, when Trinidad returned
to the United States, and throughout the 1970s, the popular sentiment
became rapidly anti-Mexican as the United States faced a severe economic recession. Between 1948 and 1965, inflation averaged 1.6 percent
annually, but by 1974 it exceeded 12 percent a year.[67] Additionally, between 1973 and 1975, unemployment reached 8.3 percent, twice the
unemployment rate of the mid-1960s, and remained high throughout
the 1970s.[68] The immigrant integration sentiment of the mid-1960s was
quickly replaced during the 1970s by anti-immigrant feelings that
echoed the earlier xenophobia that had led to mass banishments. Trinidad arrived in California when anti-immigrant laws were again being
proposed and debated at the federal and local levels. For instance, Texas
State Representative Bill Clark argued throughout the 1970s that "the
resources of a state are finite. Our boundaries are finite; there are limits
to our ability to produce food and jobs; there are limits on overcrowding
in relation to our physical and mental health."[69] The media and governmental institutions alike spread alarmist messages about a Mexican
population overflow that was leaking into the United States.[70]

When Trinidad arrived in the United States, strong anti-Mexican
sentiment was not her only challenge; she also had a weak social network. Trinidad had only her half-sister Toña, who had been banished
along with Trinidad but managed to return before her, in 1968. Trinidad's family is uncertain how Toña secured a copy of her birth certificate to return to the United States.[71] It is possible that Toña got a tourist
visa, and then Trinidad followed suit. Social networks were and continue to be important because they help migrants emigrate as well as

find housing, employment, and other resources that facilitate permanent settlement.[72] Despite the fact that Trinidad was a US citizen, her prolonged absence from her native country forced her to live that immigrant experience when she returned. Toña, who had been in the United States for only one year herself, served as Trinidad's host.[73] But Trinidad's stay was brief: she lacked the means to remain in the United States long-term, so she was forced to return to Mexico emptyhanded.[74]

As Jesús explained, his grandmother Trinidad's goal was to open immigration petitions for her two Mexican-born children and husband, so that they could resettle in the United States as a family. Jesús recalled, "In 1969, she came to the United States to try to apply for green cards for her children. She stayed here for six months, but had to return to Mexico because she did not have enough money to pay for the immigration process. She never had the chance to open an immigration petition for her children because my grandpa never sent her enough money to pay for the process. The only thing she got when she came was her birth certificate."[75] Trinidad lacked both familiarity with the US immigration system and a steady US income. Even if her husband had sent her money, his Mexican wages likely would have been insufficient to cover the legal fees to hire a US immigration attorney and file a family petition. Moreover, her family obligations and gender norms pushed her to return to Mexico, since she had household and childcare responsibilities. Mexican women who leave their homes for prolonged periods of time—even if they do so to help their family members, as in Trinidad's case—tend to be labeled "bad mothers" and "bad wives."[76] It is very likely that such patriarchal pressures made it harder for banished women to successfully return to the United States on their own.

In 1971, Trinidad tried to convince her son, Refugio, and his wife, Carmela, to leave their first-born daughter temporarily in her care so they could make their way north and settle themselves in the United

States. Carmela recounted, "She used to tell us to come like that, [without papers], and my husband told me, 'No, I won't go *a la brava* [without documents].' She used to say that we should leave my daughter [Patricia], the first one, to leave her with her. 'No,' I said I would not leave her. I said, 'No, it is better if we *don't* go.' She said, 'You should go first and leave your daughter,' to see what could be done I think, right, that is what she was thinking. . . . She wanted to send us first, that way she would have a place to come to and she would then bring my daughter, but no."[77] Trinidad's plan, while resourceful and a bit desperate, was too risky for her family. The uncertainty of the trip and the likelihood of apprehension and detention discouraged Refugio. He understood the challenges of crossing the border, because families in his hometown commonly made the trek. He was further discouraged given his mother's history as well as the portrayals of Mexicans in mainstream media, which constantly reminded Refugio of the "othering" of Mexicans in the United States.[78]

Family separation was also a major factor working against Trinidad's plan to send her son and his wife north, because Carmela's biggest fear was being separated from her daughter. She could not accept the idea of leaving her young daughter behind for an unknown period of time. The fear and guilt, common among immigrant mothers, would have been unbearable (Fig. 1.4).[79] Carmela's reservations about crossing without documents were also related to the dangers of the journey, given that she was pregnant with a second child.[80] After deciding to remain in their native town, Carmela and Refugio had a total of ten children in Mexico, including Jesús. But American influence in their lives was strong, not only because Trinidad had been born in the United States, but also because fashion, sports, and media messages crossed the border into their native Yahualica—one of Jesús's childhood sweaters, for example, featured an imitation of the Mets baseball team's logo (Fig. 1.5). The extreme measures that Trinidad proposed highlight her desperation to return to her native country to reunite with her lost kin, reclaim her US citizenship, and bequeath it to her children. Sadly, Trinidad's

Figure 1.4 Photograph of Refugio Molina and Carmela Ruano with two of their children, Patricia and Sergio, taken during Patricia's first communion, Yahualica, Jalisco, Mexico, circa 1979.

lifelong dream would never materialize. Instead, years later, Jesús and some of his siblings would enter their grandmother's native country as unauthorized immigrants. Trinidad's children and grandchildren, far from obtaining derivative citizenship, inherited a transgenerational illegality.

In 1975, four years after her last resettlement attempt, Trinidad passed away in Mexico at the age of fifty-eight. Trinidad's family believes that her banishment and lifelong inability to return to the United States contributed to her death, which resulted from complications with her gallbladder, exacerbated by a lack of appropriate medical treatment. Years later, Carmela is convinced that Trinidad could have survived if she had been in the United States, since at the time, the medical services in Yahualica, Mexico, were limited: "Well, I used to say that if she had gone to the US maybe she could have been saved. I mean because I heard that there was more aid here. I told [my husband] if she had

Figure 1.5 Jesús Molina's second-grade school photograph, Yahualica, Jalisco, Mexico, 1989.

left, [to the United States] since she was from there, maybe over there she could have been treated."[81]

TRANSGENERATIONAL ILLEGALITY AS A LEGACY OF BANISHMENT

The exclusionary immigration laws and practices of the early twentieth century have had prolonged consequences. As the Rodríguez family's experience demonstrates, transgenerational illegality has emerged as one of the legacies of banishment. The exclusionary immigration law that led to Trinidad's banishment also rendered her son, Refugio, a tourist at best and unauthorized immigrant at worst—a fate that her grandson, Jesús, also had to contend with during his stay in the United States. In 2001, after their children had immigrated to the United States without inspection, Carmela and Refugio decided to apply for B-2 visitor visas to reunite with them. Those visas allowed the Molinas to spend a couple of months a year with some of their adult children living in the United States, but they did not grant permanent residency. Only citizenship and lawful permanent residency status provide permanent residence in the United States; all other visas grant only temporary legal status.

Trinidad's gender, as a banished woman, further delayed her access to derivative citizenship rights. In the United States, citizenship has historically been linked to paternity. Though the 1922 Cable Act and its 1930s amendments granted independent US citizenship to women, derivative citizenship remained a male privilege. It was not until 1934, when Congress enacted the Equal Nationality Act, that mothers gained the right to pass on their US citizenship to their children.[82] This 1934 act and later Nationality Acts required a certain number of years of physical presence to attain citizenship. The 1940 Nationality Act held that a child born to at least one US-citizen parent had the right to derivative citizenship. The parent, however, had to have been present in the United States for at least ten years, five of which had to be after the age of sixteen and before the child's birth.[83]

The residency requirement meant that banished Mexican Americans who had not been physically present in the United States because of their banishment and delayed return would be barred from derivative citizenship rights. This legislative limitation was contested in court. *In re Juan Becerra-Torres* (1969) held that children born abroad to at least one US-citizen parent had the right to derivative citizenship, even if the US-citizen parent had not accrued ten years of physically being present in the United States.[84] The decision in *In re Juan Becerra-Torres* granted this exception when an "official error" on the part of the US government had impeded continuous residence due to "erroneous exclusion."[85] Banishment and delayed return policies had led to Trinidad's erroneous exclusion, which had prevented her from meeting the five-year physical-presence requirement after her children's birth. *In re Juan Becerra-Torres* thus provides an important legal precedent for her descendants' fight to claim US citizenship rights.

The Rodríguez family's struggle to obtain derivative citizenship has been further complicated, however, by clerical mistakes that Mexican authorities made on Trinidad's identity documents. To file an immigration and naturalization petition with claims to derivative citizenship, Refugio must first prove on paper that Trinidad is a US citizen, and that he is in fact her son. If Refugio is successful in his claim for derivative citizenship, then he can open immigration petitions for his children, including Jesús. In a 2012 interview, Jesús explained the new set of legal obstacles his family has encountered:

> We have been meeting with an immigration lawyer in Los Angeles who is helping us with this case. I first started looking into this case about four years ago [in 2008], but we first met with the lawyer about three years ago [in 2009]. It has taken very long to get the case started because there are some documents that are incorrect, so the Mexican government must fix them, and it has now been more than a year to get that fixed and it is still not done. My grandma died in Mexico, and

her death certificate says she was born in Los Angeles, California, instead of Redlands, California. It also says she died at the age of forty, but she was fifty-eight. So, if we send the death certificate with those mistakes to the immigration office, they will think the person in the birth certificate is not the same as the one in the death certificate. These two mistakes have made the process very long and expensive. My parents who live in Mexico are trying to get the Presidencia in Yahualica to fix the death certificate, but they do not know the system well, and so it is taking even longer. I wish I could go myself and try to explain the situation and have the process completed, but because I am undocumented, I cannot leave the country and come back. It is really hard.[86]

The Yahualica city council's administrative error is likely due to the relative ease of spelling Los Angeles—a Spanish name that would have been easier to write for Spanish-speaking workers at the city council—instead of Redlands, Trinidad's place of birth. The Rodríguez family's private collection includes other Mexican identity documents belonging to Trinidad that could be helpful for Refugio's immigration petition, such as her *credencial permanente de elector* (voter identification card). But this card spelled "Redlands" as "Reglas," which is the Spanish word for rulers, among other things, and a much closer phonetic spelling for the US city's English name (Fig. 1.6). Such simple clerical mistakes at the local level in Mexico have caused legal delays on subsequent generations' immigration petitions in the United States. Collectively, these clerical errors continue to uphold the status quo classification of Refugio and Jesús as "removable" immigrants in the United States, the native country of their mother and grandmother.

Jesús and his family have had to learn to navigate two countries' relatively different legal systems—Mexico has a civil law system, while the United States has a common law system—in their attempts to be recognized legally in the United States. In Mexico, Trinidad's son, Refugio, had to open a costly lawsuit against the city clerk who filed Trinidad's death certificate incorrectly. In order to verify the information in the corrections, the city must dig in the archives for the original

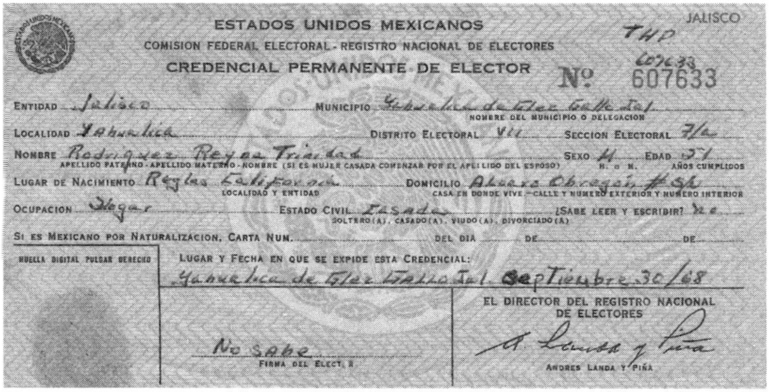
ESTADOS UNIDOS MEXICANOS
COMISION FEDERAL ELECTORAL - REGISTRO NACIONAL DE ELECTORES
CREDENCIAL PERMANENTE DE ELECTOR
JALISCO
THP
Nº 607633

Entidad: Jalisco
Municipio: Yahualica de Glez Gallo Jal. — Nombre del municipio o delegacion
Localidad: Yahualica
Distrito Electoral: VII
Seccion Electoral: 7/a
Nombre: Rodriguez Reyes Trinidad — Apellido paterno - apellido materno - nombre (si es mujer casada comenzar por el apellido del esposo)
Sexo: H (H. o M.)
Edad: 71 (años cumplidos)
Lugar de Nacimiento: Reglas California — Localidad y entidad
Domicilio: Alvaro Obregón #56 — Casa en donde vive.—calle y numero exterior y numero interior
Ocupacion: Hogar
Estado Civil: Casado — Soltero(a), casado(a), viudo(a), divorciado(a)
¿Sabe leer y escribir? No
Si es Mexicano por Naturalizacion, Carta Num. ____ del dia ____ de ____ de ____
Huella digital pulgar derecho
Lugar y Fecha en que se expide esta Credencial: Yahualica de Glez Gallo Jal. Septiembre 30/68
No sabe.
Firma del elector
El Director del Registro Nacional de Electores
A. Landa y Piña
Andres Landa y Piña

Figure 1.6 Trinidad Rodríguez's *credencial permanente de elector* (voter identification card), Yahualica, Jalisco, Mexico, 1968.

records, search local newspaper archives for mortuaries, and interview family and community members. Very little progress has been made since Refugio filed the lawsuit, and the fees and charges continue to accumulate.

Refugio and his wife have been unable to establish permanent residence in his mother's home country because there is no direct path to legalization for children of banished US citizens who cannot meet the US-presence requirement under the 1940 Nationality Act due to their banishment. Three generations later, banishment continues to enforce a transgenerational illegality on Trinidad's family, who remain separated across the US-Mexico border and must now live as a transnational family.

LIVING WITH THE LEGACIES OF BANISHMENT

The Rodríguezes often remember Trinidad during family get-togethers, when they share stories about the family's migration journeys. The passport-size photograph on Trinidad's Mexican background check has become a central part of how the family remembers her. That document, when read alongside other documents in the family's private collection, also reveals that Trinidad secured a background check in order to request her visitor visa to the United States, the one that would allow her to obtain a copy of her birth certificate from the city council in her native Redlands, California. Though she could have reclaimed her US citizenship by obtaining a copy of her birth certificate in a US consulate in Mexico, Trinidad was unaware that this was even an option. Trinidad was not alone in her struggle. In the early twentieth century, many banished people were barred from returning to the United States for decades, while others were unable to return because of bureaucratic delays.

Trinidad's forced removal decades ago not only separated her from her blood relatives, but also continues to separate her family members two generations later. Today, Trinidad's son Refugio and his wife Carmela still live in Mexico with five of their ten children. Their other five daughters and sons are now living in the United States and have formed families of their own. They remain divided by the US-Mexico border as a direct result of Trinidad's banishment and the Mexican government's legal errors after she and her children were robbed of their right to derivative citizenship. Moreover, Trinidad's multiple identities as a working-class woman of Mexican descent resulted in a triple oppression that outweighed all the benefits her US citizenship could have afforded her. While the transnational agreements between the Mexican and US governments facilitated Trinidad's banishment, decades later, legal errors by both governments continue to deny her children and grandchildren lawful recognition and integration. Trinidad's children and grandchildren inherited a transgenerational illegality that forces them to experience the legacies of banishment in the flesh.

The "Mexican problem" discourse that US officials used to banish Trinidad was directed toward mixed-status Mexican families who had conformed to Americanization pressures in the 1920s, legalized their status, and had US-citizen children. Yet no cultural adaptation, loyalty, and legal ties to the United States could prevent them from being forcibly removed from their homeland, as was the case for the De Anda family whose story we will turn to in Chapter 2. As US officials discursively racialized and legally classified all working-class ethnic Mexicans as undesirable and removable, they condemned the future family members of the banished women to a state of indiscriminate, prolonged transgenerational illegality.

CHAPTER TWO

THE DE ANDA FAMILY

Cultural Liminality

A hand-colored photograph of the De Anda family from circa 1925 captures their unity and cultural adaptation to the United States. Dimas De Anda's stylish finger-wave hairstyle, her husband's three-piece suit, and their children's shingle-bob haircuts transport the viewer to the popular fashion of the interwar period (Fig. 2.1). During this historical conjuncture, spanning the end of World War I to the start of World War II, US employers and industries identified working-class ethnic Mexicans as "desirable" in their capacity as laborers who would help industrialize the American Southwest, even as mainstream representations of Mexicans cast suspicion on their presence based on their assumed un-Americanness. Mothers often carried the responsibility to help their families navigate these contradictory social and political terrains. The De Anda family portrait and Dimas's pose in it symbolize the significant role of motherhood during the interwar period. Dimas stands with both hands slightly extended in opposite directions: her left hand rests on her daughter Guadalupe's shoulder, and her right hand gently holds her husband's shoulder. Cleto sits and holds his youngest son, Esteban, on his lap. Their three daughters stand in front of the couple from tallest to shortest: on the far right, Guadalupe holds Consuelo's arm; in the middle, Consuelo's arm, in turn, softly touches her father's left leg; and on the left, Virginia smiles as she rests her hand on her father's right knee. Their pose aptly forms a circle, representing their family unity as they hold onto each other. Dimas, as the mother and wife, stands tall in the center of the circle, visually embodying the glue that holds their family together. While the photographer likely staged the family's pose for the portrait, Dimas's role in maintaining the unity of the family was accurately captured.

The De Anda family portrait hung on their living room wall in Roseville, California, throughout the second half of the 1920s, showcasing their Americanization and hard-earned lower-middle-class status. During the first two decades of twentieth century, when the United States was reorganizing its racial hierarchies amid continuing and emerging immigration restrictions, a triad of interests—employers, restrictionists, and Americanization social reformers—championed conflicting ideological and policy positions on Mexican immigration and the place of Mexican Americans in the nation. These three groups had radically different objectives, none of which included the full integration of ethnic Mexicans into the US national fabric. Employers generally advocated for unrestricted Mexican immigration and opposed mass removals, resulting in the rapid increase of the Mexican population at the turn of the twentieth century. These tactics allowed employers to maintain a large source of cheap labor to control wages and disrupt labor strikes. Restrictionists, composed mainly of organized labor and nativists, insisted on limiting Mexican immigration and supported mass removals of ethnic Mexicans already living in the United States. Their agenda supported the mass banishment of Mexican Americans during the Depression. And social reformers, as I will explore in depth in this chapter, invested in the production of loyal and docile ethnic Mexican employees who would assimilate into American ways of life.[1]

Before arriving in the United States, Dimas and Cleto met and fell in love in their native San Juan de los Lagos in Jalisco, Mexico. Shortly after their 1918 marriage, the newlyweds emigrated and were legally admitted to the United States, where Cleto worked laying tracks for the

Figure 2.1 Portrait of the De Anda family, Roseville, California, circa 1925.

Southern Pacific Railroad in California. The family came to the United
States as part of the labor recruitments orchestrated by employers during
the first Bracero Program (1917–1921). While the Mexican government
offered repatriation to destitute ethnic Mexicans in the years following
the US economic recession in 1918, American employers still needed

cheap labor, so they organized a controlled system to recruit Mexican workers for low wages. The De Anda family, along with thousands of other recruited Mexicans, thus established themselves in the United States and had US-citizen children. These families became the focus of Americanization programs in California from 1913 to 1929. Social reformers sought to produce loyal workers, prepare women for domestic labor, and train mothers to impose American values on their children. Americanization reformers targeted Mexican women in particular because they were understood to be in charge of their family's socialization. Despite the success of these programs, the unforeseen economic downturn that spiraled into the Great Depression shifted the political pendulum toward exclusion.

The Great Depression brought the economic progress of the Roaring Twenties to a halt, which allowed the growing efforts of restrictionists to prevail over those of social reformers who advocated for Americanization.[2] Ironically, the very railroad tracks that Cleto helped build and maintain were used to banish his family by train, eleven years after they had arrived in the United States. In 1929, at the beginning of the Depression, Cleto was laid off and enlisted for removal. Because he was the head of the household, and the legacies of coverture doctrine still rendered minors and women as economic dependents of the male head of their household, the removal order meant that his wife, Dimas, and their seven US-citizen children were banished, too.

Dimas had no other option. She packed a few of her family's belongings into two large suitcases and, with Cleto and their children by her side, boarded a train bound for Mexico. Once there, they had to negotiate the pressures of assimilation yet again, but this time to become more culturally Mexican. Like many other banished families, the De Andas were shamed for their broken Spanish as well as their American fashion and customs. Schools and private citizens pressured banished families like theirs to Mexicanize. Consuelo and Virginia were only seven and six years old, respectively, at the time of their banishment. Still, they held on dearly to their memories of life in the United States, which their mother helped preserve during the next two decades they spent in Mexico.

Despite the demands of conformity, Dimas—and even more so the couple's American-born children—held on to the hope of returning to the United States, which they considered home. The De Anda sisters fought unwaveringly to reclaim their citizenship and resettle in their native California against all odds. Those plans were realized when Virginia, the third-eldest daughter, went back to the United States with the help of family and friends after spending twenty-one years in Mexico. Two years later, Consuelo joined her sister in California. They later helped their other US-citizen siblings and mother make a similar journey. But their father would not join them; he refused to ever set foot again in the country that had ousted him. Though the family never forgot the injustice of their banishment, they buried their history of exclusion and for decades kept it secret from the younger generations. They preferred to shield their own family members from the pain and alienation they had experienced in Mexico and the United States.

In the United States, ethnic Mexicans were perceived as foreigners, regardless of their legal status, cultural identity, and class status. But after they were banished to Mexico, ethnic Mexican families were labeled as foreigners yet again and had to contend with pressures to Mexicanize. This chapter draws from the oral histories of three generations of the De Anda family, their personal collection, and institutional primary sources to examine how ethnic Mexicans navigated othering and marginalization on both sides of the US-Mexico borderlands and to identify how Mexican women and their Mexican American children found ways to strategically carve out their own spaces of belonging (Fig. 2.2).

The De Anda family's story reveals how some banished women adopted both Americanization and Mexicanization as strategic political maneuvers to protect themselves and their families. Nevertheless, their Americanization did not outweigh the power of racialized claims that they were likely to become a public charge and other narratives about unemployed ethnic Mexicans that relief agencies in the United States

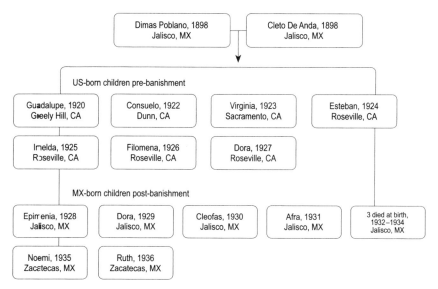

Figure 2.2 The De Anda family's pre- and post-banishment family tree. Graphic by author based on data provided by the De Anda Family.

circulated during the Depression. Similarly, Mexicanization did not guarantee their full social and legal integration in Mexico. Banishment disrupted the upward economic, social, and political trajectories of the De Anda family, who—like many other mixed-status Mexican families—were finding ways to integrate into life in US society. Indeed, their displacement racialized the De Andas as foreigners, shrouding the family in a kind of transgenerational illegality that impaired their upward mobility and interrupted the accumulation of wealth for generations of their descendants (Fig. 2.3).

The economic scapegoating of ethnic Mexicans in the United States accompanied their racialization as people who needed to be excluded for the sake of white American workers. The promise of integration for those who had followed Americanization teachings—a promise that was widely propagated during the 1920s—faded a decade later. The economic downturn during the Great Depression marked even the most

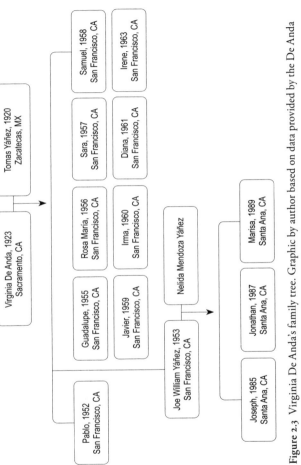

Figure 2.3 Virginia De Anda's family tree. Graphic by author based on data provided by the De Anda Family.

Americanized ethnic Mexicans with a state-imposed illegality. These racial narratives projected notions of illegality onto ethnic Mexicans, regardless of their legal status, and made them vulnerable to mass state-sanctioned banishment.

THE FIRST BRACERO PROGRAM

The De Anda family's history in the United States began in 1918, when Dimas Poblano and Cleto De Anda left Mexico to escape their families' opposition to their marriage. Cleto's family rejected his marriage to Dimas because she came from a working-class family. Joe explained that his grandfather Cleto's family was "in charge of overseeing something like ten haciendas . . . so they had a lot of money."[3] Cleto's grandparents, who raised him, wanted their grandson to marry into a well-to-do family to maintain and increase their wealth. As Virginia De Anda explained: "They met and got married, and three months later they crossed the border. My parents never planned to come here [to the United States], but they decided to migrate because of my [paternal] grandparents, who never saw my mom in a good light and always fought with her. And my mom's dad did not accept my dad as part of the family either."[4]

In the early twentieth century, Mexicans fled Mexico for various reasons, including economic and political stability, refuge from war, family reunification, and adventure. The Mexican Revolution of 1910 and the Cristero War (1926–1929) contributed to the rapid increase of Mexican refugees from diverse socioeconomic backgrounds.[5] In Dimas and Cleto's case, emigration was a revolutionary act of love. But their decision to immigrate to California was also influenced by employment recruitment under the first Bracero Program (1917–1921), which reflected the United States' need for temporary Mexican workers to address labor shortages during World War I, develop and maintain the railroad system, and industrialize the US Southwest.[6] As their story illustrates, while individual decision-making is part of the immigration journey, it is often guided by larger social and political forces. In general, upon their arrival to the United States, Mexicans—regardless of class status, educational background, and skillset—were primarily employed in the mining, agriculture, construction, and railroad industries.[7] That is, immigration to the United States regularly resulted in downward economic mobility for those who were not already lower-working-class Mexican immigrants.

When Dimas and Cleto arrived in California as twenty-year-old newlyweds, they were part of the largest wave of Mexican immigration to the United States until that time. In the years between 1910 and 1930, historians estimate that roughly one million Mexicans immigrated to the United States.[8] This large increase began as a carefully organized movement to supply the US Southwest with a substantial labor force from Mexico's central plateau region, and the first Bracero Program intensified this. The first guestworker program alone drew in approximately 73,000 Mexican men, as well as an unknown number of wives and children who followed some of them.[9] This approach to securing cheap labor became a model for establishing other recruitment initiatives throughout the first half of the twentieth century, including the official transnational Bracero Program of 1942–1964, which strengthened the disposability of this workforce. The railroad network that linked central Mexico to the US-Mexico border region, and the railroad lines that connected the border to the US interior, enabled the transnational hiring.[10] The Mexican National Railway, which was used to recruit and transport *braceros* (literally, *arm laborers*) from central Mexico to the United States, had a passenger station in San Juan de los Lagos, Jalisco, where Dimas and Cleto lived until 1918.[11] They experienced firsthand the operational processes of this organized transnational movement of workers long before they joined it.

At the turn of the century, US employers began relying heavily on contractors and *reenganchadores,* as they were known in Spanish. Before he became a social welfare worker who reported to the INS, Cleofas Calleros had worked for the Santa Fe Railroad and had personal insight into the hiring process. He explained, "*Reenganchadores* were agencies which hired Mexicans to work for the railroads, especially the Santa Fe, the Southern Pacific, and the G.H. and S.A."[12] The *reenganchadores* worked in El Paso, Texas, hiring Mexican immigrants as they exited the immigration inspection office. After they signed contracts, Mexican workers were transported to companies throughout the Southwest and Midwest. The recruitment process, however, often began with US contractors in central Mexico. A 1910 detailed report conducted by Immigration Inspector Frank R. Stone described the meticulously organized recruitment strategies that enticed Mexicans to emigrate and join the labor ranks in the United States:

> On the Guadalajara Division of the Mexican National Railway, running from Guadalajara to Irapuato, in the state of Jalisco, my investigation discloses the fact that it was a common occurrence for the labor contractor from the United States to stand on the rear platform of a North-bound train and as it passed through the various villages, at the depots of which were gathered a great many laborers employed on the adjacent haciendas, exhort these laborers to come to the United States, depicting the conditions obtaining and the comparatively high wages paid there; and this agent would later collect such peons as desired to come to the United States shipping them out in large gangs, paying their transportation to Juárez; even furnishing their bridge toll over the Rio Grande to El Paso; giving them instructions regarding the responses they should make to questions asked them by our officers.[13]

Dimas and Cleto grew up listening to the rumbling tracks, humming engine, and blowing whistle of the train as it approached their town. The buzzing activity of US recruiters and their neighbors' emigration journeys to the United States were all too familiar. Dimas and Cleto watched it all happen as children, and then they too departed on one of those trains to the United States, becoming part of this contract-labor enterprise that had deep roots in Mexico.

Laws changed quickly at the turn of the century to regulate new immigration movements and contract labor. In the early 1900s, US immigration flows shifted from northern and western Europe toward the more impoverished regions of southern and eastern Europe, prompting legislators to rethink the nation's immigration laws. The 1907 Immigration Act, which modified the 1903 Immigration Act with more immigration restrictions and regulations, cited LPC claims to make it more difficult to legally admit southern and eastern Europeans to the United States for contract work. Asian exclusion laws further contributed to labor shortages.[14] Enacted three years prior to Stone's report, the Immigration Act of 1907 made immigrants inadmissible based on ability, health, criminal record, class status (LPC), and gender (morality).[15] The new immigration law also barred "contract laborers who have been induced or solicited to migrate to this country by offers or promises of employment or in consequence of agreements, oral, written or printed, express or implied, to perform labor in this country of any kind, skilled or unskilled."[16] These restrictions, however, were principally concerned with the regulation of European and Asian immigration. Immigration officers, under pressure from employers who needed the labor, often turned a blind eye to the recruitment of Mexican immigrant workers. As F. W. Berkshire—the supervising inspector for the Immigration Service in El Paso, the major port of entry for Mexican immigrants at the time—reluctantly admitted, "The contract labor law has been flagrantly and openly violated in the past and . . . Mexican immigration was largely solicited a few years ago."[17] Immigration officers often used their discretion, not the letter of the law, to regulate Mexican immigration and labor.

A year before Dimas and Cleto immigrated to the United States, the Immigration Act of 1917 had placed significant restrictions on Mexican immigration for the first time. But persistent labor needs resulted in an official exemption for Mexican immigrants who had arrived to work in railroad, agriculture, maintenance, and mining. The waiver, in place from 1918 to 1921, permitted the heavy recruitment of Mexican immigrant workers under the first Bracero Program.[18] A 1909 report that Berkshire sent from his immigration post at El Paso, Texas, to his supervisor in Washington, DC, as well as other, similar labor data, undoubtedly informed the temporary Mexican exemption to the 1917 Immigration Act. Berkshire wrote: "We can exclude practically all of the Mexican aliens of the laboring class [on LPC grounds, yet] we know that any able-bodied man who may be admitted can immediately secure transportation to a point on the railroad where employment will be furnished him."[19] That is, though all Mexicans could theoretically be excluded under the Immigration Act of 1917, the fact that they had jobs awaiting them in the United States eliminated their likelihood to become a public charge and therefore granted them exemptions from the law. The new immigration restrictions, then, did not impede Cleto from securing a labor contract and entering the United States, in part due to the careful instructions that recruiters provided for the immigration interrogations—but they did relegate him and other ethnic Mexicans to the status of temporary and disposable workers. This process effectively marked Cleto and Dimas with an impermanent legality: while they were legally admitted into the country, Dimas and Cleto could still be removed when no longer needed. The disposability and impermanent legality of ethnic Mexicans became unstated and unofficial requirements of their legal entry.

The legal admission process was relatively easy for Mexican immigrants because the United States had become dependent on their labor. Essentially, the desirability of Mexican immigrants granted their legality even when it was impermanent. As Calleros explained, "All you had to do coming from Mexico, if you were a Mexican citizen, was to report at the immigration office on the American side—give your name, the place of your birth, and where you were going. That's all you needed."[20] Virginia further described the relative ease with which her parents, Dimas and Cleto, had lawfully crossed the US-Mexico border: "During that time, it was really easy to emigrate. The only requirement was to pay one cent that supposedly was used as a record to know how many people crossed the border into the United States. That was the only requirement, to pay one cent and to know how to read and write. . . . My dad went to school and my mom's stepmother taught her to read and write because her mom died when she was four years old. . . . So [when my parents] emigrated, they crossed the border legally."[21] Joe added, "My grandfather . . . learned to read and write. He was well educated. You never saw him without a book in his hand; it was either a book or a bible, always reading."[22]

Though the admission process was initially relatively simple, and the 1918–1921 exemption allowed most Mexicans to bypass the restrictions of the 1917 Immigration Act, the Immigration Service formalized the new regulation processes at the US-Mexico border soon after the new law went into effect. But regulation was not uniform: whether legal admission was granted fell to the individual discretion of the immigration officer on duty.[23] Dimas and Cleto's ability to read and write probably allowed them to pass the literacy test, if the inspecting officer required them to take it. The medical exam, however, was required of all working-class immigrants because the new law coincided with the outbreak of the influenza epidemic in the US-Mexico border region. The outbreak solidified fears promoted by restrictionists that immigrant bodies were associated with disease. Based on a subjective visual analysis, arriving upper-class immigrants were separated from the laboring class, and only the working-class immigrants underwent the humiliating medical examination: they were stripped of their clothing and baggage, which were fumigated while they were bathed, deloused, and vaccinated by the Public Health Service.[24] Legal admission did not guarantee equity or even humanity, a reality made clear during the degrading inspection process.

Starting in 1917, the Immigration Bureau began documenting ethnic Mexicans through identification photographs as part of increased surveillance measures at the US-Mexico border. During their 1918 immigration inspection, Dimas and Cleto were among the first ethnic Mexicans to be visually recorded (Fig. 2.4). The visual documentation system that officials used had first been tested with Chinese migrants. In 1909, federal law required photographic identification, but only for Chinese immigrants and Chinese Americans (with an exception for diplomats). Eight years later, new arrivals at the US-Mexico border were also photographed to prevent the Chinese from entering the country disguised as Mexicans.[25] These visual records positioned ethnic Mexicans as racial outsiders whose difference required state scrutiny.[26] Photographic identification became a tool to observe, regulate, and racialize the nonwhite immigrant's body. As Anna Pegler-Gordon argues, "Immigrants were photographed because they were viewed as different, but they were also viewed as different because they were photographed."[27]

The photographic record-keeping of immigrants of color became central to the "national gaze" that racialized them as the "other," and thus visually and legally equated US citizenship with whiteness.[28] Thus, as Coco Fusco has argued, "Rather than *recording* the existence of race, photography *produced* race as a visual fact."[29] The photographs were not objective visual records, but rather the very means through which racialized Mexican subjectivities were produced and reproduced. In fact, "in the Immigration Bureau's exclusionary logic of identity, one could not look both Mexican and American."[30] Thus, one's racial phenotype visually reassured or denied claims to US citizenship. To the gaze of US immigration officials, "looking" Mexican unsettled any claims to American-ness. Immigration officials and restrictions saw photographic documentation as promising visual objectivity.[31] These photographs later became one more tool in the vast official US repertoire that not only visually projected assumptions of illegality onto nonwhite people, including ethnic Mexicans, but also justified mass banishment—a removal process that happened only after the labor of ethnic Mexicans, including the De Andas, had helped to industrialize the Southwest and improve economic sectors throughout the nation.

After disembarking from the train at the US-Mexico border, and after their immigration inspection, having their photographs taken, and documented for legal admission, Mexican immigrants had to select an employer. *Reenganchadores* representing ranches and railroads waited behind the immigration office to lure as many Mexicans as possible to work for their companies. The interconnected financial interests of the agriculture and railroad industries in California, and by extension nationwide, profited from the underpaid labor of Mexican workers. A California agriculture study found that "the state ships one-third of the nation's truck crop, one-half of its fresh fruit, nearly all its dried fruit, [and] 70 percent of its canned fruit and vegetables. Of all perishables carried on the nation's railroads one-third originates in California."[32] Mexicans not only picked and canned fruits and vegetables in California; they also contributed to the development and maintenance of railroad lines that shipped this food throughout the nation.

The first Bracero Program effectively turned ethnic Mexicans of diverse socioeconomic backgrounds, skillsets, and educational levels into underpaid laborers who enriched multiple US industries with their hard work. This highly lucrative venture on the American side produced an intricate labor recruitment process. As an official from El Paso described it, after arriving immigrants applied for admission, "guards would escort the men outside to the rear of the building and line them up. The agents representing the railroads and the ranches would make speeches about the delightful quarters, good pay and fine food they would have if they went to work for their company. When the promising was over, the agents would shout, 'This way for the Santa Fe,' 'This way for the Southern Pacific,' and so on, the men following the agent they thought offered the best of most benefits."[33] Once immigrants selected an employer, the railroads transported them across the entire Southwest and Midwest to fulfill their roles as members of a profitable labor force. All Mexicans recruited to work in the United States under this labor enterprise were thus racialized as immigrants fit only for backbreaking and seemingly unskilled occupations.

The hiring method used from 1910 to 1929, the years leading up to and shortly following the first Bracero Program, helped determine the settlement patterns of Mexican communities in the United States. The railroads transferred workers and their families by the trainload from the border to places like California, Arizona, Kansas, and Illinois.[34] A man from Jalisco and one from Aguascalientes, for instance, were hired as *traqueros* (trackmen) by *reenganchadores* and sent to Arizona. One explained, "the work was heavy, but we got used to it."[35] The other disagreed: "The work was so hard that I thought I was going to die."[36] The demanding labor forced some to find alternative employment prospects, while others managed to remain in the railroad industry for prolonged periods. Of the numerous Mexican immigrants sent to California to lay tracks and construct roadbeds, many remained in the region to fill track-maintenance positions, while others later found employment in mining and agriculture.[37] Cleto and Dimas followed the California route and stayed in the railroad industry for a few years before finding alternative employment. As Virginia recalls, "I used to hear that when they first arrived in the US [my dad] worked laying tracks . . . in Northern California."[38] During the years that Cleto worked laying tracks for the Southern Pacific Railroad, Dimas made a home for their family in the boxcar that the company had assigned them.

Dimas's experience as the wife of a railroad track worker signaled a key difference from earlier recruitment practices that initially required Mexican male workers to leave their families behind. During the late nineteenth and early twentieth centuries, Mexicans recruited to lay and maintain tracks mainly arrived as unaccompanied men. The company gave railroad workers free train passes to go see their families in Mexico twice a year, but not until they had provided at least six months of service.[39] At the turn of the century, however, it became customary for Mexican railroad workers to arrive in the United States with their families. The Dillingham Commission, established by the US Senate to study immigrant conditions at the national level, examined hiring practices for railroad workers. Based on data collected from nine railroads in the West Coast, the commission found that between 1907 and 1909, 58.2 percent of Mexican wives were living with their railroad-employed husbands. This was an extraordinarily high percentage compared to European and Asian railway workers in the same region and period. The study concluded, based more on racial biases than actual evidence, that "the conditions under which section hands live are less uninviting to the Mexican women than to the women of any other race."[40] These types of immigration studies, frequently conducted at the turn of the century, helped cement stereotypes about Mexicans having lower expectations for living standards, wages, and labor conditions. Guided by the need to generate a continual supply of dependent workers, US employers hired men accompanied by their families, particularly during the early 1900s.[41] Employers were banking on the key assumption that a head of household's concern with providing for his family would make him less likely to leave a job, even when the wages and conditions were undesirable. Biases in immigration studies conducted by the federal government, along with employers' recruitment tactics, confined Mexican immigrants to the cheap labor sector. Their wives had to make ends meet with their husbands' low wages and make a home in substandard living conditions.

Like agricultural laborers, railroad workers led migratory lives. Track laborers and their kin moved from one boxcar community to the next, following the labor demands along the train lines.[42] Calleros recalled that starting in the early 1910s, "families that went along with their husbands were given old boxcars, which were converted as living quarters. They were called bunk houses, and the railroad usually had them in isolated whistle stops."[43] The isolation of these boxcar communities made workers and their families reliant on services the employers provided. Families purchased their provisions from the commissary and obtained healthcare from company doctors, for prices that were usually inflated. Mexicans were promised a good salary, food, and shelter to work as *traqueros*. In fact, as one of the workers recalls, "the food was scanty and poor and we were all crowded in a [box]car, we were like pigs. Then, I found out that the foreman robbed all the workers of their money by means of the commissary store and that whoever got mad or complained was locked up and beaten."[44] Track families could easily become trapped in debt peonage and labor abuse. Saving money to buy land or moving to a different job were challenging, especially because occupation advancement was limited for Mexicans. For instance, train mechanic and crew boss positions that paid higher wages were usually reserved for white Americans.[45]

While their husbands built railroad tracks, Mexican women constructed communities of resiliency. Women relied on the support from their families and their *comadres* to make ends meet. The wives of railroad workers contributed to their household incomes through informal markets. Dimas and many like her took up sewing, gardening, and laundry jobs to supplement their husbands' salaries. Other women opened their homes to boarders and worked as wet nurses. Sometimes two families would live in a boxcar or a couple of single men would rent a room from a railroad family. Women often leaned on their farming knowledge, which they acquired while living in rural communities in Mexico or working in US agriculture. Women and children tended to vegetable gardens and barnyard animals, which provided fresh produce, dairy, and eggs. The food that women and children produced reduced their families' dependency on the commissary. *Comadres* traded food from their gardens with each other and came together to raise their children in community. When one matriarch was in need, other women from the railroad community came to her aid. Migrant families survived and thrived in part due to the unsung contributions of women.[46] Dimas's resiliency and informal labor allowed her husband to save a portion of his wages to invest in their future.

After five years of migrant work as a railroad family and having saved some money, the De Andas decided to find a place to settle permanently. The birth of their three daughters in different locations across the state reflected their migratory labor experience: Guadalupe was born in Greeley Hill, California, in 1920; Consuelo, in Dunn, California, in 1922; and Virginia, in Sacramento, California, in 1923. The De Andas chose Roseville, California—twenty miles northeast of Sacramento—

as the place to raise their family. The ongoing industrialization of the US Southwest was transforming Roseville when they settled there. In 1905, it was a mere railroad junction of the northbound and eastbound lines of the Southern Pacific Railroad, but by 1920, Roseville had become the most important shipping terminal of the Southwest.[47] In 1913, Roseville was selected as the home of the Pacific Fruit Express building, the "world's largest ice manufacturing plant," which manufactured the ice used to refrigerate railroad cars that carried produce such as peaches, pears, and plums nationwide. The plant had an approximate storage capacity of 11,000 tons of ice, with the potential to produce two hundred tons a day.[48] Cleto was employed at this ice plant. According to Joe, after his grandfather left his railroad position, he worked "at an icehouse for a while and then he worked at a mine, a silver mine."[49] By 1923, California agriculture had significantly expanded, and specialty crops produced in the Imperial, Coachella, and Salinas Valleys were in demand by Midwest and East Coast markets. The use of refrigerated railcars allowed the transportation of diverse crops like lettuce, potatoes, beans, carrots, celery, artichokes, and broccoli through the railroad system that connected the West and East Coasts.[50] As California became the primary supplier of US food, ethnic Mexicans who worked for the railroad, agriculture, and the Pacific Fruit Express helped feed the nation.

In 1923, the De Anda family deepened their US roots when they bought a house in Roseville, California. By then, Charles Decater, a Roseville house-moving and real estate businessman, had relocated numerous houses within the town to make way for the construction of new railroad tracks. Decater, who was in business from 1906 to 1940, also moved houses from other towns to rent and sell to the large number of workers who came to Roseville during the town's economic boom.[51] Dimas and Cleto purchased a relocated house, likely moved by Decater's company. As Joe explained, "The house had been brought from some other location and they put a foundation, and then put the house down, and my grandfather bought it. But, for [my mom], it was like a palace because she can still describe all the fruit trees in the back and the entrance with the flowers as you came in."[52] Virginia added with great enthusiasm, "It was so pretty! An excellent house. It had three rooms and a restroom."[53] Eventually Dimas and Cleto had one son and three additional daughters, for a total of seven US-born children. Their decision to become homeowners symbolically marked their settlement and claims to belonging in their children's native country. Virginia and her siblings cherish the memories of their Roseville home because it granted a sense of stability. Emblematic of their integration, they removed the identification photograph that captured Dimas and Cleto's 1918 arrival to the United States from their immigration document and hung it on the living room wall of their new home.

Families often challenged the authority of immigration photographs by using the pictures for their own purposes. The photographic identification requirements imposed by the US Bureau of Immigration also became evidence of a person's migration across the border, since everyone who was photographed was given a copy of the image. In some cases, those snapshots included family members, since the bureau photographed entire groups of families who crossed together. These images became central to the families' visual and archival record of migration. Often, they provided the only evidence and reminder of loved ones and their fateful journey across the divide. The immigration photo of Cleto and Dimas in 1918 is one of the few surviving images of them together. In it, the couple appears side by side, with heads slightly touching, making for an intimate picture of the newlyweds (Fig. 2.4). Dimas's hair is pulled back and both she and Cleto look directly at the camera. The photograph, meant to freeze in time every detail of their "racial otherness," also manages to convey their humanity and history. As of this writing, more than one hundred years later, the picture is treasured by the family as a special part of their shared history. Exceeding the frame of a state-controlled visual record, this identification photograph from the De Anda family's private collection not

Figure 2.4 Immigration photograph of Dimas Poblano (*left*) and Cleto De Anda (*right*) at the US-Mexico border, 1918.

only dates the beginnings of the family's roots in the United States, but also reminds the family of their parents' love story and why they came to this country.

Photographs as visual records capture and help recall numerous stories passed on from generation to generation in the form of oral traditions. As oral historians have demonstrated, the photography-memory relationship can inform the writing of history, because photographs are essentially linked with memories.[54] Dimas and Cleto's image, too, has helped family members to recall, connect with, and preserve the family history. When I talked with Virginia and her younger sister, Consuelo, about their family's history of migration and banishment, they brought out their parents' photograph and placed it on the table. In many instances, the picture seemed to refresh Virginia and Consuelo's memories about their parents' migration and the family's subsequent banishment. They often pointed to it as they recounted specific moments of their parents' experiences. In the oral history context, photographs can become powerful descriptors of the past and bring their subjects into the present.[55] Visually and symbolically, this image of Virginia and Consuelo's parents became part of the interview process and the perpetuation of the family's history.

GENDERED APPROACHES TO AMERICANIZATION

While employers heavily recruited Mexicans to the United States, social reformers coordinated their amalgamation into the "melting pot." Official Americanization programs emerged at the turn of the century as a development of the Progressive Era's reform movements.[56] Social reformers were primarily middle-class and affluent white Protestant women driven by the social settlement and social gospel movements. They viewed education as a tool to convert immigrants into English-speaking, Americanized, and highly patriotic new citizens. These women embodied their presumed God-given role as social moral guardians.[57] The Americanization programs were originally designed to help millions of allegedly unassimilable immigrants from southern and eastern Europe become more American in behavior and culture. In 1912, New York established the Bureau of Industries and Immigration, becoming the first state to regulate the domestic behavior of immigrants. While Americanization efforts began on the East Coast, they reached California in 1913, at a time when both the Mexican American population and Mexican immigration to the region were on the rise. California's demographic shift made it a perfect case study for Americanization initiatives driven by state, religious, and private organizations.[58] Social reformers viewed Mexican women as central to the family unit, and thus key to ensuring their families' cultural allegiance to the United States given their assigned roles as the transmitters of culture and values.[59] Reformers invested in the social integration of immigrant families, but only when the economy was stable or on the rise. As a result, ethnic Mexican social and legal integration was impermanent, with ethnic Mexicans welcomed as desirable only when conditions were good but derided as undesirable and foreign during economic crises. In the early 1900s, the United States enjoyed a strong economy. Thus ethnic Mexicans were considered suitable members of the nation, but only if they Americanized.

From 1913 to 1929, Americanization efforts in California focused on immigrant women as a way to assimilate entire family units. The De Anda family and hundreds of other mixed-status Mexican families were the targets of these Americanization efforts. Social reformers aimed to eradicate the "Mexican problem" by offering work trainings, teaching Protestant religious values, and implementing lessons in hygiene, citizenship, and civics. The 1910 California election of progressive governor Hiram W. Johnson helped to institutionalize Americanization programs in the state. He had the support of most of the state legislature, whose majority comprised progressive Republicans and pro-labor Democrats.[60] In 1913, Governor Johnson followed New York's lead by establishing the California Commission of Immigration and Housing (CCIH) under the Department of Industrial Relations, charging it with investigating "the conditions under which immigrants are housed and employed."[61] But the CCIH's investigative powers extended to "all things affecting immigrants within the confines of the State, particularly their care, protection and welfare."[62] The paternalistic mission created a hierarchical relationship with the communities they served, yet the efforts continued in earnest with the support of local and state leaders. To cover its wide scope, the CCIH opened offices in Los Angeles, Fresno, Sacramento, and San Francisco, but the commission conducted studies and provided services in urban and rural areas across the state. The CCIH—composed of five unpaid commissioners—operated with a generous allocation of $50,000 in state funds for their initial assignments from 1913 to 1915. An executive officer ran the San Francisco office and oversaw the taskforce by implementing the commission's recommended policies.[63]

California soon surpassed Americanization efforts in New York and other states by developing a strategy that brought together government, business, and private citizens to assimilate ethnic Mexicans.[64] After conducting a series of studies, the CCIH recommended and implemented English lessons, adult education, and recreational activities, transforming California into the national leader in Americanization efforts.[65] The CCIH recruited academics, religious social workers, government representatives, and middle-class volunteers to help the commission on its mission to remove immigrants' "handicaps incidental upon their ignorance of language, laws and customs and to see to it that the immigrant and his family are given every opportunity of acquiring education, security, and eventually citizenship."[66] Unlike during the social-settlement response to European immigrants prior to World War I, the CCIH did not highlight the "immigrant gifts" that Mexicans brought to American society.[67] Instead, the commission, employers, and legislators often described Mexican immigrants with derogatory language, as evident in the CCIH mission statement.

Ethnic Mexican families' economic and living conditions were often blamed on their social behavior, as opposed to their exploitation as workers. In one of its first studies, the commission examined the living quarters that employers provided for migrant families. A 1914 camp inspection revealed that housing arrangements were "unspeakably bad throughout the state" due to contaminated water supplies, unsanitary toilet facilities, and limited or no heating, cooling, or ventilation.[68] The report also revealed that camps were often located in areas prone to flooding and infestations. The commission lacked legal enforcement authority at the time and could not effect change based on its pressing findings. But in 1915, the California legislature "amended the Labor Camp Sanitation Law and placed its enforcement into the commission's hands."[69] That same year, the commission inspected agricultural labor camps and boxcar communities in the railroad industry. The study produced similar findings to those reported in 1914. Nonetheless, the commission decided to relinquish its newly acquired enforcement powers and instead acted "in its original capacity of adviser and co-operator."[70] That is, the commission simply recommended—rather than enforced—sanitation improvements to prevent disease and poor quality of life in housing quarters. Employers were not eager to cooperate with the CCIH recommendations because they assumed that if "laborers had always lived so—why should any change be made?"[71] Not surprisingly, then, three years later, in 1918, Dimas and Cleto encountered similarly abysmal living conditions upon arriving at their boxcar community in Northern California.

The commission experienced significantly less opposition to its education initiatives than to its labor and housing recommendations. The CCIH focused its efforts on Americanizing male workers through evening schools that emphasized the acquisition of trade skills, children through public education and day nurseries, and teenagers through continuation schools. Yet the commission soon realized that they had "reached out for every member of the family except the mother."[72] Commissioner Mary Simons Gibson, the only woman on the committee, took it upon herself to champion home instruction for immigrant women.[73] To do so, Gibson listened to Pearl Ellis, a social reformer who worked with Mexican girls in Southern California. Ellis believed that to "assimilate the countless number of Mexicans that cross our southern border, either legally or otherwise, to better their condition in a new land, we must begin at the basic structure of their social order—the home."[74] Gibson's plan was well received, and in 1914 the CCIH drafted a bill "providing for home teachers to bring immigrant mothers in contact with and make them a part of American social and civic life."[75] The bill was introduced under the endorsement of the Women's Legislative Council. Commissioner Gibson, with the help of women's organizations, persuasively lobbied for the bill, and on April 10, 1915, Governor Johnson signed Senate Bill 427, the Home Teacher Act, into law.[76] The Mothers Congress, State Federation of Women's Clubs, Daughters of the American Revolution, and Parent-Teachers Association were essential to this effort.[77]

The Home Teacher Act not only allowed the commission to focus on immigrant mothers for the first time, but also invited the state to intervene in and regulate the private sphere of the immigrant home. The law called for "home teachers to work in the homes of the pupils, instructing children and adults in matters relating to . . . sanitation, in the English language, in household duties such as purchase, preparation and use of food and of clothing and in the fundamental principles of the American system of government and the rights and duties of citizenship."[78] While the act named adults and children generally, the CCIH used the law to Americanize immigrant women specifically. They rationalized the redirected effort by explaining that "the mother always shares gladly with her children, and so will be in this case."[79] Inevitably, lack of childcare meant that many Mexican mothers participated in classes organized by home teachers with their children by their side (Fig. 2.5). The goal was not only to Americanize Mexican women. Instead, home teachers trained immigrant mothers to raise their US-citizen children with American values and traditions in order to assure the second generation's political loyalty to the United States. During World War I, new anxieties had emerged regarding the loyalty of immigrants during wartime and their political subversiveness in labor organizing.[80] As I discuss further in Chapter 4, immigrant workers in California unionized to demand better wages and labor conditions. This presented unwelcome challenges to employers, who wanted to keep wages low.

Social reformers, then, trained immigrant women to produce respectable American households and raise their children to become loyal citizens and obedient workers. An Americanization home teacher stressed the importance of targeting mothers to ensure the loyalty of subsequent generations: "'Go after the women' should become a slogan among Americanization workers. The children of these foreigners are the advantages to America, not the naturalized foreigners. These are never 100 percent Americans, but the second generation may be."[81] This teacher's comment underlined the direct link between the push for Americanization and the "100 Percent American" movement, which called for immigrants' unconditional loyalty during

A class of Mexican immigrant women, with their babies and small children. This class was organized by a Home Teacher in Los Angeles. The women in the picture are holding copies of the Commission's Home Teacher manual, containing lessons in English. (Copy of Home Teacher manual, opposite page 148.)

Figure 2.5 Mexican women and their children posed after a class organized by a home teacher, Los Angeles, California, circa 1916.

the war. The teacher not only had no faith in the immigrant generation; she was not even certain that the second generation—that is, Mexican American children—could be 100 percent American. This widespread distrust of ethnic Mexicans and the new approach to Americanization put Mexican mothers in an impossible position. If they adhered to the Americanization trainings, immigrant women ran the risk of appearing as traitors to their own ethnically Mexican communities and of denying their own rich history. But if they rejected the pressures of Americanization, then white reformers labeled them as unassimilable menaces to society.[82] Faced with this very choice as a Mexican mother, Dimas found a pragmatic middle ground. She opted to selectively adopt Americanization teachings to protect her family, while also teaching Mexican culture and Spanish to her children. In doing so, Dimas strategically chose to navigate both worlds and engage in what historian Vicki L. Ruiz has called cultural coalescence—a dynamic process of cultural exchange specific to many Mexican American experiences.[83]

Though social reformers focused on women in their efforts to assimilate Mexican immigrant families, it was Cleto who spearheaded the De Anda family's Americanization by adopting a new religion. As Virginia recalled, "My dad decided to change religions; he was Catholic. Dad comes from a very, very Catholic family, strong believers. Once here, he changed religions. I don't even know what religion it was, but we belonged to that church."[84] It turned out to be the Protestant church, a religion that social reformers reinforced through their educational trainings. Cleto was likely introduced to the Protestant church through the evening classes that CCIH offered to Mexican workers. Education was one of the numerous tools used to convert ethnic Mexican families, but religion also played an important role in Americanization efforts. Aware of the discriminatory nature of the distribution of public services, mixed-status Mexican families selectively aligned themselves with the ideals and practices of the Protestant churches to access the health-care benefits and food assistance they provided.

Clinics run by nurses and Methodist missionaries, with the assistance of local physicians, offered prenatal exams, medical screenings, and pediatric services; some even had a maternity ward. Prenatal classes, pregnancy tests, and infant immunization were offered free of charge.[85] During the 1920s, Catholic and Jewish organizations established similar health clinics to compete, given the high rates of Protestant conversions. These clinics could be found in California, throughout the Southwest, and in Midwest states where Mexicans were concentrated. In Southern California, the Los Angeles Section of the National Council of Jewish Women (founded in 1909) offered Americanization and other civic classes; they also started a health camp in 1928 for underprivileged girls. In Denver, Colorado, also in 1928, the

Diocesan Council of Catholic Women and the Catholic Daughters of America offered a free clinic at the St. Cajetan's Church and provided sewing, cooking, and home economics classes as part of their Americanization programs.[86] In 1920, Dimas became pregnant with her first child, Guadalupe, at the age of twenty-two and later gave birth to six additional children. When Guadalupe was born, Cleto worked for the Southern Pacific Railroad, where he earned a low salary without medical benefits. The health services provided by Protestant missionaries in Northern California were likely a key factor in the family's religious conversion and Americanization.

While Cleto made the decision to convert, it was Dimas who performed the learned lessons at home and imparted Americanized ideals to her children and husband. In 1923, when the De Anda family bought their home and moved to Roseville, California, they lived eighteen miles away from the CCIH's Sacramento office. The large number of immigrant families who moved to Roseville to work for Pacific Fruit Express Company undoubtedly meant that home teachers also entered that community. Mexican mothers' traditional roles, which usually confined them to domestic duties, have been read as a limitation to their influence within the family unit. From the private spaces of their home, however, women have been actors of change. As historian Monica Perales has shown, ethnic Mexican women often used Americanization trainings to empower themselves and their communities.[87] While the De Anda family is unsure if Dimas participated in lessons provided by home teachers, the family's memories of her role in the home imply that she did. Dimas, like many other ethnic Mexican women, influenced her family's Americanization through her domestic roles of cooking, storytelling, and playing games. Consuelo explains that her mom stopped using corn tortillas, and they became "accustomed to only eating flour tortillas and bread."[88] This dietary shift reflects the American cooking lessons that insisted on using flour instead of corn. According to Americanization program recommendations, for example, modern Mexican women were expected to substitute tortillas with bread, broil instead of fry their food, and serve lettuce as an alternative to beans.[89] In making these changes, Dimas had a strong influence on her family's cultural development through her dominant role in the kitchen. No one in Dimas's family, not even her husband, would question her cooking. Thus, while this domestic role appears to be a subtle one, it was actually an important and powerful way for women to intervene in the shaping of families and communities at the turn of the twentieth century.

Social reformers charged Mexican mothers with teaching their children English to Americanize the family, as a continuation of the language instruction that women received from home teachers and that children acquired in school. The CCIH designed English lesson plans for home teachers, some of which mirrored curricula for kindergarten and first-grade children. The lessons included the days of the week, numbers from one to one hundred, and vocabulary to form short sentences.[90] Thus mothers could practice their lessons while also helping children learn English. Research studies in the 1920s and 1930s contributed to the widespread belief that speaking Spanish was a hindrance to educational attainment for Mexican American children. In 1933, the *Mission Times* newspaper reported on the findings of a Spanish-language study: "A language handicap is partly responsible for the lower scores Mexican children sometimes make on intelligence and achievement tests."[91] The study recommended a separate-but-equal approach to educating ethnic Mexican children by endorsing segregation in schools based on English-language ability.[92] Some mothers thus had their children practice English at home so that they would not be segregated in school. In fact, Mexican parents would eventually organize to overturn the separate-but-equal doctrine in California that placed their children in Mexican schools or segregated classrooms, which had limited resources and outdated textbooks compared to the white-only schools or classrooms.[93]

While Dimas was not fluent in English, she asked her children to practice it at home. Virginia recalls that everyone else, including her siblings, her father, and herself, learned English: "We used to speak basically only English, me [and my siblings], only the [four of us] who attended school. . . . My dad learned a bit [of English], but my mom not so much."[94] Though Dimas knew only basic English words, she was extremely influential in encouraging her children to learn the language. Home teachers used music and games to teach women English. For instance, one of the CCIH lessons included learning the song "Home, Sweet Home."[95] Similarly, children also were taught songs at school to help them retain specific vocabulary. Dimas was thus equipped to use songs to help her children practice English. Virginia remembers that her mom used to insist that they sing in English: "She used to tell us to hug each other and 'sing that one that says Old McDonald had a farm.' She used to say, 'I like it so much!'" Gid Tanner & His Skillet Lickers, a widely recognized band in the "golden age" of country music, popularized this song in 1927, when the De Anda family were immersed in Americanization programs.[96] As María Herrera-Sobek reminds us, songs and games are a "cultural reflection" of the people who produce them.[97] Beyond simply practicing English by singing "Old McDonald Had a Farm," the De Anda sisters were also learning to embrace rural white American traditions, just as Americanization efforts intended.

Americanization was an uneven process. It was not always enforced as a top-down decree from government agencies and officials; it also occurred naturally given the fluidity and malleability of culture. Indeed, the imperative to "become American" came from lots of different places. Mexican immigrant parents and their children were influenced by American music, films, fashion, and consumer culture, traces of which are evident in the De Andas's family portrait (Fig. 2.1). Families absorbed American fashion trends and culture through visual and printed media. For instance, *La Opinión,* the oldest running Spanish-language newspaper based in Los Angeles, contained fashion advertisements as well as hygiene and health advice columns that informed the cultural behavior of their Mexican readership.[98] Children also absorbed American culture from their classmates and friends. Consuelo attended first and second grade in the United States, and Virginia attended first grade there. Even this limited exposure had a lifelong influence on the De Anda sisters, who maintained their American identity. Even after her family's banishment, Dimas's hope of eventually returning to the United States pushed her to continue Americanization practices. As Virginia recounted, my mom "used to make us sing my dad's church's English chorus," to which Consuelo added, "so that we would not forget how to speak English."[99] Consuelo, Virginia, and their mom did eventually return, but at a later age, and they were never able to fully relearn their native language. "We do not know a lot of English," Virginia explained, "but the little that we do know we pronounce it without a problem."[100] It may be that Dimas tried to help her daughters retain English so they could prove their American identity once they eventually returned to their native country. At home and in their communities, the De Anda sisters also received daily messages about Mexican culture and traditions that helped them to achieve cultural coalescence.[101] This merging of cultures allowed the De Anda sisters to adapt to life in both the United States and Mexico, even when the process was painful.

FROM AMERICANIZATION TO BANISHMENT

Notwithstanding the increasing vigor of Americanization programs, with the catastrophic economic decline of the 1929 stock market crash, demands for the assimilation of Mexican immigrants were replaced with calls for their removal. Americanization programs, historian George J. Sánchez argues, "had no place in an economically depressed America."[102] In fact, the most progressive goals of the programs—full integration of Mexican immigrants that would have put them on more equal footing with their white counterparts in US society—were never implemented because they were not supported by the government or business interests behind the CCIH.[103] The decisions they made imposed illegality onto ethnic Mexicans instead of integrating them legally and socially into the fabric of the country. By 1927, the nativist loyalties of social reformers had become apparent as they sided with businessmen to champion immigration restrictions at the expense of immigrant communities in California. That year, in their annual report, the CCIH acknowledged that Mexicans were "doing much of the common labor in the fields and railroads and seem almost essential," at the same time that the commission accused Mexicans of "causing an immense social problem in our charities, schools and health departments."[104] The essential-worker narrative that proclaimed the need for ethnic Mexican workers during labor shortages, only to then present them as a social problem during economic crises, gave way to ethnic Mexicans' impermanent legality and disposability. Consequently, the image of Mexican migrants as essential workers that employers propagated to recruit thousands of Mexicans to the United States dissipated as the restrictionists' fight to include Mexico under US national-origin quotas gained momentum. The commission, caught in the middle of the intensifying immigration debate, produced findings that would contribute to mass banishments two years later. Indeed, the 1927 CCIH report proffered a damning forecast: Mexican laborers once considered essential were now "almost essential," and the "Mexican problem" had become all but intractable. Banishment appeared to be the only solution.

As US officials considered elusive solutions to the economic crisis, the priority became to "get rid of the Mexicans," as Cleto De Anda learned firsthand.[105] During the Depression years, jobs were usually reserved for white Americans. Employers began laying off Mexicans and Mexican Americans to create vacancies for so-called more deserving US citizens.[106] Relief assistance became associated with "women's and people of color's dependence, laziness, opportunism, and pathology."[107] Facing unemployment and unable to apply for relief because it would have drawn attention to the family for removal, Cleto and his family had no option but to leave the United States. As Virginia explained years

Later, "[We left] because they were going to take [my father's] job away and he had to go because they were going to pay for the entire family's train transportation expenses."[108] Even if they were not on relief rolls, unemployed, or undocumented, Mexicans were targeted for removal. Cleto's employer gave him an ultimatum: either accept paid transportation to take his family to Mexico, or be fired. These circumstances did not give the De Anda family the option to *choose* to leave; instead, they were effectively coerced into banishment. As the economic recession worsened, and the Great Depression roiled the US economy, Mexican immigrants and Mexican Americans faced similar overt forms of discrimination and threats of racial violence throughout the country. Ethnic Mexican railroad workers in Terre Haute, Indiana, for instance, had to surrender their employment when a hundred men and women surrounded their work camp and ordered them to resign immediately or face the consequences. In a similar racial attack against Mexican workers in Malakoff, Texas, "a gang of ruffians bombed the headquarters occupied by the Society of Mexican Laborers. Signs were displayed warning Mexican residents to leave town."[109] Such hostility mocked the very ideals of the Americanization programs and their promises of integration.[110]

Indeed, ethnic Mexicans were no longer seen as essential laborers; instead, they were now understood as a threat to the white Americans who were supposedly more entitled to what limited jobs were available during the Depression. The threat that Cleto received from his employer in 1929 became a common one for ethnic Mexican workers across the country.[111] Even when more jobs were created through federal programs, local "counties did everything possible to keep minority nationals from C.W.A. [Civil Works Administration] jobs."[112] Because local and state agencies implemented President Franklin D. Roosevelt's federal New Deal policies, they often used their discretionary power to exclude Mexican workers from the CWA jobs program. In 1931, California formalized this practice in the Alien Labor Act, which made it illegal for any business working with a government agency to employ unauthorized immigrants on public works jobs in the state. Just a year later, in 1932, the General Consul of Mexico reported that California's implementation of the 1931 Alien Labor Act made it virtually impossible for so-called foreigners to secure employment in construction sites, highways, schools, government office buildings, and other public works executed by both government agencies and private contractors.[113] The inability to find jobs forced many displaced workers to accept banishment offers. Those who decided to remain in the United States struggled to survive without financial income, and many were inevitably removed on LPC grounds.

Unemployment investigation reports during this time documented anti-Mexican sentiment in the workplace, often citing discriminatory hiring practices by employers that favored whites over ethnic Mexican workers. San Bernardino County in California, for instance, had an estimated 10 percent unemployment rate in 1931.[114] For ethnic Mexicans, however, unemployment rocketed to 30 percent in that same period.[115] A special investigation on unemployment rates by the Mexican General Consul on January 6, 1931, reported that the drastic unemployment rates were a direct result of the rampant campaigns against ethnic Mexican workers. The consul explained: "The intense campaign that is being promoted by governmental authorities, Chambers of Commerce, and Civic Associations, against the Mexican worker, [is] a campaign that has resulted in the displacement of our laborers in order to provide employment to Anglo-Americans even at the cost of efficiency at the worksite."[116] Ethnicity—not efficiency—had become the major factor in determining who had the right to employment and relief benefits during the interwar period.

The anti-Mexican campaign permeated social, cultural, and legal life: propaganda circulated anti-Mexican sentiment and local laws led to anti-Mexican regulations. US citizens and lawful and long-term residents of Mexican origin were not only denied the right to WCA employment opportunities, but also fired from their current jobs. After hundreds of ethnic Mexicans had been fired and banished, employers replaced them with Anglo-American workers. Anti-Mexican messages were regularly produced in political discourses, which were heavily circulated in newspapers. This propaganda resulted in material action against Mexicans and their US-citizen children. A 1932 report published by the General Consul of Mexico documented the conditions of Mexicans and Mexican Americans in California. It emphasized the coerced nature of banishment by stating that although destitute ethnic Mexicans had long enjoyed the right to food and shelter assistance granted by the Charity Department, "the only help they can now expect from the same department is to be repatriated to the nearest border."[117] When food and shelter were denied to ethnic Mexicans who had been suddenly fired from their jobs, "opting" into banishment became their only way to survive. This forced choice coerced thousands to leave the United States.

The LPC clause was used to remove the De Anda family, but it was used unfairly, without following its own provisions. Dimas and Cleto had resided in California for eleven years and their children were US citizens. In fact, most banished Mexican families had established residence—often beyond the minimum three years required—in the United States, and most of them did not volunteer for departure.[118] Moreover, some removed families, including the De Andas, did not apply for relief assistance. Nevertheless, neither proof of relief assistance nor any other evidence was needed to expedite banishment. After years of informal banishment processes, US Under Secretary of State Sumner Welles finally outlined a formal process for the removals. He explained: "It is probable that many of the heads of these families and their dependents will prima facie be eligible for removal under Section 23 of the 1917 Act as amended, and so their signed application on Form 543 should be obtained, but the record in each case may be forwarded after departure and decision will be made in the Central Office nunc pro tunc. In other words, removal should not be delayed until complete investigation has been made and the approval and issuance of the removal order obtained from this office."[119]

In the rush to remove Mexicans and Mexican Americans, officials relied on a process that assumed entire groups of people to be eligible for removal, even without evidence; only later did the INS offer a nunc pro tunc ("now for then") procedure whereby banished mixed-status Mexican families could request that the "procedural error" of their own banishment be rectified. This approach of "banish first, fix later" not only sanctioned the indiscriminate banishment of ethnic Mexicans, but also placed the burden on them to file legal claims to challenge their removals. In the eyes of the law, anyone of Mexican origin—without regard to citizenship, dependence on public assistance, or desire to remain in the United States—was suitable for removal. An assumed homogeneity of the richly diverse Mexican population in the United States guided these mass removals of ethnic Mexicans, as explained in a 1931 *El Defensor* newspaper editorial: "The classification of 'Mexican' [is] applied to us without distinction, [they] consider us all racially, morally, socially, and to an extent even economically, identical."[120] These broad assumptions contributed to the justification of mass-banishment raids that ignored the legal status, length of residence in the United States, and economic status of those being removed. Such tactics led to a state-imposed illegality that racialized all ethnic Mexicans as removable foreigners.

Under these circumstances, Mexican parents often fabricated "family vacation" narratives to help their children deal with the trauma of their sudden displacement. Unable to explain to their children the racial tensions that had resulted in their banishment, Cleto and Dimas decided to tell them that the family was going on vacation to San Juan de los Lagos, Jalisco, Mexico. Virginia, who was six years old at the time, believed them. She had no reason to question her parents. Instead, she was excited about the trip. The fact that her family left most of their belongings behind re-affirmed the vacation narrative. As Virginia remembered, "We only took two big suitcases, it must have been only clothes."[121] The family of nine left their home, furniture, and most of their clothing, pictures, and other belongings. The children—perhaps the parents, too—believed that they would return home after a short stay in Mexico.

The reality of leaving their native country became apparent to the De Anda children immediately after the train crossed the border. Years later, Virginia recalled that moment with sadness and resentment: "When we crossed the border, I saw everything was different. I saw people dressed badly, and we didn't like anything. I didn't like [the vacation] anymore. After we crossed the border, I didn't like it anymore!"[122] Almost immediately, Virginia noticed the sharp distinction in resources between the United States and rural Mexico. The global reverberations of the Great Depression had devastated what would become—unbeknownst to her—her host country for the next twenty-one years. Consuelo, a year older than Virginia, had a similar reaction. She recalled, "The train and trip were very pleasant. We got to see many places we had not seen before. However, the place we arrived to was no longer pleasant."[123] Virginia's shock at the poverty her family encountered in rural Jalisco quickly broke the enchantment of her vacation fantasy. It became clear that life in Mexico would not match what Dimas and Cleto had built for their children in the United States. As Virginia recalled about their US home: "My dad was a really hard worker, he bought a home, and we always attended school. . . . I still remember my teacher's name, Ms. Parrish."[124] The De Anda sisters cherished their memories of life in the United States, where the family had reached lower-middle-class status and achieved homeownership. More than eighty years later, Virginia—eighty-nine years old at the time of our interview—still remembered her first-grade teacher's name, an indication of the significance of that period of her life, which had ended abruptly with her family's banishment.

When they arrived in Mexico, the De Anda family barely had any money; the suddenness of their removal had forced Dimas and Cleto to sell their home for a pittance. In fact, the rushed sale meant that Cleto had received only an advance on the house before they left for Mexico; the buyer had promised to send the rest of the payment to Cleto in

Mexico, but never did. Virginia explained, "My dad made a deal to sell the home, but they only paid him [a portion] of the price and they were supposed to have sent him the remaining [in monthly payments] to Mexico. The man who bought the home was going to take the payments to the bank and then the bank would send the payments to my dad, but for a while they did not send him the money because the man disappeared. We later found out that he had lost his job [during the Depression]. Those were our days of suffering."[125] Though the deal was rushed and risky, the De Andas had agreed to it because they knew that if they did not, then the bank, city, or county would confiscate or otherwise take possession of the home to allegedly recoup the cost of the family's banishment transportation and any other charity they had received. Such appropriations of property that banished ethnic Mexicans had left behind were common practice at the time.[126] Fortunately, Cleto owned a small house in Jalisco, Mexico, which he had inherited from his grandfather before he married Dimas. His plan was to go to that house and wait for the sale of his US home to go through, so that he could then invest in a small family business to make a living. But when the buyer did not follow through with the payments, the De Andas were left with few means to establish themselves in Jalisco. They would have to make do with what little remained and adjust to their new life after their banishment.

LIFE IN MEXICO AND MEXICANIZATION PRESSURES

Contrary to the opportunities promised in Mexico, many banished people encountered extreme poverty and homelessness. Not only did the De Andas not receive any governmental support in Mexico, but they were shocked to discover upon their arrival in Jalisco that the house Cleto had inherited from his grandfather was no longer in his name. Virginia described their astonishment: "[My parents] lived here [in the US] for eleven years, and my dad *never* knew that his aunt had sold his land and house without his permission. . . . And what a surprise, [my dad] found that he had nothing!"[127] But even with no means to care for their children, Dimas and Cleto did not despair. Instead, they improvised and "built a small *jacal* [hut] made of branches" to shelter them.[128] Sadly, the family's post-banishment experience in Mexico was not uncommon. Historian Camille Guerin-Gonzales reminds us that "repatriates often found that economic conditions were as bad as or worse than those they had experienced in the United States."[129]

Hunger and infant mortality were common among banished families in Mexico.[130] Consuelo remembered her family rationing their food: "We had a really rough time because they would give us only one and a half tortillas to eat."[131] Often it was the children, not the government, who carried the burden of helping their families secure food during the Depression. Joe grew up listening to his mother and aunt's stories of resilience and ingenuity, and as he recalled, "*Mi tía* Consuelo and my mom would go out and hunt for rattlesnakes. They said that for months one of the things they ate the most was rattlesnakes! [They] would [also] hunt . . . birds, they'd go catch fish . . . they learned to hunt to survive."[132] The older children adopted to the tough conditions, but not without prolonged health and emotional consequences. For babies in particular, malnutrition proved deadly. Dimas and Cleto had nine additional children in Mexico, but sadly seven perished either at birth or in early childhood. Virginia recounted: "Of the [siblings] who were born in Mexico, only the two youngest survived. The rest died at very young ages."[133] Joe added, "As soon as they got there [to Mexico], the food just didn't settle well with none of them, and specially the babies. They tried to feed them, but everything they would give them, they would throw it up and they were just not accustomed to it. I don't know if it was an illness, but they just couldn't hold any food down."[134] While the food made the children sick, the lack of medication and the general conditions of poverty, more generally, likely contributed to their illness. The anguish of banishment intensified with the death of the De Anda babies, the hunger, and the homelessness—all collateral effects of coerced displacement and the ill-planned mass removals. While the De Anda sisters found ways to adapt to their new reality and survived hunger, they also had to navigate assimilation pressures. Ironically, in the United States they had been trained to Americanize, and then once they were in Mexico, they encountered similar demands to Mexicanize. Somewhat reminiscent of approaches taken by social reformers in the United States, a group of Mexican citizens—mostly college professors— orchestrated Mexicanization efforts under the sponsorship of the Mexican government.[135] In May 1934, the newspaper *El Universal* reported on the School for the Mexicanization of Immigrants in Mexico City, and its plan to assimilate wealthy immigrants:

> There are now in Mexico around 200,000 foreigners who hold in their hands a great part of the national wealth and who, nevertheless, continue to retain their customs, their language, and in general, all their manner of living, without preoccupying themselves with their positive integration to Mexico. For this reason, a group of Mexicans, under the auspices of the Ministries of Public Education, Interior, Foreign Affairs, National Economy, the Central Department of Civil Retirement Pensions, have founded the School for the Mexicanization of Immigrants, which is an institution where foreigners residing in Mexico will be able to learn the language, history, geography, and folklore of the country.[136]

Unlike the Americanization efforts that targeted working-class immigrants, Mexicanization was originally carried out to integrate influential foreign investors residing in Mexico. Nonetheless, both programs relied on education to convert immigrants into trustworthy members of society. Lessons on language, history, culture, and civics were used on both sides of the political divide to assimilate immigrants. The Mexicanization efforts were originally concerned with establishing the national loyalty of wealthy foreigners so that they would think of Mexico not as a temporary colony, but as a permanent home.

More informal Mexicanization efforts were then used on the thousands of banished families arriving in the country during the 1930s, as the communities they were settling in began demanding their assimilation. Mexicanization for working-class banished families took place in overt as well as subtle forms, with Mexican American children feeling the effects on the playgrounds and schoolyards.[137] Consuelo recalled vividly how the other children in the rural town teased them about their American fashion: "They ridiculed us because we arrived with bob haircuts. They used to call us shorn sheep because all the girls had long braids and we had very short hair. Yes, we were from here [the United States]!"[138] The De Anda sisters' short hair defied Mexican gender and cultural norms. Working-class women and girls in Mexico were expected to have long, braided hair, a symbol of their femininity. Short hair was associated with masculinity and far removed from the feminine ideal. Consuelo resented the mockery and insisted that she was a Mexican American who liked popular US fashion. Joe recalled his mother's and aunt Consuelo's stories about their initial inability to conform to the Mexican cultural dress codes, which were more conservative than those in the United States. Joe explained, "They talk about how all the kids made fun of them because their dresses were short, and everyone else's were long. They were just the opposite; their dresses were too short, and their hair was too short! Everyone had long dresses and long hair."[139] The De Anda sisters had not been accepted in the United States as full-fledged Americans, while in Mexico they were seen as too American.

The disconnect led Mexicans to read the newly arrived US girls and women as liberal and improper. Virginia recalls that her mother was accused of disrespecting her husband with her perceived indecent American clothing styles, which did not abide by Mexican gender norms. After the women in Dimas's rural Jalisco neighborhood strongly criticized her for her too-liberal style, she used patches of fabric to lengthen her knee-high dresses so they went down to her ankles.[140] When short hair and short dresses first became a trend in the United States, they were also seen as indecent. In Mexico, how-ever, these styles were read as not only improper but also foreign. In other words, the fashion of banished women and girls did not align with Mexican cultural politics. On both sides of the US-Mexico border, it was the De Anda women, not the men, who were criticized for their fashion and cultural customs. It was also the women who were expected to impart the Mexicanization lessons to their families. On both sides of the US-Mexico divide, assimilation ideologies glo-rified the role of women in shaping the future political citizenry of the nation.[141] Their experiences also illustrate how Mexican American children had to navigate the often-contradicting terrains of their lim-inal identities.

Years following their relocation to Mexico, the De Andas received a message that offered a glimmer of hope. After Cleto lost contact with the person who bought his family's US house, he assumed that the un-paid balance was lost, but he eventually heard from the bank that processed the sale. Virginia recalled, "The bank took a very long time to find the new owner and it repossessed the house. It took many years for the bank to send the remaining money to my dad. I don't remember if they sent the remaining amount in full, but they eventually sent the money to my dad. My dad used that money to buy his ranch in the state of Zacatecas."[142] In all likelihood, the bank kept most of the profit from the repossession. But the funds Cleto received allowed him and Dimas to move their family to the neighboring state of Zacatecas and provide their children with economic stability. As Joe explained, "When the money finally arrived, my grandfather was able to purchase land in Zacatecas. . . . On this land in the town of Seis de Enero, he built a large home with adobe. . . . He later added a small store in the front where he sold . . . rice, beans, cookies, candies, and sodas that would sit in a tin bucket filled with water to keep them below room temperature."[143] Consuelo and Virginia helped their parents raise cows, pigs, and donkeys in their new home in Seis de Enero, in the municipality of Fresnillo, Zacatecas. While the family was no longer impoverished and enjoyed some sense of normalcy, the De Andas sisters held dear to the hope of returning to their native California.

RESETTLEMENT AS A LIFELONG DREAM

The poor economic conditions and cultural alienation that banished Mexican Americans encountered in Mexico often became their main reasons for wanting to return to the United States. After witnessing the dire conditions in Jalisco, Cleto tried to return to the United States to find work that would give him the opportunity to send for his family later. Virginia recalled her father's desperate attempt: "Soon after we arrived, he tried to return once he realized that he had nothing, that he did not have his land, he did not have his little house anymore. He asked for a loan to return, but there was no one to lend him money."[144] Despite Cleto's attempts, and those of many others who sought to return, it was nearly impossible for banished families to be readmitted to the United States during the 1930s. The De Anda family was banished in 1929 during the second period of removals, but immigration policies during the 1930s decreased the possibility of returning to the United States. Many were turned back when they were unable to convince immigration officers that they were not likely to become public charges. Banished children were more successful in their attempts, but not until decades later, because as adult US citizens they were not held to inadmissibility based on LPC regulations. Virginia's desire to return began when she was only eleven years old, but her parents opposed it because they had no family or means of support in the United States. Cleto warned his young daughter of the potential difficulty of life in the United States, remembering his own experiences moving from place to place following the crops: "You are going to suffer, you will be going from home to home."[145] Despite his protests, Virginia was determined to return and was encouraged to do so by the stories she read in letters her dad received from a highly esteemed *compadre*. He had managed to escape the mass banishments and remain in California during the

Depression. Virginia remembered, "[The *compadre*] used to always write to my dad, and I used to read the letters and saw the beauty in what he said. Besides my own memories of my life here, which I never forgot. [He also shared stories] of having two houses, and that they lived in South San Francisco, and that his wife also worked."[146] These romanticized stories sustained Virginia's desire to resettle in her native country, regain middle-class status, and enjoy the economic independence that the letters alluded to.

Despite Virginia's urge to return to the United States, her parents' opposition, as well as gendered expectations, made it difficult for her to leave the household as a young, unaccompanied, single woman. Her parents refused to give her their blessing or any money. At the time, in the 1940s and 1950s, most working-class Mexican women left home only through marriage or the Catholic nunnery.[147] This gendered restriction slowed resettlement for banished women. Virginia remained patient but focused on her resettlement goal. Eventually, Mexican demographic and economic shifts likely persuaded Virginia's parents to allow her to return to the United States. During the period that Virginia and Consuelo lived in Mexico, rapid population growth resulted in increased internal migration as people moved from rural to urban areas in search of labor opportunities with better economic prospects. Mexico's population skyrocketed from 16 million in 1934 to 32 million in 1958.[148] Mexicans often first opted for internal migration only to later emigrate to the United States when labor prospects were not as promising in Mexican urban centers. Virginia and Consuelo, however, could skip the internal migration step because their US citizenship allowed them to enter the United States legally.

Finally, in 1950, once her parents had recovered a semblance of economic stability and owned their home and a small grocery store in Zacatecas, Virginia—at the age of twenty-seven—left Mexico to resettle in the United States as a single woman. She had been dreaming of returning for decades: "I thought of coming back all the time. I did not return sooner because my mom and dad did not allow me, and they would not give me any money either. In the evenings, to escape the daily routine, [my dad] used to leave me in charge of the small [family] store. Since they would not let me return, one day I told them: 'I am going to steal the money [from the store] and leave without warning you!'"[149] Virginia's threat showed just how determined she was to fulfill her dream of returning to her native country. It was only then that Virginia's parents agreed and helped her. Cleto, with his wife's consent, asked his *compadre* to accompany Virginia on the trip back to the United States. Once they had crossed the border, he also hosted Virginia, opening his home and offering the family's support in South San Francisco until she could afford a place of her own. Virginia was not alone for long; two years later, she helped Consuelo, other siblings, and her mother resettle in the United States.

Virginia served as an important link in the social network, guiding and hosting her family's travel and readjustment upon their resettlement in the United States. When her sister Consuelo resettled in 1952, it was a more complicated process because she had five Mexican-born children and was trapped in an abusive marriage. Ever resourceful, Consuelo devised a plan to return to the United States to carve out a new life for her and her children, who she would eventually bring over to join her. Consuelo explained, "One time Virginia was visiting, and I decided to come back with her, and I tricked [my husband into believing] that I would come back for him in three months. Three months later, I sent him a letter telling him that he would never again have me in his claws!"[150] Consuelo's ability to leave her abusive spouse came from her conviction that she could have a better future in the United States.

Consuelo and Virginia's US citizenship granted them the lawful capacity to cross the border into the United States, but only after border restrictions had been relaxed for Mexicans. For the De Anda sisters, as was the case for Sara Marie Robles in Chapter 3, resettlement in the United States was relatively easy after the border was reopened because they had access to their US birth certificates. Others, like Trinidad Rodríguez, found it far more difficult because they did not have access to their documents and were unable to prove their US citizenship at the border. Once back in the United States, Consuelo never remarried.

Instead, she devoted her time and energy to working and saved her wages to open immigration petitions for her children. With Virginia's assistance, Consuelo succeeded: all of her children eventually entered the United States as lawful permanent residents, and are now thriving members of their communities.

When Virginia and Consuelo returned to the United States in the early 1950s, progress had been made toward racial equality. In the 1930s and 1940s, civil rights organizations increasingly fought for the rights of Latinas and Latinos throughout the United States. For instance, the Alianza Hispano-Americana, in Los Angeles, California; the Liga Protectora Latina in Phoenix, Arizona; the League of United Latin American Citizens (LULAC) in San Antonio, Texas; and the Liga Protectora Mexicana in Kansas City, Kansas, advocated for the improvement of social and economic conditions of their members as well as the protection of their civil and political rights. These efforts increased from the 1940s to the 1960s, but while important advancements were made, Mexican immigrants came under attack yet again.[151] In addition to attacks against pachucas and pachucos during the 1940s, anti-immigrant fears increased significantly during the Cold War, which exacerbated xenophobic immigration policies.[152] The Immigration and Naturalization Services organized a large deportation campaign, known as Operation Wetback, which once again targeted Mexican immigrants. The operation began in 1954 and used fear tactics that resembled the mass removals during the Great Depression. The mass deportations under Operation Wetback began in the Southwest but soon extended across the United States. By the end of 1954, more than one million people had been apprehended and removed to Mexico.[153] This must have been deeply upsetting for the De Anda sisters, who likely recalled their banishment traumas when they listened to the news of this episode of mass removals.

Such emotional wounds were likely not prioritized since the banished women had to learn how to survive in their new realities. Many of their actions post-banishment mirror feminist behavior, tactics they likely learned to navigate new social norms. For instance, the De Anda sisters'

Figure 2.6 The De Anda sisters, Virginia (*left*) and Consuelo (*right*), Hemet, California, March 3, 2012.

experiences with banishment and their ability to negotiate and challenge power structures demonstrate the feminist goals of woman- and community-centered empowerment. While they do not identify as feminists, their actions highlight the force of their independence and persistence despite the social, cultural, economic, and legal obstacles they encountered as banished Mexican American women. Virginia and Consuelo lived about two hundred miles away from each other when I interviewed them, but they visited frequently and continued to care for each other until they passed away (Fig. 2.6).

CONFRONTING BANISHMENT

Later in life, Virginia openly shared with her children stories about her birth, life in the United States, and banishment, but for a long time she did not talk about her experiences in the United States. Joe, Virginia's son, did not know about her life-altering experience until recently, and he discovered it nearly by accident (Fig. 2.7). Joe explained, "I found out about five years ago [in 2007], when Senator Dunn had a meeting here at the *LA Times* building to discuss his plan to have the state of California apologize for the repatriations. That's when I found out from my mother. . . . I mentioned [the event] to her and found out that she had been repatriated. So, we took her [to a second event], and once we took her, then all of a sudden, she started to have memories of the time, and of course we had a lot of questions."[154] Until that time, the De Anda

Figure 2.7 The Yáñez brothers, Joe (*left*) and Pablo "Paul" (*right*), Hemet, California, July 16, 2024. The picture was taken after they shared new photographs and documents with me.

sisters had never talked about their banishment, probably to suppress the shame and pain they endured. Joe always knew his mother was born in the United States, and that the family had moved to Mexico when she was a child. But he simply assumed that her family had returned to Mexico because his grandfather missed his country of birth. In reality, Dimas and Cleto had adapted well to their host country. They not only actively engaged in Americanization trainings as a family, but their labor also contributed to the industrialization of California. The De Andas had even managed to save some of their wages to purchase a home and secure a higher socioeconomic position. Banishment disrupted all these achievements and replaced the prospect of transgenerational wealth with the penumbra of transgenerational illegality.

Third-generation members of the De Anda family, the furthest removed from the banishment experience, began to uncover this family history only through their participation in the research that led to this book. Their American birth did not preclude them from knowing their history, but their grandmother had kept it from them. As a result, the third generation—Virginia's grandchildren—know very little about their grandmother's banishment history. As Marisa Yáñez, Virginia's granddaughter, explained, "I don't know if we don't talk about it because it is painful or just because it was so far removed from me. You know, I was not even born."[155] Since Marisa and her father, Joe, did not have to go through the ordeal of family separation and immigration—as was the case with other families in this book—they did not delve into Virginia's history of displacement and resettlement. Marisa revealed, "I have never heard [my grandmother] talk specifically about it. I have only heard what my dad has told me about it, and even then, it's not too much. I only know that her family and her were forced to go back to Mexico, even though she was a citizen here."[156] When we spoke, Marisa was a medical student and very busy with her studies. Since her grandmother did not live close by, the stories she knows about Virginia's banishment are the few that her dad has only very recently passed on to her. The pain of recounting their traumatic history likely kept Virginia,

Consuelo, and other banished US citizens from talking about their experiences. Their silence about their banishment may have served as a shield from their painful past, which they are still healing from decades later.

In 1952, Virginia married Tomas Yáñez, a Mexican citizen in San Francisco, California, where their children were born with birthright US citizenship. Virginia's children, in turn, also had their own children, born and raised in California—that is, all three generations in Virginia's family were born in the United States. Consuelo had a different resettlement experience. She had Mexican-born children who did not benefit from derivative citizenship, because she was unaware of that legal right. Instead, Consuelo opened family-based immigration petitions for her children, who are now naturalized US citizens. Because they took that route, Consuelo paid unnecessary legal fees, and her children had prolonged adjustment processes. Sara Marie Robles, whose story we will encounter in Chapter 3, also had to endure drawn-out, expensive legal processes and prolonged family separation, though unlike Trinidad Rodríguez, she succeeded in passing on her US citizenship to her children.

CHAPTER THREE

THE ROBLES FAMILY

Transnational Motherhood

At the tender age of two, Sara Marie Robles sat on a park bench in Pasadena, California, as she posed for a picture. The small black-and-white photograph captures Sara Marie sitting in the center of the bench with a line of palm trees in the background. Sara Marie holds her hands gently on her lap as she gazes timidly at the camera's lens. This image was meant to safeguard the memory of her childhood in her native city. Little did her family know that this photograph would be the last one taken of Sara Marie as a child in the United States (Fig. 3.1). This portrait, her birth certificate, and other documents in the family's private collection bear witness to Sara Marie's 1928 birth in California and her short-lived childhood experience in the United States. The Robles family now sees this photo as a visual record of Sara Marie's US birth and the family's removal to Zacatecas, Mexico, in 1932. It serves as a stark reminder of her family's banishment history when she, at the age of four, along with her Mexican immigrant parents and three US-born siblings, were sent to Mexico. After their banishment, the Robles family settled in the municipality of Valparaíso, Zacatecas, Mexico, in a small town called Potrero de Gallegos. Sara Marie became one of the hundreds of thousands of banished Mexican Americans that the United States and the Mexican governments failed to protect.

Figure 3.1 Sara Marie Robles in Pasadena, California, circa 1930.

Shaped by particular local, regional, and national conditions, banishment unfolded differently in the United States and Mexico for households like the Rodríguez, De Anda, Robles, and Espinoza families. At the turn of the twentieth century, the United States was restructuring itself along racial lines, while Mexico was developing a nation-building project through agrarian reform. As a result, ethnic Mexicans were simultaneously being expelled from the United States and recruited by the Mexican government. This meant that anti-Mexican discourses and other hostilities in the United States, along with particular forms of othering in Mexico, shaped the experiences of transnational marginalization for banished ethnic Mexicans, disempowering them in distinct ways on both sides of the US-Mexico borderlands. Banished women were marginalized in Mexico, as rights and public aid were assigned to male heads of households with the assumption that wives and daughters would indirectly benefit. In the long shadow of banishment, women's ethnicity, working-class status, limited labor experience, gender, and Spanish monolingualism meant that their experience of resettlement in the United States would resemble, in some ways, that of unauthorized immigrants. In addition to whiteness, English-language use became another symbol of American citizenship, which caused those Mexican Americans who spoke only Spanish to be further relegated to a position of foreigner.

Despite these conditions, displaced communities remained politically engaged in demanding inclusion and found creative ways to assert their rights and claim belonging on both sides of the border. Overall, the process of being marginalized and fighting for one's place in each country had long-lasting effects on family separation, motherhood, and childhood across the US-Mexico borderlands. Sara Marie's complex family history—narrated against a backdrop of banishment and return—captures the ways in which banished women who held US citizenship inhabited distinct legal, economic, and social positions. Her experience also provides an example of how banished Mexican American women who managed to resettle in the United States negotiated gender-based expectations and stereotypes as they crossed the US-Mexico border, grappled with motherhood, and managed transnational families.

The oral histories of banished returnee Sara Marie Robles, her children Guillermina and José Isabel, and her granddaughter Sara Veronica provide further insight on the strategies that banished women used to return to their native country and to resettle decades after they had been expelled. Guillermina and José Isabel—or "Chabelo," as the family calls him—shared their experiences living as a transnational family divided across the US-Mexico border, while Sara Veronica spoke to the process of breaking the silence surrounding banishment. The Robles family's memories and their private collections, along with other US and Mexican institutional sources, uncover how some banished survivors challenged and circumvented the gendered restrictions on movement that both their families and immigration policies imposed on them. Sara Marie's banishment experience forced her to build a life in Mexico. While there, her father, and then her husband, managed her life decisions and kept control of her US birth certificate, the very document that granted her mobility and legal reentry into her native country. Thirty-three years after her banishment, Sara Marie managed to convince her husband that it would benefit them economically if she returned to the United States. In this way, her story illustrates how the birthright US citizenship of banished women shifted traditional Mexican migration trajectories. As US citizens, banished women could legally enter the United States to file immigration petitions for their Mexican-born nuclear family. This distinctly gendered legal capital facilitated the creation of a particular type of Mexican American transnational family and increased the frequency of a particular type of transnational motherhood, as returned banished women created or maintained families across national borders.

In this chapter, I recover some of the history of banishment in relation to gendered migrations and transnational families. In doing so, I shine a light on gendered and racial immigration policies of exclusion, particularly the development of the "Mexican American problem"— an expansion of the "Mexican problem" and its scapegoating of Mexican immigrants as outsiders who were burdening the US economy— as a xenophobic political discourse against US citizens of Mexican descent. As Sara Marie's case illustrates, despite the exclusionary policies, Mexican American women did not remain silent, passive victims. They came up with creative political strategies to exercise their right to return to the United States, maneuvering through legal bureaucracies and social hierarchies to convince government representatives and their own husbands to support their decision to resettle in their country of origin. Sara Marie's story epitomizes the resilience of banished women who insisted on demanding their civil and legal rights as US citizens for themselves and their nuclear families. It also highlights the prolonged effects that Mexicans and Mexican Americans in general, and women and their families in particular, endured. Confronting the legacies of banishment and its attendant transmission of transgenerational illegality, Sara Marie—navigating gendered and racialized expectations, constraints, and assumptions across both the United States and Mexico—imagined new possibilities for her family and then made them a reality.

THE "MEXICAN AMERICAN PROBLEM"

Following in the spirit of exclusionary US immigration laws that restricted immigration to the United States from Asia and eastern and southern Europe, US policymakers, officials, and other stakeholders developed the concept of the "Mexican problem" to discursively link illegality to ethnic Mexicans and justify the mass expulsion of Mexican immigrants. Immigration restrictionists then transitioned from addressing the "Mexican problem" to explicitly focusing on the "Mexican American problem." The exclusion of immigrant parents extended to their US-born children to an even larger extent, because during the 1930s a significant increase occurred in the second-generation population of all races and ethnicities. The Chinese American population doubled from 20.9 percent in 1910 to 41.2 percent of the ethnic Chinese population in the United States in 1930. Japanese Americans, who accounted for 30.1 percent of the ethnic Japanese population in 1920, increased to 49.2 percent of that population in 1930. The Mexican American population also grew from 34.79 percent of ethnic Mexicans in 1920 to 56.6 percent in 1930.[1] The inclusion of "Mexican" as a racial category on the 1930 Census generated Mexican-specific data for the first time; in 1930, Mexicans ranked as the third largest "racial" group in the country behind the white and Black populations. The attention to regulating Mexican immigrants shifted to their US-born children, in part because the Mexican American population surpassed foreign-born Mexicans that year. The census counted 43.4 percent (616,998) foreign-born Mexicans, 38 percent (541,197) second-generation Mexican Americans, and 18.6 percent (264,338) Mexican Americans of the third generation and beyond.[2] As historian Natalia Molina has argued, "By the 1930s it was not just immigrants that needed to be governed, but their children, who were US citizens by birth though still perceived as not American enough."[3] US-born children of immigrants, a group with access to more legal rights because they are citizens, became a new threat to those invested in a white racial order.

Mexican American children and women were at high risk of removal, despite their US citizenship, because they were perceived as legal threats. During a congressional hearing on immigration in 1933, for instance, representatives expressed frustration about birthright citizenship. Representative William Traeger from California complained that "[Mexican] nationals remained in Los Angeles County long enough to produce children. Those children naturally, being born on the soil of the US or under its jurisdiction, became citizens of the US."[4] During the same hearing, Representative Charles Kramer from California also complained about Japanese American children's birthright citizenship: "We have Japs [sic] . . . boys and girls attending the public schools. . . . We are obliged to educate these Japs [sic] because they are born here and they become American citizens."[5] These ideas were reinforced during hearings throughout the 1930s and into the 1940s. Absent official banishment legislation, these political speeches guided the discretionary power of immigration officials who removed Mexican Americans from 1921 to 1944, and who used the racist statement "a Jap is a Jap [sic]" to justify the incarceration of Japanese Americans from 1942 to 1945.[6] The US citizenship of both Japanese Americans and Mexican Americans was disregarded during the processes of mass incarceration and banishment.

Toward the end of the decade, in 1939, Joseph A. Facci, an information consultant to the Farm Security Administration (FSA) under the New Deal, sounded the alarm about banishing US citizens and expelling long-term residents who did not meet the LPC requirements outlined in the 1917 Immigration Act. Facci wrote a report titled "The Problem of the Mexican Americans" in which he stated: "We are chiefly concerned here . . . with the welfare of families which have been in the United States, and particularly in California, for ten, fifteen, twenty or more years, with children born here and who are American citizens, who are part, even if an unfortunate part, of the American life. . . . American youghs [sic] of Mexican origin, who have been victims of a tremendous erosion from the very day they were born."[7] Facci, in his attempt to defend the rights of Mexican Americans against banishment, also depicts the deep-rooted xenophobic tensions that animated American culture in the 1930s. While he condemned the "tremendous erosion" of Mexican American youth, he also categorized Mexican Americans as an "unfortunate part of the American life." This contradictory representation contributed to the marginalization of Mexican Americans across the US-Mexico borderlands.

Amid the mass removals, the ability of banished citizens to resettle was already a concern for some government officials. During the same period that Sara Marie and her family were banished from the United States, Representative Traeger condemned Mexican American children's birthright citizenship as interfering with the intended permanence of banishment: "Those children, born in LA County, will remain in Mexico until there is some way of getting them back into the US. Suppose the female of the family remains in Mexico long enough to raise her own family. Then she is entitled to bring all of those back to the US when they return."[8] Indeed, in the decades that followed, banished US citizens of Mexican descent would use this legal entitlement to make the case for their return. Sara Marie was entitled to open US immigration petitions for her Mexican-born children, and succeeded in helping them to become naturalized US citizens, though the process involved legal fees and delays that separated the family for over a decade.

COLLABORATIONS BETWEEN FEDERAL AND LOCAL AUTHORITIES

By 1932, when the Robles family was banished, debates over relief aid, unemployment, and immigration quotas in relation to the economic crisis had cemented the idea that Mexican men were temporary laborers likely to become a public charge (LPC) and should be removed along with their dependents. When the US federal government used mass deportations as an alleged solution to the unemployment crisis, local governments were influenced to do the same through so-called repatriation campaigns organized by relief officials. The Bureau of Immigration approved deportations grounded in the recently enacted 1924 Immigration Act, a revised version of the 1917 Immigration Act, which left removal decisions up to the discretion of immigration officers. In 1930, President Hoover appointed William N. Doak as secretary of labor. Doak immediately publicized his solution to the national unemployment crisis: "oust job-holding undocumented immigrants to provide work for unemployed [white] Americans." According to Doak, there were 400,000 immigrants "illegally residing in the United States," and "under current immigration laws, 100,000 were deportable."[9] President Hoover openly granted Doak his complete support, authorizing "245 more agents to assist in the deportation of foreigners"; these agents helped raid community and private spaces throughout the country from Los Angeles to New York.[10] Hoover also granted financial support to the Bureau of Immigration's budget by allocating an additional $500,000 in funds during the 1932 fiscal year.[11] Social workers, immigration officers, and charity employees collaborated with local governments to replicate the federal removal campaigns. These removals included banishments and deportations, but banishments were merged and masked under the term repatriation. Both Mexico and the United States were invested in their political priorities, not the protection of citizens.

Los Angeles County officials, for their part, requested assistance from the federal government to remove ethnic Mexicans from their region, while concerned civic and business leaders responded to President Hoover's Emergency Committee for Employment (PECE) by creating a local citizens committee led by the Los Angeles city and county governments. In December 1930, following Doak's announcement, Charles P. Visel was appointed coordinator of this group, called the Los Angeles Citizens Committee for Coordination of Unemployment

Relief. Its purpose was to "contact all government, industrial and private sources of labor with a view toward creation of employment."[12] Just one month after his appointment, on January 6, 1931, Visel sent a telegram to Colonel Arthur Woods, the national coordinator of PECE. In the telegram, Visel, aware of Doak's announcement about the 400,000 immigrants living in the United States, claimed that in Southern California there were an estimated 20,000 deportable immigrants.[13] This exaggeration effectively created the conditions for removing Mexicans and Mexican Americans. In his communication to Woods, Visel asked for federal assistance: "We can pick them all up through police and sheriff channels. Local US Department of Immigration personnel not sufficient to handle. You advise please as to method of getting rid. We need their jobs for needy citizens."[14] Two days later, on January 8, 1931, Woods sent a zealous reply directing Visel to contact Labor Secretary Doak. "There is every willingness at this end of the line," affirmed Woods, "to act thoroughly and promptly."[15] Visel immediately contacted Doak, urging him to send immigration agents to create a "psychological gesture . . . to scare many thousand alien deportables out of this district which is the result desired," to which Doak agreed.[16] Visel suggested that widely publicizing deportation in local newspapers, along with carrying out actual arrests and deportations, would coerce ethnic Mexicans into leaving the country.[17]

The racialized discourses cemented the idea that ethnic Mexicans did not deserve relief assistance and justified their banishment. In January 1931, Bureau of Immigration Supervisor William Watkins arrived in Los Angeles with eighteen immigration agents, who began arresting and pressuring ethnic Mexicans to accept "voluntary departure," which was often not voluntary. Watkins soon realized Visel's exaggeration about the number of deportable immigrants, but that did not impede the raids. In February 1931, Watkins wrote to Assistant Labor Secretary Robe Carl White with his concern: "I am not overly sanguine of our ability to pick up contraband aliens in large numbers or groups."[18] This did not stop Watkins. On the contrary, he reported an alternative to continue the raids: "I do believe from what I have observed since arriving here that there are many aliens hereabouts amenable to the immigration laws. In my opinion the situation will ultimately resolve itself into one involving relentless and diligent effort on the part of our officers to locate and apprehend the class of aliens sought."[19]

Less than a week later, five additional immigration officers arrived in the city and staged a raid in El Monte, California, with the assistance of the local sheriff's office. Three hundred people were stopped and interrogated, and thirteen were jailed, twelve of them Mexicans. One had been in the United States for thirteen years and was removed, even though the law protected immigrants from deportation if they had a long-term residence in the country. Another was classified as an "American-born Mexican," pointing to the person's birthright US citizenship, which the immigration officer ignored.[20] This banishment case was not an isolated incident. As the removal raids continued in California and throughout the country, cost became an issue. As James L. Houghteling, immigration commissioner of Chicago, explained to San Francisco's district commissioner Edward W. Cahill: "I am sure it would be of no avail to secure [federal] funds for the removal . . . of US citizens, which would be necessary in respect of the American-born children of Mexican nationals." But, Houghteling explained, "the state or municipal organizations called upon to support destitute Mexican nationals would be glad to provide funds to pay the transportation of American-born children of Mexicans whom the Federal Government repatriates."[21] Under these local-federal orchestrated efforts, ethnicity outweighed citizenship, and immigration officials found ways to sponsor Mexican American banishments.

The usual fear-based tactics of removal relied on violence and what one local government official referred to as *scareheading*—conducting one large, highly publicized raid and warning there would be more.[22] Raids "assumed the logistics of full-scale paramilitary operations," during which "federal officials, county deputy sheriffs, and city police cooperated in local roundups in order to assure maximum success."[23]

Immigration officers went door to door, demanding—without search warrants or probable cause—that residents in Mexican communities produce proof of legal status. Those unable to produce documentation were coerced to leave or removed under false pretenses. A 1933 report on US-Mexico border conditions found that patrol inspectors would "enter houses and make arrests at all times of day and night without warrants; advises the Mexicans that they are here illegally and railroads them across, with jail threats, or secure 'voluntary departure' agreements, as the accused are ignorant of their rights."[24] Ethnic Mexicans were scapegoated at all levels of government and expelled en masse because many were unaware of their civil and constitutional rights. Hoover explained his generalization of immigrants during his administration in his 1952 memoir: "In view of the large amount of unemployment at the time, I concluded that directly or indirectly all immigrants were a public charge at the moment—either they themselves went on relief as soon as they landed, or, if they did get jobs, they forced others onto relief."[25] Their perceived immigrant status—not their indigency or likelihood to become public charges—provided grounds for removal.

Regardless of the concerning reports about unjust removal processes, the raids continued throughout the United States with praise from the Bureau of Immigration and the secretary of labor. Visel credited Doak with success, emphasizing that the bureau had completed the removals with "efficiency, aggressiveness, [and] resourcefulness," and boasting that the "exodus of aliens deportable and otherwise" had opened many jobs for US citizens. The communication affirmed that deportation drives also expelled those who were not deportable, but Visel remained committed to his goal.[26] Between 1930 and 1939, ethnic Mexicans accounted for more than 46 percent of all those removed, even when they represented only 1 percent of the US population.[27] The Bureau of Immigration became the most heavily criticized agency in the federal government for its reprehensible raids, but despite investigations, the removals continued without obstruction.[28]

The local-national efforts soon became a transnational collaboration between Mexican and US authorities. In a desperate effort to reduce the number of enlisted relief beneficiaries, Rex Thomson, the newly appointed director for the Welfare Department of Los Angeles County, rapidly became a self-proclaimed "expert on repatriation" by promoting and overseeing removals, though he had no formal immigration training.[29] Thomson was an engineer who worked as a mining project supervisor and cement salesman. He had retired from the California Taxpayers' Association, where he had administered governmental funds to construction projects like the Los Angeles General Hospital. It was then that Thomson became acquainted with the Los Angeles County Board of Supervisors. In 1930, he was brought out of retirement to reform the social services operation in Los Angeles County. With little understanding of US immigration laws and practices and a focus on cutting costs by any means, Thomson and many other county relief directors expedited the removal of destitute, working-class ethnic Mexicans who were on relief rolls. As Thomson explained in a 1976 interview, "I was always saying every time you take a man off relief you made a tax payer, and a man that has his self-respect back again."[30] He believed that relief should not be provided to "the ones that are lazy."[31]

Destitute ethnic Mexicans in need of relief after losing their jobs were labeled lazy and blamed for their misfortune, then their alleged dependency became the basis for their expulsion. Thomson—who in 1934 served as the superintendent for the Los Angeles County Board of Supervisors, which oversaw the Department of Charities for the County of Los Angeles that led the banishment drives—explained his role in the mass removals during the Depression: "I employed social workers that were Americans of Mexican descent but naturally fluent in the language, or that were Mexican nationals fluent in the language, to go out and . . . offer repatriation to these people." Once they had gathered enough people, Thomson explained, "We would send out four trains in the morning every week—twice a week . . . and eventually we started to pick up, at their request, the 'repatriados' from Arizona and Texas. . . .

When we got to the border then we turned them over to the Mexican Central or El Paso or Nogales Southern Pacific of Mexico."[32] In this transnational effort, US and Mexican authorities bore the expenses of relocating ethnic Mexicans across national borders for their own gain. The United States paid to transport ethnic Mexicans to the border, and the Mexican government financed their passage into the interior of Mexico. The United States reaped the benefits of ethnic Mexican labor, then orchestrated ways to remove these "foreigners" when they were no longer needed. After their removal to Mexico, the Mexican government, in turn, used them to advance agrarian reform and populate border towns in Mexico. This transnational process of banishment effectively displaced and marginalized ethnic Mexicans on both sides of the US-Mexico border. No matter which side of the border they were on, ethnic Mexicans became entangled in a distinctly racialized, gendered, and transnational cycle of displacement and marginalization.

TRANSNATIONAL REMOVAL AND
THE BURDEN OF RETURN

The Mexican government welcomed the mass removals for its nation-building project, as Chapter 4 will examine in even more detail. While political discourses in the United States centered around the "Mexican American problem," Mexican politicians described the newcomers as "loyal compatriots." On September 1, 1932, the year Sara Marie and thousands of other Mexican Americans were banished, Mexican President Pascual Ortiz Rubio addressed the thirty-fifth national Congress of Mexico and cited among his government's achievements "repatriating 125,000 Mexican citizens from the United States, where the economic crisis had made it difficult for them to live. . . . These Mexicans are now being taken home and without any appreciable drain on the national treasury."[33] President Ortiz Rubio perceived the so-called repatriation efforts as a success that came to be understood as a "patriotic duty" for both the government and returnees, turning a blind eye to the injustice of banishment and forced returns. His emphasis on the insignificant effect of the relocation efforts on the national treasury directly contradicted the US portrayal of ethnic Mexicans as a drain on government funds. Situating the Mexican government as a helping hand became an important political strategy. Mexican officials at all levels of government popularized the idea of helping Mexicans abroad as part of their patriotic obligation, while relocated ethnic Mexicans were expected to prove their loyalty to the country by supporting the nation-building project of agrarian reform.[34]

Support throughout Mexico spread rapidly, as it did in the United States. For instance, in 1933, Mexican senators and deputies agreed to "pay 50 pesos ($14.80 USD) each to a fund to care for Mexicans who are being removed from the United States. Their contributions [would] aggregate almost $3,000 [pesos]."[35] Additionally, state governments followed President Ortiz Rubio's lead by having "the governor of nearly every state in Mexico" pledge anywhere from "10,000 to 100,000 acres of land for use of repatriates and [the] unemployed."[36] While Mexico promoted the relocation of mixed-status families for its nationalistic project, men were the primary beneficiaries of the agrarian reform. Land grants were awarded to male heads of household under the assumption that wives, daughters, and minors were indirect beneficiaries.[37] Employment offers were also largely reserved for male heads of household and single men who were assumed to be better equipped for physical labor.[38] Banished women in Mexico continued to be understood as dependents, as they had been in the United States. Thus the sexist frameworks of governmental programs and policies on both sides of the US-Mexico border continued to echo coverture doctrine that limited women's social, economic, and political advancement.

Throughout the 1930s, the Mexico-sponsored removal drives continued to target destitute ethnic Mexicans, including US citizens of Mexican descent. In 1938, Manuel Gamio, head of the Demographic and Repatriation Department, informed Mexican nationals in the

United States that all they needed to qualify for the Mexico-sponsored repatriation campaign was to "prove to the consulate" their "Mexican nationality and indigent status."[39] The Mexican authorities went further this time by addressing the long-overlooked issue regarding US-citizen children in mixed-status families who were entangled in the removal raids. The communication claimed that "children born in the United States of Mexican parents are Mexican citizens and would be entitled to repatriation irrespective of their dual nationality."[40] The parents, however, needed to register the US-citizen minor with the Mexican consulate to be eligible for Mexican nationality. While the United States banished Mexican Americans who were not removable under the LPC clause, Mexican authorities assumed that removal financed with non-US funds was in the US-citizen children's best interest—assumptions that did not consider the needs or desires of US-citizen children and women.

Soon after the announcement, Mexican nationals began contacting their consulate offices with return requests. Some—like Manuel Rodríguez and Pedro E. Gonzáles from Robstown and Barstow, Texas, respectively—reached out to the consulate simply to ask for more information regarding the repatriation offers.[41] Flores y Ropon from Arizona, for example, asked for "assistance to return to his native Zacatecas," and Villareal Silva from Wisconsin requested "repatriation and employment in Mexico."[42] Some who were already in Mexico contacted their consulate office for help. In one case, José Cruz Chávez wrote to the consulate office to request the Mexican president's intervention. Cruz Chávez explained that the border customs of Sonorita, Sonora, had "created many obstacles when attempting to import his belongings from American territory," even as he was returning to Mexico as a "repatriate."[43] Mexican President Lázaro Cárdenas attempted to address some of these concerns by establishing an agreement with the Ferrocarriles Nacionales de México (Mexican National Railroad Company) to grant a "60 percent discount on incoming tickets and a 75 percent discount on the excess of luggage" to "indigent Mexicans, repatriates or deportees by foreign authorities, following the tradition established since the year 1931."[44]

Despite some initial interest, the late-1930s efforts did not remove as many ethnic Mexicans as compared to the second and third periods. In 1939, Ramón Beteta, undersecretary of foreign relations, asked Mexican consuls in the United States to conduct a census to enumerate people interested in "repatriation." The census, compiled by the Foreign Relations Ministry, surveyed communities in New Orleans, Denver, Salt Lake City, Oklahoma City, Kansas City, Saint Louis, Chicago, Detroit, New York, Mobile, and major cities in California, Arizona, and Texas. The results showed that only 565 families were interested in the so-called repatriation offer, totaling 2,785 people.[45] Mexican and US officials, however, moved forward with their plan to remove approximately 100,000 Mexican citizens, a process that continued to coerce mixed-status families into banishment based on LPC claims.[46] As ethnic Mexicans in the United States learned of the dire situation in Mexico, which included extreme poverty and hunger—as the De Anda family had experienced—their hopes for new opportunities after their relocation quickly diminished. Banished mixed-status families in Mexico continued to face hunger, unemployment, family separation, ineligibility for land grants, and other broken promises.[47] Some border towns, where banished families resettled, were plagued with sickness, starvation, and death.[48] Reports of these conditions, particularly starvation, among those removed began to surface. In Hermosillo, Sonora, expelled ethnic Mexicans were reported to be in "such a lamentable state that many [had] taken to eating grass as their only means of sustenance."[49] This dissonance led to a sharp increase in reverse-migration attempts during the second and third periods of removals.

Not surprisingly, banished US citizens started asking for assistance to return to their native country. After becoming unemployed, Juan Terriquez, a Mexican national, left New York City for Guadalajara, Mexico, with his American wife Marrion Terriquez, and their four US-citizen children. Marrion, who had teaching experience and was bilingual in English and Spanish, claimed in a 1933 letter to President Roosevelt that she was denied employment as a teacher in Mexico because she was an American and asked him for help to return to New York.[50] Similarly, Samuel Andrade agreed in 1934 to a repatriation offer from Milwaukee, Wisconsin, under the condition that his wife, Soledad Gutiérrez, and eight children be allowed to remain in Wisconsin for a year until he was able to find employment in Mexico.[51] In 1935, Andrade wrote to the consulate office in Milwaukee, which in turn contacted the office of Mexican President Cárdenas, with his request for assistance to return to the United States in light of his inability to find employment in Mexico after his removal. He wanted to find work in the United States to provide for his family in Milwaukee.[52] As was the case with many of these petitions, the Mexican government denied Andrade's request, citing lack of funds and blaming Andrade himself for his inability to secure employment.[53] Andrade's family, however, was allowed to remain in the United States, likely because Soledad secured employment to provide for her children and reduced LPC concerns. Nonetheless, Andrade's denied return request turned them into a transnational family.[54] Terriquez faced a similar response from the US government, which claimed that she would become a public charge if allowed to return and cited a lack of funding to help "destitute Americans stranded abroad."[55] Thus countless removed Mexicans and Mexican Americans became resigned to remaining in Mexico, while those who did manage to return to the United States had to wait for decades.

Enrique Vega and his extended, mixed-status family were relocated to Zacatecas, Mexico, in 1932 with the assistance of the Mexican Council. Vega remembers that about ten members of his family were moved, some of whom were US citizens, including his "married sister . . . with all her children."[56] They departed using their private vehicles, which some banished mixed-status families did to avoid having to leave their prized possessions behind. Vega explained, "We drove down in a car, we had a car and a truck. We carried everything, all our belongings. It took us about ten days. . . . From Juárez to Zacatecas there was no highway, just a trail."[57] Both Enrique and Sara Marie's families were removed from California and sent to Zacatecas, but unlike Sara Marie and some of his siblings, Enrique was born in Mexico. He returned to the United States in 1942, a decade after his removal, because he was able to prove he would not become a public charge. As Vega explained, "I had to get a sponsor. You would get a definite promise of a job, [and prove] you were not going to be a public burden."[58] This LPC clause of the 1917 Immigration Act included in subsequent immigration acts continues to be used to determine admissibility for immigrants. Though US citizens do not carry the LPC burden of proof for admissibility, returning unaccompanied Mexican American women were often understood to be likely to become public charges because of their assumed economic dependency on husbands or fathers. This was the case for Marrion Terriquez, who as a banished US citizen was denied resettlement assistance on LPC grounds.

Returning banished women also encountered other obstacles. Emilia Castañeda de Valenciana was banished by train in 1935 from her native Los Angeles after her mother died and her father was unable to secure employment. In 1944, after living in Mexico for almost a decade, Castañeda de Valenciana, with a copy of her US birth certificate in hand, finally returned to California. In some cases, Mexican Americans were required to pay unexpected legal fees upon their return. Castañeda de Valenciana recalled returning to the United States by train, just as she had left, and being required to pay a tourist fee: "When I was close to the border, Mexican Immigration boarded the train and asked if you had your tourist card. So, I had to pay the money for a tourist card because, according to them, I was a tourist [in Mexico]."[59] In this and countless other ways, both the Mexican and US governments imposed an "otherness" on Mexican Americans that relegated them to the margins of the national body.

Governmental officials on both sides of the border placed the legal and financial burden of return on banished people, blaming them for their situation and shirking all responsibility for the mass removal raids.

Through their discourse, policies, and practices, authorities in both the
United States and Mexico were complicit in reproducing and expanding
the ways in which banishment further entrenched banished Mexican
American women and their families in a state of transgenerational illegality. By blaming and otherwise marginalizing ethnic Mexicans in
the United States and Mexico, these officials and their actions (or their
refusals to do anything) not only allowed for the juridical and discursive imposition of unauthorized status on the banished families that
catalyzed their removals in the first place, but also continued to insist
on their illegality over time and even as banished Mexican American
women attempted to return. The refusal to facilitate return migration,
as well as the legal and financial barriers imposed on expelled US citizens, effectively extended the detrimental impacts of banishment. To
confront this transgenerational illegality, reclaim their US citizenship,
and pass that citizenship on to their Mexican-born children, women
like Sara Marie Robles would have to learn to navigate two legal systems in order to reverse a banishment that, as Cahill had made clear,
was intended to be permanent.

THE ROBLES FAMILY'S BANISHMENT

Sara Marie Robles was born in 1928 in Pasadena, California, to Mexican immigrant parents. In 1932, she was banished, along with her three
US-citizen siblings and their parents, to Zacatecas, Mexico. Robles
was one of an estimated 77,453 to 80,648 ethnic Mexicans who were
removed in 1932.[60] Chabelo Villegas grew up not fully understanding
the conditions of his mother's arrival to Mexico. He explained, "I knew
that she had been born in the United States, and for a long time that's
as far as I went, as far as the details of why she ended up back in Mexico
with her parents. . . . Many years went by, and I only found out more
after my sister told me. . . . And then, more time went by and then
I started to wonder, if she was a US citizen, why did she have to go

through all the trouble of getting us all the green cards a few at a time? I learned that if you are a US citizen, your descendants, your kids automatically are US citizens. But we were seen as your so-called regular immigrants."[61] Unaware that the rules for derivative citizenship would have granted her children automatic US citizenship, Sara Marie relied on a paralegal's advice and filed lengthy and expensive US family immigration petitions.

This apparent legal contradiction—a US citizen filing petitions as if she were an immigrant to the United States—highlights two key ways in which impermanent legality unfolded over time in the lives of banished women and their families. In the 1930s, the US officials who facilitated Sara Marie's banishment rendered her US citizenship impermanent through various racialized and gendered assumptions about ethnic Mexican women. And in the 1960s, Sara Marie's filing of immigration petitions to bring her family members to the United States indicates how the assumptions of illegalized outsider status that made her banishment possible reappeared in the legal classification of her family members as "immigrants." Guillermina Hinojos, Chabelo's sister, remembered her mother's banishment as an act of humiliation: "I only remember that, well, she only used to tell us stories about how they *kicked them out* of here. She doesn't know how to explain how it all happened, but she says that they were *kicked out* of here, so they had to leave."[62] Guillermina learned from her mother, Sara Marie, that her grandparents returned to Mexico with their four US-citizen children because of the politics of the time—in other words, the anti-Mexican discourse that was fueling banishment and other exclusionary policies and practices. Sara Marie did not have the vocabulary to explain exactly why the family was forced to leave, so she used the phrase kicked out, hinting at the injustice and imposed illegality of the process.

While immigration officials underscored the illegality of banishing US citizens and legal residents under the expulsion raids, in practice they often ignored the legal status of those removed. As historian Camille Guerin-Gonzales contends, local agencies established campaigns

to "ostensibly repatriate Mexicans," but the removal raids "made no effort to distinguish between immigrants and US-born Mexicans and,
in fact, set numerical goals that included both groups."[63] Similarly, at
the federal level, the INS commissioner in Washington, DC, informed
local immigration district directors that "those whose birthplace is
shown as the United States" in departure records "will not be considered for removal," but that stipulation was often overlooked. For instance, when Clyde Campbell, INS district director in San Antonio,
was asked to report admission records for removed Mexican nationals,
he explained: "Full information was not secured with respect to whether
there was a record of admission." This oversight, Campbell continued,
"was due to the short time allowed and the resultant rush to get the repatriation party under way."[64] This was not an unusual experience,
since the removal processes were often rushed, and all ethnic Mexicans
were regularly assumed to be foreigners even when legally admitted or
born in the United States. Government officials readily engaged in these
racialized assumptions of illegality. This wholesale imposition of unauthorized status onto all ethnic Mexicans—regardless of their actual
legal status—paved the way for the continued juridical and discursive
linking of illegality to banished Mexican American women and their
families, not only at the moment of banishment, but also for many
years afterward.

Investigations of US citizens' removals were conducted, but little was
done to correct the violation of citizens' legal and civil rights. A 1934
"State Committee on Mexican Problems" report, delivered by the US
Catholic Conference Department of Immigration, investigated the conditions of Mexicans in relation to the mass expulsions. In its comparison of Texas to its neighboring state of California, the report found that
"Los Angeles County had paid the way of the majority" of so-called
repatriates "into Mexico and that they were American citizens."[65] It also
stated that the main goal appeared to be "to get rid of persons of Mexican descent regardless of their condition in life or anything else."[66] Sara
Marie and her family were banished in 1932 during the second period

of removals, but the government's indifference regarding the unjustness of the process continued, as this report conducted during the third period of removals shows. The banishment would continue unquestioned during four successive periods, building and cementing the social construction of Mexican illegality that later prevented the resettlement of banished Mexican Americans.

It was under these circumstances that Sara Marie, at the age of four, began her life in Mexico despite being a US citizen. After the Robles family's banishment from Pasadena, California, they settled with kin in Potrero de Gallegos, a pueblo in the municipality of Valparaíso, Zacatecas, Mexico, where Sara Marie's parents—Roque Robles and Teresa Gamboa—were born. She grew up there in a mixed-status family composed of Mexican-born parents and US-born children (Figs. 3.2, 3.3). Sara Marie's extended family provided Teresa and Roque with the means to rebuild their lives and support their children. As Guillermina

Figure 3.2 Sara Marie Robles (*left*) pictured with her sister-in-law Emilia (*right*), Zacatecas, Mexico, circa 1944.

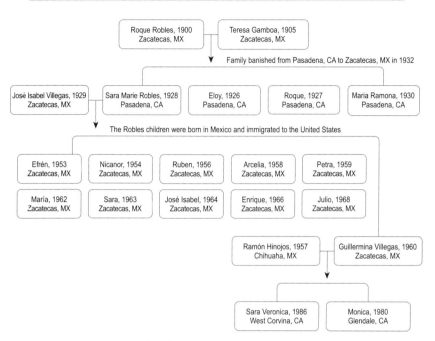

Figure 3.3 Sara Marie Robles's family tree. Graphic by author based on data provided by the Robles Family.

recounted, "[My great-grandparents] had cattle, that was what they used for their income, and they owned land, that's all they had on both sides of the family. Besides, [my maternal grandfather] went on to work as the sheriff of Valparaíso, Zacatecas. That is to say, he used to work for the government . . . he also had cattle on the ranch."[67] Unlike other banished families who arrived to nothing, the Robles family transitioned reasonably well economically—a benefit that not many banished mixed-status families enjoyed.[68] The Robleses became one of their rural town's well-to-do families, and Sara Marie's father, Roque, gained the town's respect as sheriff.

Although the family gained status and influence, their living conditions remained simple due to the town's limited infrastructure. Sara

Marie's experience was not very different from those of women in lower social classes in Mexico at the time. She recalled, years later, that washing clothes was no easy task: "I remember I used to fill a washtub with water, put one of those washboards made of wood in it, and pile bed sheets on one side . . . and that's where I kneeled to do the washing. . . . I had to wash and iron it all by hand, all of it."[69] Sara Marie's banishment not only relegated her to gendered, labor-intensive housework, but also denied her opportunities for formal education, which she likely would have enjoyed in the United States. "Just imagine, I never went to school there [in Valparaíso]," she explained, "because there were no teachers on the ranch where we lived. But I did learn to write my name, some small words too, and to read."[70] Despite her hardships, Sara Marie eventually formed a family of her own in Mexico. In 1951, at the age of twenty-three, she married twenty-two-year-old José Isabel Villegas. His family also owned land and cattle, and after their marriage, José continued working on his father's property. In time, Sara and José raised eleven children in Valparaíso, Zacatecas, including Chabelo and Guillermina.

Sara Marie experienced gendered restrictions in her own household, too, where her husband made the decisions for the family and kept her US birth certificate. After Sara Marie married José in 1951, her father gave her most important legal document not to her but to her husband. "My dad came by . . . and I remember that my husband was there with him and then [José] came in. I said, 'What did my dad want? Why didn't you invite him in?' 'No,' he said, 'he only said he was coming to give me your birth certificate in case one day we wanted to go to the United States.'"[71] Sara Marie responded, "Let's go!"[72] José immediately rejected the idea, telling her, "You go, I'm not crazy."[73] This conversation took place on the eve of significant political and economic upheaval in Mexico. The egalitarian goals of the Revolution, particularly the elevation of the *campesino* (farmer) in the countryside, were becoming a faint memory, especially as internal migration from rural to urban areas increased in Mexico. In fact, one of the main strategies for development under President Miguel Alemán's administration involved the "massive transfer of resources from the poor to the rich and from the country to the city."[74] Shortly thereafter, "the top 10 percent of the population, which enjoyed 49 percent of the national income in 1950, would accrue an even larger slice of the pie, while the bottom 20 percent would lose even more of the 6.1 percent it held that same decade."[75]

Despite this emerging, drastic national economic shift, José's reaction discouraged Sara Marie. She did not mention emigrating to the United States again for another fourteen years, after the new economic reality had taken a toll on her family. José had made it clear that "he did not want to come over here [to the United States], never," Sara Marie remembered sadly.[76] Sara Marie endured the legacies of coverture on both sides of the border.[77] In the United States, outdated coverture practices guided her banishment and once in Mexico it granted her husband authority over her decisions, which delayed her return to the United States. In many ways, the sadness in her voice reflected her frustration with having to depend on her husband to make important decisions. But it was a frustration she later turned into action, because she believed her family could have a better life in the United States. Though her return was delayed for over three decades, her legal status as a US citizen eventually made it possible.

USING LEGAL CAPITAL TO RESETTLE

Immigration scholars cite social capital as a central tool for emigration, but in the case of banished Mexican Americans, it was legal capital—US citizenship—that facilitated return migration to the United States.[78] This legal capital also disrupted gendered migratory patterns. While men traditionally emigrated from Mexico to the United States first and then sent for their families, the legal capital of banished US-citizen women often allowed them to sidestep gendered restrictions and initiate migration. Indeed, the husbands and fathers of US-citizen women generally understood and acknowledged, although not always without hesitation, the women's lawful ability to return to the United States, work legally, and petition for their nuclear family members' legal adjustment.[79] Thus men often eventually agreed to allow their wives and daughters to lead the family's migratory journey as unaccompanied women, in a reversal of traditional gendered immigration patterns.[80]

Sara Marie negotiated her subordinate gendered position with her husband through the discourse of the "American Dream," which she argued would enable them to climb the economic ladder and gain personal advancement.[81] As a woman without a formal education living in a Mexican rural town during the late 1950s, Sara Marie was not expected or even allowed to work outside the home. Aware of such socially imposed gendered restrictions, she imagined that the US labor force would be more equitable for women. So she made the case to her husband that the United States would provide better opportunities for their children, and that once she was there, and working, she could petition for his US lawful permanent resident status. She made it clear that her primary motivation to leave the nucleus of the home was her children's needs. Finally convinced, José decided to hand over her birth certificate.

In Sara Marie's view, the resettlement process forced her to make many sacrifices, but they were worth enduring for her children: "You see, I had the courage to suffer everything I did [upon returning to the United States] so that [my children] wouldn't suffer over there [in Mexico] by themselves. I knew how much the older ones suffered with my husband's brother. He treated them very badly and used to make them work a lot."[82] Sara Marie reflected, almost in disbelief, "And to think that I came back, after having eleven children, I came back."[83] Sara Marie strategically navigated gender norms to pass on the privileges of US citizenship to her children and husband. In this way, banished women like Sara Marie mobilized their gendered legal capital to facilitate their return to the United States—and in the process created, as transnational mothers, distinct transnational family formations.

In 1965, thirty-three years after her banishment, Sara Marie returned to her native Pasadena, California, where immigration politics continued almost unchanged. She reestablished herself there, leaving her children and husband behind. Two of her sisters who had already returned to the United States helped her find a job and a place to live. Sara Marie returned in the wake of the civil rights movement, a time when the virtues of multiculturalism were celebrated but racial hostility was still rampant. The year she returned, the US Congress passed the Hart-Celler Act, also known as the Immigration and Nationality Act of 1965, which curtailed legal immigration from the Americas. It specifically included a limit on the number of Mexicans who could legally immigrate to the United States, thus reinforcing the link between ethnicity and illegality.[84] These limits meant that all ethnic Mexicans, regardless of their legal status, would still be perceived as unauthorized immigrants because the high demand for immigration led many Mexicans to enter the United States without documentation. The racial and social tensions remained very much unchanged from the 1930s, when Sara Marie had been banished. Only after the Hart-Celler Act established a new preference system that favored family reunification for US citizens could Sara Marie continue with her plans to reunite her family.[85]

Under the preference system, Sara Marie was able to file family-based immigration petitions and bring her children to the United States, two at a time. During this twelve-year process, they lived as a transnational family and had to learn ways to maintain their intimate connections across national borders. As anthropologist Lynn Stephen has described, transnational families must "construct space, time, and social relations" to create community in "specific locales, but also through interlinked networks in the United States and Mexico."[86] Like other members of transnational families, Sara Marie worked to create strong economic, familial, and cultural ties between California and Zacatecas.[87] The separation of their family, though necessary, resulted in a painful sense of abandonment among some of Sara Marie's children—a devastating yet common consequence of immigration for transnational families.[88] These challenges led Sara Marie to find creative ways to negotiate gender relations and intimacy with her children and husband across the US-Mexico border.

Once in the United States, Sara Marie's lack of formal education, work experience, and English-language skills limited her labor opportunities. It was her domestic experience sewing her children's clothing while in Mexico that would help her transition to the labor market in the United States. This experience is captured in a family photograph taken in Zacatecas a couple of years before she left to resettle in California. Like her childhood photograph, this image captures Sara Marie gazing directly at the camera—but this time, she is sitting in front of her sewing machine as she holds a piece of fabric with both hands (Fig. 3.4). Given her lack of paid employment history, Sara Marie's work prospects were limited to being a low-paid sweatshop worker in the garment industry. "When I returned [to the United States], I began working in sewing factories, using machines like these ones," Sara Marie recalled as she pointed to the sewing machines in the room where we were talking during her oral history interview.[89] She continued, "My work was so hard. . . . At first, when I began working in the sewing industry, I was paid fifty dollars a week. That was nothing! And they did not pay me by the hour, but by the piece."[90]

Sara Marie's weekly earnings for five eight-hour days included three hours of working at home, which her employer required her to do without additional pay. Sara Marie recalled, "They used to give me [textile] rolls and when I did not finish them . . . I would bring them [home] . . . and I would sew for three hours at night."[91] The labor experiences of Sara Marie and other banished women mirrored that of their undocumented colleagues, in that they were deprived of basic labor rights, including a minimum wage and overtime pay. This, too, was a consequence of the banishment: the impermanence of citizenship had prevented Sara Marie and other banished women from learning English, securing labor experience, and obtaining a formal education.

Figure 3.4 Sara Marie making clothes for her children, Zacatecas, Mexico, circa 1963.

Furthermore, her line of work did not guarantee social mobility, because she and her peers lacked opportunities for wage increases or promotions. She worked in the sweatshop for sixteen years until she retired. The economic opportunities and gender-equitable society she had imagined accessing in her native country proved to be an illusion. Instead, Sara Marie's Mexican ethnicity and inability to speak English continued to mark her as a foreigner who should be relegated to low-paying jobs. Whiteness and English-language dominance were still socially understood as prerequisites of US citizenship.

The perception that Mexicans were a source of cheap and disposable labor dominated in the United States throughout much of the twentieth century. Historians have argued that unauthorized immigrants of all backgrounds became dispensable in the United States because they were relegated to low-paying service-sector jobs.[92] While this argument still holds true, banished Mexican Americans, like working-class unauthorized immigrants, have also been thought of as cheap and disposable labor (more on this in Chapter 4). In 1965, as much as in 1932, US labor was racialized into two major categories: (1) permanent or (2) fluid and unstable. "Skill labor and permanent common labor is American, white, as a rule," explained George P. Clements, Los Angeles Chamber of Commerce's Agricultural Department Manager, in a 1929 report on Mexican immigration. "Casual labor," he continued, "must be fluid and is therefore necessarily un-American. This labor amounted to about 80 percent and was supplied mainly by Mexican and Filipino workers."[93] The same xenophobic labor rhetoric that marked casual, contingent labor—and the workers that worked those jobs—as "necessarily un-American" remained in the American psyche even decades later, when Sara Marie entered the employment sector in the United States.

When Sara Marie returned to the United States in 1965, she encountered a country once again polarized around the role of immigrants. Immigration debates in the 1960s and 1970s replicated the same exhausted stereotypes that portray immigrants as an influx that usurps limited employment opportunities and public goods. In a 1976 debate on immigration, US Senator Strom Thurmond, a Republican from South Carolina, claimed, "America is, in reality, still a land of opportunity and the most generous Nation in the world. However, our wealth is not boundless . . . domestic unemployment clearly shows that we do not have a general excess of available jobs."[94] Speaking in support of immigration restriction, the American Federation of Labor and Congress of Industrial Organizations (AFL-CIO) declared, "Illegal immigrants have for years been taking jobs from American citizens . . . and are all too frequently a drain on the welfare resources of the communities where they live."[95] Mirroring the racialized anti-Mexican discourse of the Depression era, these immigration debates portrayed ethnic Mexicans as a collective economic burden that disrupted employment prospects for US citizens and unauthorized immigrants alike. Even as a US citizen, Sara Marie found that she was racialized as a specific type of worker; the only work she could find was reserved for immigrants and considered "casual labor."

The racialization of this work as both "casual" and "immigrant" marked her and her labor as cheap, disposable, and un-American. Years later, Sara Marie continued to resent the prolonged consequences of banishment that had limited her labor and economic opportunities. As she explained, "I, with no formal education, without knowing how to read, I had to come [to the United States] and work. . . . I suffered a lot!"[96] While Sara Marie enjoyed the legal right to work in her native country, her banishment had deprived her of an education and the language skills that would have given her better opportunities in the United States, opportunities that were further limited by pervasive xenophobia.

Though Sara Marie suffered many hardships in the apparel industry, her position as a wage earner, along with her status as a US citizen, shifted the gender dynamics in the household. Unable to immigrate legally and work in the United States, José now depended on Sara Marie to provide for the family. But the subverted gender relations did not equalize the gender dynamics in their marriage. Women's employment advantages—and in Sara Marie's case, her added legal capital—often inflamed rather than quelled family tensions as well as household inequalities in immigrant families.[97] In fact, gendered power dynamics rarely change with immigration. For example, immigrant women, as "good mothers," are expected to send money home, while men, as "good fathers," are not always expected to do the same; in fact, over time, some men are even excused from doing so.[98] Moreover, women are usually expected to maintain relations with their children and continue their caretaking roles across borders, even as their family members tend to evaluate them more critically.[99] A lack of intimacy and strong relations with children is labeled "bad" mothering.[100] Sara Marie's decision to emigrate did not bring "freedom" from traditional gender constraints. On the contrary, José became even more controlling than before. His exaggerated sense of authority likely resulted from a loss of masculinity and power given the shifting gender roles.[101]

Despite José's attempt to enforce his will, Sara Marie challenged the restrictions he imposed, even after she established residence in California. For instance, in 1966, a year after Sara Marie's return, the petitions by her husband and son for US lawful permanent resident status were approved. They made plans to meet in Tijuana, where Sara Marie was going to deliver their "green cards" (lawful permanent resident documents). With their lawful resident cards secured, the three of them would enter the United States and make their way to Pasadena. Those plans were put on hold, however, when her son Nico's immigration petition was granted but her husband's was delayed. After waiting in Tijuana for more than two months, José's patience wore thin; he wanted to go back to Zacatecas. Sara Marie worried because she knew this could mean that she might not be able to stay in the United States as she had originally planned. Undeterred, she quickly devised a plan that convinced him not only to wait for his lawful permanent resident card, but also to immigrate to the United States to join her permanently. Sara Marie explained how she used her legal status and guardianship of her son to challenge her husband's attempt to dictate her future: "One day [my husband] called me [from Tijuana] and said, 'You know what? I am leaving.' He told me, 'You have to come,' and he asked me to bring him something from [the United States], but I did not want to leave. He said, 'Bring our son and let's go.' Well, I did not take him, I left him here with someone, I only took what he had asked for and some money too. He said, 'Where is the boy?' I told him, 'Well, I did not bring him.' He said, 'Well, I changed my mind, I am not leaving after all.'"[102] Though a potentially risky move, Sara Marie knew that her husband would be unwilling to leave Tijuana and return to Zacatecas without their son. A few weeks later, José received his lawful permanent resident card and immigrated to Pasadena.

As Sara Marie's experiences show, the gendered legal capital of banished women proved to be one way for them to find their way back to the United States. The decisions that Sara Marie made as a US citizen enabled her to get a job in the apparel industry and navigate the shifting gender dynamics of her marriage once she returned. Her US citizenship provided her with the legal right and mobility to cross back and forth between California and Zacatecas, facilitating her role as a transnational wife and mother. But her resettlement was limited by the prolonged effects of banishment. When she returned to the United States in 1965, Sara Marie encountered a resurgence of the same xenophobic political discourse used during the Great Depression to justify the banishment of ethnic Mexicans, which further complicated her resettlement process. Resettlement in her native country also did not grant Sara Marie direct, immediate access to upward socioeconomic mobility; instead, because Sara Marie's removal from the United States had robbed her of English-language skills, formal education, and employment experience, she was forced to take disposable jobs often reserved for unauthorized immigrants. Thus, after successfully overturning her banishment by resettling back in California, Sara Marie, like many other banished women, essentially became an immigrant in her own native country, forced to function as a transnational wife and mother.

TRANSNATIONAL MOTHERHOOD AND CHILDHOOD

The actions of nation-states can have direct consequences on individuals and entire families, as they did in the case of the banishment drives. As Deborah Boehm argues, the US state "can impact, construct, define, (re)produce, reunite, and / or divide families."[103] For banished mixed-status families, the state-sponsored mass removal that they endured, and their eventual return to the United States, gave way to a new construction of the family, shifting it from a nuclear family formation in which everyone lived together under the same roof to a geographically separated family with members living across national borders.[104] Such transnationality "results in new kinship configurations and ways of caring for children, as well as a diverse range of experiences that shape children's lives."[105] That is, the roles of motherhood and childhood change, as transnational mothers and children learn to negotiate the terms of their new family formation. The term *transnational motherhood* refers to the experience of "women who work and reside in the United States while their children remain in their countries of origin."[106] Similarly, I use the term *transnational childhood* to refer to the experiences of children who stay behind in their country of origin while one or both parents emigrate. These shifts, while facilitated by citizenship and naturalization laws, exact a toll on family members. As Marjorie Orellana and her colleagues remind us, "Families do not move easily through transnational circuits; on the contrary, the borders of nation-states are real, and they exert social, emotional, and financial costs on those who cross them."[107] While every family member likely feels the emotional and physical drain of functioning as a transnational family, children are the most affected, and mothers are often blamed for leaving.

Indeed, the emotional pain of negotiating transnationality profoundly affected the Robles family. Once Sara Marie had secured US lawful permanent resident status for her spouse, José, both could cross the US-Mexico border more easily. This allowed them to return to Mexico on a yearly basis to retrieve their children, two at a time, as their immigration petitions were approved. Sara Marie and José took turns working in the United States to save money for the immigration fees. Sara Marie recalled, "He [my husband] came to work here in Oxnard, [California] . . . in the agricultural fields. I used to go back to Mexico to file immigration documents [for my children]. . . . How could I have brought them all at once?"[108] Sara Marie's gendered obligations as a mother required her to spend time in Mexico with her children, all while continuing to file immigration petitions for them. By doing so, she learned to navigate the immigration legal system on both sides of the border.

Though an apparently seamless process, the yearly visits and family separations were fraught with emotional labor and turmoil. Sara Marie had to demonstrate their ability to financially provide for each petitioned child and was unable to do so for all eleven children simultaneously, given her and José's meager salaries. She would return to the United States to work while her husband stayed in Mexico to care for their children. Other times, both worked in the United States while the children stayed with their grandmothers or aunts until their mother could prove to the INS that they were not likely to become public charges. The same public-charge regulation of the 1917 Immigration Act that had banished Sara Marie and her family, and is still in effect, delayed her ability to reunite her family in the United States. Guillermina Hinojos, the sixth of Sara Marie's eleven children, recounted her living arrangement during her mother's absence: "I used to live with my [paternal] grandmother. . . . She lived not too far from us . . . about seven houses, so I went to live with her. But sometimes, I would go to sleep with my sisters [at my parents' house]. . . . At first my dad stayed [in Mexico] with us while my mom left [to the United States]."[109] Divisive forces, including immigration policies as well as economic and political conditions, have long made families of color in the United States struggle to live under the same roof.[110]

In this situation, transnational children have had to mature rapidly to adjust to their new family formations. Children are socially and legally understood as "economic and emotional dependents in need of adult care, labor, and economic provisioning."[111] Children are also "defined and positioned by laws" as dependents of adults in regard to "citizenship, child labor, parental obligation requirements about school attendance, and eligibility for government programs."[112] In an idealized childhood, the parents will provide for their children economically and nurture them emotionally; they will allow children to fulfill their intellectual curiosity through games and formal education without imposing taxing family or financial responsibilities on them. Children in transnational families, however, particularly impoverished ones, are not always protected by the law nor are their parents always physically present in their home to care, work, and provide for them. This often means that transnational children must mature quickly and contribute to the household through their physical and emotional labor. They also cannot always express the pain they endure.[113]

Guillermina Hinojos recalled the loss she felt when the family splintered: "I remember I used to cry. . . . I would be asleep, I remember that I was laying down by my father's feet because my dad was there, meaning that my mom had come [to the United States], and at the beginning my dad stayed behind. That's the only thing I remember—that I used to cry and cry and then my dad would say, 'Who's crying?' No one would answer. I remember that I simply . . . held back my tears so that he would not hear me. But I used to cry for my mom."[114] Families often become transnational because prolonged immigration-adjustment processes, or the lack thereof, divide them across national and emotional borders. Guillermina was five years old when her mother returned to the United States, and she felt her absence as a profound loss. Despite the pain, she buried her feelings to prevent any remorse her parents might have felt. Protecting immigrant parents is not uncommon for transnational children, who often refrain from expressing their emotions to lessen the burden on their migrant family members.[115]

Sara Marie's ninth son Chabelo experienced similar pain and longing. He was one year old when Sara Marie returned to the United States the first time, and twelve years old when he finally joined his family there. Chabelo, like his sister, had to mature at an early age. Starting at the age of six, he worked alongside his father in the corn fields and helped with the cattle (Figs. 3.5a, b). These expectations, in addition to his responsibilities as a student, steered him away from an idealized childhood. Chabelo, now a husband and father of two, compared his childhood in Zacatecas to that of his own children in California, emphasizing the clear differences in responsibilities imposed on transnational children in Mexico compared to middle-class children in the United States: "I remember helping my father in the field planting corn before school. It was a different life there. Here, you wake up your kids at seven, 'Come on guys, wake up, get your backpacks' . . . have breakfast, then you go to school. There, when I was in first [up to] my

Figure 3.5a Guillermina Hinojos on horseback with her sister María riding behind her. Standing in front of the horse are two of their sisters, Petra (*left*) and Sara (*right*), and their cousin Ana (*middle*), Zacatecas, Mexico, circa 1975.

sixth grade of school, I would have to get up at five or six in the morning, go out to the fields, bring the cows home, then have breakfast, then go to school!"[116] Transnational children from working-class families manage busy schedules that include physical and emotional labor as well as their school responsibilities, often without hesitation, because such routines are necessary for the survival of the family and so become normalized.[117] For Chabelo, it was not until he had a point of comparison with his own children that he realized the drastic difference in responsibilities.

Cultural and religious gender norms dictated that Sara Marie, as a mother, bore the responsibility of childrearing. As the only US citizen in her immediate family, however, she positioned herself as the leader in

Figure 3.5b José Isabel "Chabelo" Villegas (*left*) with his sister Arcelia (*right*), in Zacatecas, Mexico. This photograph was taken in 1977 when Sara Marie Robles went to Zacatecas to take Chabelo and his brother Enrique with her to the United States. They were the last two of Sara Marie's children to make the journey to the United States during the family's resettlement process.

her family's migratory journey to the United States, which transformed her into a transnational mother. Sara Marie recalled, "Just imagine, I came here [to the United States] and left all my daughters. . . . I used to ask my God, the Father, to look after them. I was not here for pleasure, but I had to be here because they asked for letters [for proof] of employment and so I was required to work."[118] This reflection on her role as a mother and conduit for lawful status suggests how guilty she felt leaving her children behind. To justify that decision, Sara Marie highlighted the fact that she did not come to the United States for leisure or self-indulgence. She had to come for the sake of the family. Mothers who have transgressed gender boundaries and cultural norms by emigrating alone often share this guilt.[119]

BREAKING THE SILENCE

Sara Marie's determination to resettle in her native country after her banishment required her to challenge the social and cultural gender-based restrictions imposed on her as a wife and mother. She developed creative ways to navigate the gender and racial constraints to maintain a sense of intimacy with her husband and children, even when they were divided across national borders and had to function as a transnational family for twelve years. Her family history highlights the prolonged effects of banishment on multiple generations, and her story is just one of many like it, including the others in this book, that helps us better understand the legacy of banishment today. But these histories could only be documented once banished survivors and their families decided to speak about their removals.

Once in Mexico, Sara Marie's parents rarely, if ever, talked about their life in the United States. Perhaps the humiliation the Robles family experienced prevented them from recounting their removal story. The subsequent generations, then, did not learn about their family's banishment history until decades later. Once they finally did, it was the family's personal narratives that provided the rich hidden histories that written records could not capture. Documents are impersonal and, while important, they usually do not depict the nuances of lived banishment experiences. As oral historian Alessandro Portelli argues, the researcher must work within the intersections of factual evidence and collected narratives, the referent and the signifier, past and present—as well as the spaces in between.[120] It is in these in-between spaces—these interstices of historical memory and meaning—that the Robles family's stories reveal unexplored histories of gendered formations and negotiations across the US-Mexico border.

Sara Veronica, Sara Marie's granddaughter, became curious about her family's immigration history when she began learning about Mexican migration as a college undergraduate (Fig. 3.6). Sara Veronica first learned about her grandmother's banishment unexpect-

Figure 3.6 *Left to right:* José Isabel "Chabelo" Villegas, Sara Marie Robles, and Sara Veronica Hinojos, Pasadena, California, circa 2019.

edly from her mother, Guillermina: "I remember saying something along the lines, to my mom, about my grandmother being an immigrant. My mom was like, 'Oh, she is not from Mexico,' you know, almost like insinuating something. And I'm like, 'What do you mean?' My grandma only speaks Spanish. She doesn't understand English."[121] Sara Veronica always imagined her maternal grandmother as a Mexican immigrant because of her Spanish monolingualism. In fact, she grew up thinking that her family's US history began with her parents' immigration to the United States. Sara Veronica's confusion points to a broader social assumption that links language to citizenship. Constructions of "natural" US citizens presume not only that they are racially white—as the mass removal raids in the wake of the Depression and the accompanying anti-immigrant discourse clearly demonstrated— but also that they are English-only, or at least English-dominant, speakers.

These racialized assumptions about who "belongs" in the United States, and who does not, highlight the relative ease with which Sara Marie's ethnic Mexican identity became linked to notions of illegality. Guillermina corrected her daughter, exclaiming, "No, she was born here. Her name is Sara *Marie*," stressing her Nana's anglicized middle name. For the family, her name accentuates her heritage as a US citizen by birth, since she is the only one in their family with a non-Mexican name.[122]

Sara Veronica's initial conversation with her mom about her grandmother's birth in the United States led her to ask more questions and examine family pictures more closely. Photographs often invite questions about the past and closer visual analysis.[123] Sara Veronica cited the black-and-white picture, the last photograph taken of Sara Marie in the United States prior to her banishment, in particular (Fig. 3.1). "I remembered [my Nana] has this picture when she was little and she's sitting at a park bench and she's like three or four. It's so weird to see your family history in black and white. For some reason I felt like I belonged to history. When I think of black-and-white pictures, I think of old white people like in the 1920s," she said, laughing.[124] This picture became a tool for remembering and breaking the silence. It is also visual proof of Sara Veronica's family roots in the United States dating back to the early twentieth century.

A photograph like this, taken when cameras had become more readily available, can legitimize a history in ways that are legible to a family regardless of their formal education and literacy. Photographs allow the viewer to imagine the oral histories that family members share, and make new connections to the faces and landscapes on view. As historians Alexander Freund and Alistair Thomson remind us, for oral historians, photographs are powerful signifiers of an important past, of history. Although "albums seldom make their way into archives," by conducting an oral history that engages with family pictures, "the oral historian can ensure they enter the historical record."[125] For Sara Veronica, then, this black-and-white photograph of her grandmother as a child in the United States legitimized her family's rooted US history, served as a tool to remember, and invited historical inquiry into the Robles's banishment history.

Now, as a college professor of media studies, Sara Veronica includes topics of immigration in her lessons, including the history of mass removals during the Great Depression. She shares her maternal grandmother's banishment story with her students and highlights the silence, sadness, and paradoxical limitations that banished people faced: "I just remember thinking about the pain she had to go through. And then, the fact that, like, you're a natural-born citizen and then you don't have access to the language. So, when I talk about my grandma in class, I always tell my students she's a natural-born citizen, but she doesn't speak any English. So, I think [there's] just like this sadness about what had happened. And the fact that . . . a lot of people don't know that they sent back citizens. Like, 'What? How can they do this?' [There] was just a silence around the whole thing."[126] When she shares these histories with her students, Sara Veronica emphasizes the silence around her family's banishment, which came from an enduring sense of shame and pain.

Indeed, a breadth of emotions—including shame, pain, and sadness—accompanied the transmission of transgenerational illegality in the Robles family. While Sara Marie's banishment invoked feelings of inferiority and shame for being targeted as an "outsider," there was also sadness in being denied access to opportunities in one's own native country as a Mexican American. Sara Veronica also feels a sadness that comes from the pain that her grandmother, along with thousands of banished people, had to endure, compounded by the heartache of not knowing this history. For a long time, Sara Veronica imagined her Nana as part of the immigrant experience, a feeling that was socially legitimatized by her ethnicity, while her mother, Guillermina, kept quiet about her family's long-rooted, troubled history in the United States. It was not easy, but Sara Veronica's insightful questioning of her family's migration history opened the conversation, as painful as it might have been, that has allowed the three generations to safeguard this history through their collective stories. They shared memories of pain, anger, and frustration, and in those conversations, they also found a sense of validation. In breaking decades of silence around their banishment experiences, members of the Robles family also generously contributed their painful history of removal, survival, perseverance, and the gendered tactics that banished women used to reclaim US citizenship and challenge their imposed illegality during the Depression. While their perseverance and successes are critical to acknowledge, we cannot forget, as Sara Marie's story also illustrates, how the prolonged consequences of legal impermanence marginalized women in terms of the work they could perform on both sides of the US-Mexico border. As I will explain in Chapter 4, other Mexican American women who were removed from the United States because of their disposable status were allowed to return, but only to fill labor shortages during World War II. Their imposed illegality followed them for decades.

CHAPTER FOUR

THE ESPINOZA FAMILY

Impermanent Legality

In 1932, Felicitas Castro packed ten years of her family's life in two large trunks and boarded a train with her four US-citizen children in tow, including her daughter Ramona Espinoza, who was born in San Dimas, California.[1] At the young age of six, Ramona witnessed Felicitas carefully select family photos, important documents, clothing, and other essentials as they prepared to depart the United States after receiving a "repatriation letter" ordering their family's banishment from their home in Los Angeles, California. When they arrived in Mexico, they experienced danger, homelessness, and hunger. Notably, it was the generosity of residents, not the government, that helped them during the transition.

As soon as the Espinozas reached La Ilama, Sinaloa, Ramona's mother started saving for their return to the United States. As Ramona recalled, "When we first arrived in Sinaloa, my mom started planning our return because they told her that she could return a year later."[2] But even though US officials promised banished families that they could come back a year after their removal—supposedly once the economic crisis had stabilized—Felicitas and her children were among the many who were denied reentry. The family ended up in the border town of Mexicali, Baja California, in hopes of eventually returning to

California. In 1941, during World War II, Ramona, now almost sixteen, was finally admitted into the United States with her birth certificate, but only to toil as a seasonal farmworker in the fields of California's Imperial Valley. Two years later, the Thornton Canning Company in Stockton, California, recruited Ramona, other banished Mexican Americans, and locals living in Mexican border towns for seasonal employment. Thus Ramona was forced to leave her native country only to be recruited back nine years later to fill demands in the United States for cheap and temporary labor. The temporary recruitment of Ramona and other ethnic Mexicans to fill the labor shortage reveals the ways in which legal status was granted conditionally and contingently on the labor they could provide—and only when it was needed. It was not until 1948, sixteen years after her banishment, that Ramona resettled permanently in the United States as a twenty-two-year-old married woman.[3]

In the United States, the lack of a clear national policy for what was referred to as Mexican repatriation made banishment a highly discretionary process and gave considerable decision-making latitude to local charities, social workers, and Bureau of Immigration officers, all of whom often operated with anti-Mexican stereotypes.[4] On the other side of the border, during the three decades ranging from the early 1910s to late 1930s, Mexico underwent a nation-building project centered around agrarian reform.[5] Mexican governmental officials and consulate offices promoted "repatriation" as a "patriotic duty" and an opportunity for Mexicans abroad to return home and help rebuild the nation by colonizing redistributed land.[6] Then, in the late 1930s and early 1940s, banished Mexican Americans were recruited back to the United States to perform their "patriotic" duty as US citizens: filling labor vacancies during World War II. Thus, the US and Mexican governments both called on the loyalty of Mexican Americans, even as each nation continued to marginalize and displace them.

Multiple displacements on both sides of the US-Mexico borderlands robbed Felicitas and her children of most of their belongings. While the Espinoza family has a rich documentation of their banishment history, they do not have photographs of the family in the United States prior to their removal, as was the case for other participating families in this book. Still, the transgenerational oral histories and private collections of Ramona, her daughter María Guadalupe Espinoza, and her grandson Arturo Espinoza—as well as the expansive archival sources about her family's banishment that Guadalupe has recovered—provide a window into the process under which ethnic Mexicans of varying legal statuses have been historically demoted to so-called immigrant jobs characterized by low wages, limited labor protections, and no benefits.[7] In the early twentieth century, this practice trapped ethnic Mexicans in disposable employment positions and rendered them vulnerable to unemployment during the interwar period, as previous chapters have shown. As a result, unemployed and destitute ethnic Mexicans turned to relief assistance, leading social workers to advocate for mass removals that portrayed all Mexicans as "likely to become a public charge" (LPC). In the early 1940s, the United States suffered labor shortages resulting from those mass ethnic Mexican removals (as well as from Filipino repatriation, expanded Asian exclusion laws, and World War II enlistments). White migrants who moved to California and other parts of the Southwest during the Dust Bowl soon filled the labor demand. But they commanded higher wages as well as relief aid during the low labor season, creating extra expenses for both employers and local governments. Ironically, US companies then turned to Mexicans, including banished Mexican Americans, as a cheaper, and therefore preferable, source of labor for agriculture and canning.

Ramona Espinoza was one of the thousands of banished US citizens recruited for temporary labor in the late 1930s and early 1940s. As her story shows, Mexican Americans' inability to access full US citizenship—and the ways that impermanent legality always qualified and weakened their claim to belonging in the United States—effectively made banished returnees into temporary immigrants in their own country and continued to relegate them to low-wage employment. Even in the shadow of banishment, Ramona and her family members experienced firsthand how this illegality showed up differently across generations (Fig. 4.1). In this chapter, I examine banishment through a close

Figure 4.1 *Left to right:* Arturo Espinoza, Ramona Espinoza, and María Guadalupe Espinoza at Chicano Park in front of a Coatlicue (Earth Goddess) mural, San Diego, California, 2018.

analysis of racialized allocations of relief aid, the LPC clause of the 1917 Immigration Act, and local-federal removal efforts. The Espinoza family's stories help us understand the complexities of employment racialization processes and abuses that entangled banished Mexican Americans in impermanent legality, in part due to the oscillating desirability of Mexican labor in the United States at various historical conjunctures. Indeed, the Espinoza family's story reveals the racialized and gendered discourses, processes, and dynamics that enabled their banishment and historically trapped banished ethnic Mexicans in a cycle of continual displacement, dispossession, and economic marginalization everywhere they went.

RACIALIZATION OF PUBLIC ASSISTANCE AND LABOR

The racialization of banishment became apparent when ethnic Mexicans were targeted for their alleged dependency on social benefits. In a 1932 special report on Mexican conditions, the Mexican consulate in San Bernardino cited an estimated 50,000 Mexicans living in San Bernardino and Riverside counties, accounting for 15 percent of the total population for that consulate district.[8] While unemployment records in this district reported a rate of 10 percent among people of all nationalities, Mexican unemployment was disproportionately higher, reaching 25 to 30 percent.[9] Many of these unemployed ethnic Mexican families had to rely on public and private charities for assistance. In Los Angeles, the unemployment and relief statistics told a similar story. While Los Angeles public relief—assigned based on an unofficial white racial prerequisite—increased rapidly from 18,650 in the 1928–1929 fiscal year to 25,913 in 1929–1930, the proportion of Mexicans on relief decreased from 21.5 percent in 1928–1929 to 12.5 percent in 1930–1931.[10] It is estimated that Mexicans received only $38,000, equivalent to around 2.5 percent of the total $1,509,780 that Los Angeles County spent on relief per year. These statistics reflect the exaggeration of the "Mexican problem" that called for the mass removals of ethnic Mexicans. In fact, these figures challenge the veracity of county officials' claims that repatriation, and by extension banishment, would save the county $2,400,000 a year in relief expenditures.[11] Nonetheless, the racial exclusion of ethnic Mexicans continued in the processes of both mass removal and aid distribution.

Cultural pride and fear of removal can help explain the low numbers of Mexicans on relief rolls. Culturally, Mexicans generally took great pride in their ability to provide for their families. Therefore, asking for aid represented a failure of their role as providers.[12] Additionally, the threat of removal associated with asking for relief discouraged most ethnic Mexicans from seeking or obtaining aid, so as to avoid any unwanted attention that could lead to banishment.[13] Mexicans who had no other option but to use public assistance also encountered unequal distributions of aid. White families, for instance, received a basic grant of thirty dollars a month, while Mexican families were given only twenty dollars a month regardless of family size. The difference in dollar amounts was based on governmental officials' belief that "Mexican families had a lower standard of living and could get along on a cheaper diet."[14] The assumption that Mexicans could survive on lower-quality food was also extended as the reason for paying Mexicans lower wages. Both governmental officials and social workers in private organizations had similar views on ethnic Mexicans.

On June 26, 1934, Texas officials convened a State Committee on Mexican Problems to provide recommendations to deal with the so-called social, economic, and political problems that Mexicans represented. Out of this meeting emerged a notable claim that Mexicans should be given a cheaper diet in their relief packages. This conclusion was based on misguided studies carried out at local food markets on the consumption habits of ethnic Mexicans that reinforced stereotypes. The committee organizer, Cleofas Calleros, claimed that Mexicans were getting too much pork and flour. Such foods, Calleros argued, were not part of their diet, so the food assistance was a waste of resources.[15] In reality, however, working-class ethnic Mexicans did not buy inexpensive foods or eat less because they were culturally satisfied with such inferior goods or limited quantities; on the contrary, they did so because they lacked the economic resources to buy larger quantities and higher quality food. Juanita Barbolla, a member of the State Committee on Mexican Problems, corrected Calleros's racialized assumption: "Mexican people should have just the same thing the American should. They like fruit, vegetables, and cereals. . . . To say that the Mexicans should be satisfied with potatoes, beans, and coffee does not mean to say that he should have nothing better but beans. All growing children should have fruits and vegetables."[16] Despite the debates, the racialized and uneven distribution of social benefits by private and public welfare organizations continued at the local and national levels, marking ethnic Mexicans, regardless of legal status, as outsiders and thus less deserving of public relief. This racial construction of ethnic Mexicans as fundamentally different from and inferior to white Americans paved the way for US officials to link ethnic Mexican identity to the notions of excludability that made the mass banishments possible.

From 1929 to 1933, during the second period of removals, when Ramona and her family were banished, US officials orchestrated the mass removals of some 400,000 Mexicans and Mexican Americans. Not everyone supported these mass removals. The agricultural sector strongly opposed them because it depended heavily on Mexican families for labor. Women and children often worked alongside their fathers and husbands in the fields, and growers expressed concern about the effects an ethnic Mexican labor shortage would have on agricultural production if entire mixed-status Mexican families continued to be banished. During a March 1930 meeting of the Rio Grande Valley Potato Growers Association, Sam Robertson of San Benito explained that the "continued deportations of Mexicans will likely result in a labor shortage which may be felt during the potato harvesting season."[17] The secretary of the Western Growers Association, C. B. Moore, similarly warned that the "vegetable and fruit growers of Southern California and Arizona have become alarmed over the incessant stream of Mexicans pouring over the border into their native lands."[18] While some politicians and social workers saw mass removal efforts as a tool to solve unemployment and reduce relief expenses, growers, including Robertson and Moore, anticipated that mass removals, far from helping the economy, would hurt agricultural labor and production. "Americans are so far removed from the class of the work Mexicans do in the fields," Moore complained, "that a labor shortage during the summer harvest time is sure to result."[19] Notably, even though he opposed these removals, Moore—not unlike the social workers and representatives who championed banishment—operated with specific Mexican stereotypes in mind. In his claim that Americans are not fit for agricultural labor, Moore assumed that Mexican bodies were equipped to endure backbreaking labor conditions and would unquestionably accept low wages. These stereotypical perspectives largely drove growers to protest mass removals as they continued to exploit Mexican labor. Nevertheless, the pressures for ethnic Mexican expulsions were stronger, and support for those measures spread rapidly across the United States and Mexico with the help of government officials, social workers, and private parties.

THE ESPINOZA FAMILY'S BANISHMENT

The Espinoza family's history in the United States began in 1922, when Felicitas, after marrying Emilio Castro, emigrated from La Ilama, Sinaloa, Mexico, to Lamanda Park, a neighborhood in Pasadena, California. Felicitas and Emilio separated shortly afterward. Felicitas remained single for a few years and earned a living by working at a restaurant. While employed as a waitress, Felicitas met Pilar García, who was a frequent customer. In 1925, after dating for a while, Felicitas and Pilar began raising their family in the Sawtelle area of West Los Angeles (Fig. 4.2). Ramona was born in 1926, the first of four of their US-born children.[20] Ramona recalls being excited by the prospects of attending school in 1932, at the age of six, "I remember when my mom

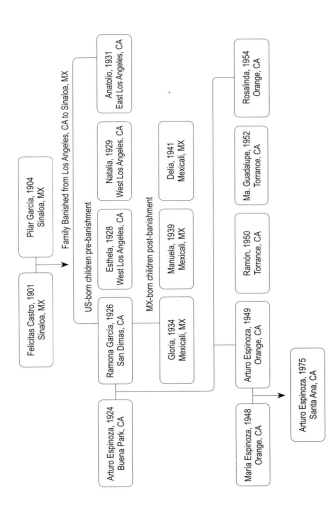

Felicitas Castro, 1901
Sinaloa, MX

Pilar Garcia, 1904
Sinaloa, MX

Family Banished from Los Angeles, CA to Sinaloa, MX

US-born children pre-banishment

Esthela, 1928
West Los Angeles, CA

Natalia, 1929
West Los Angeles, CA

Anatolio, 1931
East Los Angeles, CA

MX-born children post-banishment

Arturo Espinoza, 1924
Buena Park, CA

Ramona Garcia, 1926
San Dimas, CA

Gloria, 1934
Mexicali, MX

Manuela, 1939
Mexicali, MX

Delia, 1941
Mexicali, MX

Maria Espinoza, 1948
Orange, CA

Arturo Espinoza, 1949
Orange, CA

Ramón, 1950
Torrance, CA

Ma. Guadalupe, 1952
Torrance, CA

Rosalinda, 1954
Orange, CA

Arturo Espinoza, 1975
Santa Ana, CA

Figure 4.2 Ramona Espinoza's family tree. Graphic by author based on data provided by the Espinoza Family.

took us to get vaccinated. . . . I think my mom was getting ready to send me to school because we were already attending catechism."[21] This excitement was abruptly interrupted when Ramona and her family were banished. Guadalupe, Felicita's granddaughter, researched her family history in order to reconstruct her family's presence in the United States prior to their banishment. During her investigation, Guadalupe found Felicitas's 1922 US legal admission record, her home address at the time, and other archival records, and she had the documents certified. "I have my Nana's record with a seal and a ribbon that makes it a legal document," she explained (Figs. 4.3a,b).[22] Guadalupe found tangible, legal proof that corroborates her family's banishment memories, alongside other evidence, to bring a forgotten history back into existence.

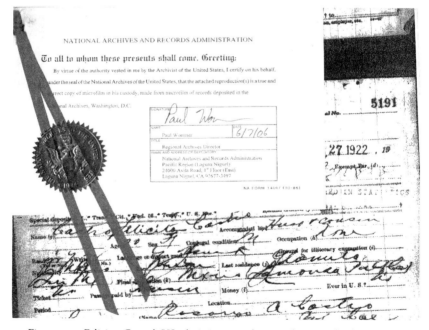

Figure 4.3a Felicitas Castro's US admission record stamped in 2006 by the National Archives and Records Administration, June 7, 2006.

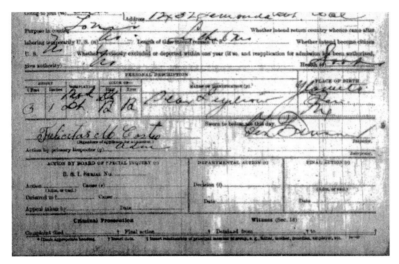

Figure 4.3b Felicitas Castro's US admission record (*close-up*), July 27, 1922.

Ramona considers the Los Angeles General Hospital as the place where her family's banishment originated. From mid-1931 to early-1932, Felicitas took her children there to get vaccinated. Then, in early 1932, Felicitas received a letter saying that the family was enlisted for so-called repatriation. In 1932, when the family was banished, both the Los Angeles General Hospital and Department of Charities were administered by Rex Thomson. As previous chapters have shown, Thomson widely used the LPC language of the Immigration Act of 1917 to encourage the removal of ethnic Mexicans who requested charity or medical services.[23] Ramona's General Hospital card shows her name and address on the front and her four visits ranging from June 1931 to January 1932 on the back (Figs. 4.4a,b). Thus, according to Ramona, "It was there [in the hospital] where they tracked our address to send us the repatriation letter. They used to send a letter that said when you had to leave the country. . . . It had a date and the time when your train would depart. . . . If you did not leave on the date listed on your letter

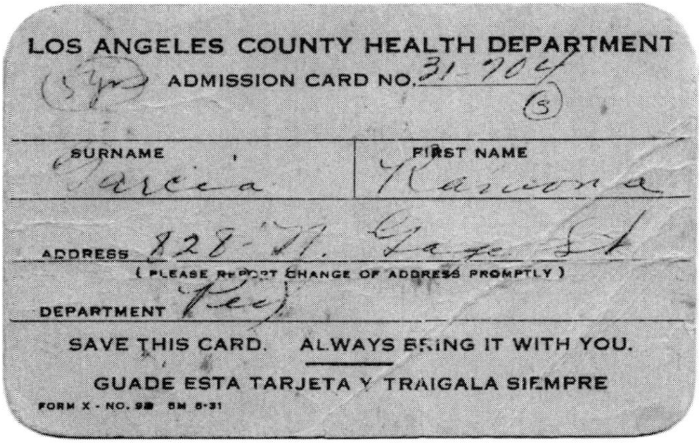

LOS ANGELES COUNTY HEALTH DEPARTMENT

ADMISSION CARD NO. 31-704

SURNAME Garcia

FIRST NAME Ramona

ADDRESS 828 N. Gage St

(PLEASE REPORT CHANGE OF ADDRESS PROMPTLY)

DEPARTMENT

SAVE THIS CARD. ALWAYS BRING IT WITH YOU.

GUADE ESTA TARJETA Y TRAIGALA SIEMPRE

FORM X - NO. 9 5M 5-31

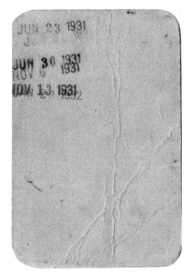

Figure 4.4a Ramona's admission card for the Los Angeles County Health Department (*front*), 1931–1932, showing her full name and address.

Figure 4.4b Ramona's admission card for the Los Angeles County Health Department (*back*), 1931–1932, listing the dates that she was treated.

they would come, and they did not let you take anything, they would just take you."[24] Felicitas feared the possibility of an abrupt expulsion, which was common during immigration raids at the time, and of potentially being separated from her children. She had no option but to follow the instructions in the letter.

Felicitas and her children were classified as LPC and banished, not due to their immigration status, but because she was a Mexican working-class single mother of four. Guadalupe discovered that Felicitas and Pilar had been separated for six months in 1931, which she attributes to Felicitas's banishment: "Women that were needy, women with marital problems, women that were single moms, were targeted. The most vulnerable of all. Single women with children, US citizens who needed the help of their government were just sent to Mexico."[25] Indeed, some social workers, politicians, and immigration officers saw the reproductive power of working-class women of color as a threat to the desired middle-class white racial order. Mexicans were not racially excluded from US citizenship, as was the case for Asians. Yet Mexican women and their Mexican American children were understood as undesirable because of their ethnicity and class status.[26] For nativists, ethnic Mexican women and children were economic burdens given their alleged LPC status.[27] Thus it became common practice for state-funded services to routinely report recipients for removal on LPC grounds, regardless of legal status.[28] As Ramona recounts: "My mom was legally admitted to the US. . . . And we were born here [in the United States]. Nonetheless, they kicked us out."[29] Despite the family's rooted and legal presence, Felicitas was forced to select only a few of her family's belongings and pack their entire lives into just two trunks.

The train ride marked a significant turning point in the lives of banished families. This moment is still imprinted in Ramona's memory: "I remember when we boarded the train and when we were about to arrive in Sinaloa where my grandfather lived. . . . The train took us all the way to Los Mochis. . . . For a long time, I cried when sharing these stories, but over time you become stronger."[30] As the transgenerational stories in this book attest, a sense of loss often defines banishment across generations—not only for the dispossession of material things, but for the erasure of home and belonging. It was often generous residents facing similar circumstances, not the government, who extended a helping hand to recently arrived mixed-status Mexican families who had been banished. After disembarking the train in Los Mochis, the Espinozas found their own way to La Ilama, Sinaloa, where Felicitas's father lived. Unable to cross a river on the route to La Ilama because rainy conditions had made the current too dangerous, Felicitas had to find temporary shelter for her family. Ramona recalled that they stayed in "a store that belonged to a Mexican woman who was married to a Chinese man. . . . My grandfather was friends with the man, and he told my mom to go to that store. . . . During that time, they were removing Chinese people and sending them to China. The lady was on her own and had small children. So, the store was closed. . . . We stayed there for more than a week."[31] By 1926, the Chinese population in Mexico had reached 24,218, making them the second largest immigrant group in the country and a target for removal during the Depression.[32] The store owner sympathized with the Espinozas, because her husband had also been removed from Mexico under similar circumstances.

During the second half of the nineteenth century, following US Asian exclusion laws, a significant number of Chinese people (mainly men) moved to Mexico in hopes of eventually returning to the United States.[33] The exclusion regulations, however, ended up lasting over sixty years. Thus Chinese men and some women settled in Mexico permanently, and some married Mexicans, giving birth to generations of Chinese Mexican children. When the United States expelled thousands of ethnic Mexicans during the Depression, Mexico implemented an almost identical approach to remove ethnic Chinese from Mexico. The Mexican government argued that the newly arrived Mexicans needed jobs and resources that the ethnic Chinese were taking. Yet many of the removed Chinese were Mexican citizens themselves who had married Mexican-citizen women and had Mexican-born children.[34] Ultimately,

Chinese Mexican families who had themselves experienced firsthand the injustice of forced relocation often came to the aid of Mexican Americans banished from the United States.

Like the ethnic Chinese, banished mixed-status Mexican families settled in Mexico with the hope of soon returning to the United States. After all, government officials had told ethnic Mexicans that their removal was temporary. According to R. J. Norene, an INS divisional director who studied the "Mexican repatriation process," displaced ethnic Mexicans could supposedly return after a year, despite the lack of clear national guidelines around such returns: "The American immigration authorities have instructions from their main office at Washington to repatriate Mexicans. . . . Even though these cases do not have the nature of a deportation, they do restrict the rights of the repatriated person to return to this country until a year has elapsed."[35] Ethnic Mexican removals thus functioned as deportations in all but name—at the same time that authorities mischaracterized them as voluntary, temporary, and benevolent. As Ramona's family soon discovered, the claim that ethnic Mexicans could return after a year proved to be misleading. As Guadalupe explained, her grandmother Felicitas had complied with the removal because of the one-year provision and thus immediately began planning her return: "They stayed [in Sinaloa] for a year. And then my grandmother tried to come back. She raised pigs to make money and sold property that she had inherited."[36] Felicitas was determined to return to raise her children in their native country. Ramona remembers that in 1933, after spending one year in banishment, her mom "was convinced they would let us back in, so we took a train again from the station in Los Mochis [Sinaloa] all the way to Nogales, Sonora. When we wanted to cross in Nogales, Arizona, they didn't let us in because they were still repatriating families."[37] After selling their belongings and traveling 481 miles, Felicitas and her children were turned back from the inspection site in Arizona. The misleading information the Espinoza family received when banished and the continued removals during the second period meant that they were forced to remain in Mexico. With their return thwarted by US border officials, they had to come to terms with the fact that they had been banished from their native country.

The anti-Mexican sentiment in the United States promoted by nativists during the peak of the Depression intensified, even as the economy began to recover. In 1935, Willard F. Kelly, supervisor of the Border Patrol, warned that economic recovery would increase return migration: "We estimate that between 200,000 and 350,000 Mexicans, repatriated after being domiciled here, are ready to return to this country illegally."[38] The promise that banished Mexicans could return to the United States after a year quickly gave way to propaganda around an alleged "alien influx" threat.[39] For banished Mexican Americans, their legal status as birthright US citizens was of little help at the border; instead, they were considered foreigners in part because their Mexican-ness was read as irrevocably "other." In 1933, when Ramona's family requested readmission, INS Commissioner George L. Coleman reported, "Mexican-Americans . . . were hindered and insulted by our immigration officers when they tried to return. . . . At times immigration officers refused to accept birth certificates. . . . In one such case an inspector stated that a birth certificate meant nothing to him."[40] Some immigration officers, informed by US anti-Mexican sentiment, felt entitled to abuse their authority by denying admission to Mexican Americans despite proof of US citizenship. Immigration inspectors also routinely used LPC as grounds for inadmissibility.[41] Felicitas, who never stopped trying to return to the United States, attempted via other inspection points. As Ramona explained, "We also tried to enter through Calexico . . . and Mexicali, but they did not let us in either." Felicitas was likely not readmitted to the United States for the same reason that her family was banished to Mexico. After Felicitas separated from Pilar in 1931, she became a destitute, single mother of four US-citizen children, which labeled her as LPC. As Guadalupe concluded, Felicitas and her children "got stuck in Mexicali."[42] In this notable instance of impermanent legality, a Mexican American woman's access to US citizenship and legal status was once again rendered conditional on the basis of ethnicity, class status, age, and gender. Like many others in her shoes, Felicitas had been deceived into believing that she and her children would be readmitted to the United States after a temporary removal, but instead their banishment was intended to be permanent.

GENDERED EXPERIENCES IN A MEXICAN COLONIZATION PROJECT

Some of the banished families who were denied return entry into the United States settled in colonization projects near the US-Mexico border. Ramona and her kin became one of the many displaced families who spent a significant part of their lives in these colonization projects. After Ramona's family was denied admission in Nogales, her mother learned about a transportation service that took people from the border to Pueblo Nuevo, a colonization project in Mexicali, Baja California. Ramona vividly remembers her family's 1933 journey from Nogales to Mexicali: "There was a transport, as mom used to say, that would take people from Nogales to Mexicali, all the way across the desert. It was a black car. . . . My mom paid for the tickets. . . . Then, she put two sets of clothes on each of us . . . she had to leave the trunks behind . . . [we] could only take whatever we had on. They packed the car with as many people as possible."[43] Not only did Felicitas have to pay additional unplanned fees to transport her family from Nogales to Mexicali, but she again had to leave most of her belongings behind. Every time Felicitas's family was displaced, they became more destitute—an experience all too familiar among banished mixed-status families.[44] Felicitas and her children arrived in Mexicali with only the clothes on their backs. This relocation of Mexicans to colonization projects was part of the greater national project of agrarian reform and land redistribution, but it was a gendered one that benefited Mexican men in particular.[45] As a woman, Felicitas had to fight for her right to buy land and make a home for her family when they arrived in Pueblo Nuevo.

Agrarian reform was used as a tool to unify the nation and create a modern state in the two decades following the Mexican Revolution of 1910. In the years leading up to the revolution, anarchists, magonistas, and agrarian movements promoted the slogan "Tierra y Libertad" (land and liberty) to refer to the redistribution of land from domestic and foreign ranchers to peasants under the idea that *la tierra es de quien la trabaja* (the land belongs to its workers).[46] When the subsequent agrarian reform movement coincided with the banishment of mixed-status Mexican families from the United States, in 1931, Mexican President Pascual Ortiz Rubio promoted the return of Mexicans to the motherland to help reconstruct the nation.[47] In 1934, Mexican President Lázaro Cárdenas also supported land redistribution and oversaw studies conducted to establish *ejidos* (communal holdings) for banished and repatriated people.[48] During the overlap of mass ethnic Mexican removals from the United States and land redistribution in Mexico, officials on both sides of the border identified male heads of mixed-status banished households as the perfect candidates for colonization projects. Men with US agricultural experience were portrayed as crucial contributors to the development of a modern Mexican agricultural industry. The plan was soon put into action. In 1935, in a transnational arrangement, Dr. C. N. Thomas, a California civic worker, and Mexican officials allocated a ten-thousand-acre tract for a colonization project in El Valle de las Palmas, Baja California, for "35 Mexican repatriates, men, women, and children" who were part of a larger group of "60,000 Mexicans who left Southern California . . . on special trains."[49] Physician Dr. Crotty, surveyor John Jamieson, and overseer Captain Knute Knudson escorted the group and remained in Mexico until they became self-sufficient, a paternalistic strategy to prevent the newly arrived from returning.

The romanticization of agrarian reform and the rapidly increasing number of new arrivals led to the creation of a national committee to assist banished mixed-status families. In October 1932, Eduardo Vasconcelos, the Mexican secretary of the interior; Alfonso Fabila, an anthropologist who specialized in migratory problems; and Jorge Ferretis, a writer and journalist, organized a series of meetings with governmental officials and influential businesspeople to create a committee to address the difficulties that banished ethnic Mexicans were facing. In November 1932, the Comité Nacional de Repatriación, Acomodamiento y Reincorporación (national committee of repatriation, adaptation, and reincorporation) was founded.[50] The committee launched a national campaign to raise half a million pesos to help transport banished mixed-status families from the border to the interior of Mexico, create employment opportunities, and develop colonization projects.[51] Eduardo Vasconcelos launched this national effort, known as the "Campaña del Medio Millón" (the half-million campaign), on December 10, 1932.[52] The committee asked Mexican governors for their "patriotic and humanitarian cooperation for this fundamental case for civic and racial solidarity."[53] Governors and representatives at all levels of government across Mexico organized collection drives by hosting rodeos, carnivals, and theater festivals.[54] In July 1934, Alfredo Levy, vice president of the committee, announced that a total of 300,000 pesos had been collected. While the amount fell below the committee's goal, it was a significant sum at the time, especially during a global depression.[55] The collection campaign's nationalistic discourse also temporarily succeeded in unifying a divided nation by turning attention away from internal conflicts and focusing it on the injustices that banished mixed-status Mexican families were facing.

For women, colonization became another form of marginalization; women generally and single-mother households specifically received minimal support. While presumed repatriated Mexican men were idealized as model laborers, their wives and children born in the United States tended to experience hostility.[56] Some locals perceived them as foreigners and thus rejected and harassed them. Article 27 in the 1917 Mexican Constitution laid out the foundation for the agrarian reform, one of the first of its kind in Latin America, by committing to "an equitable distribution of public wealth."[57] Women on both sides of the US-Mexico border, however, were understood as economically dependent on fathers and husbands. Echoing the legacies of coverture doctrine, priority for land, supplies, and other support was given to male-headed households, with the assumption that this aid would indirectly benefit wives and daughters.[58] The gendered policies on both sides of the national divide thus contributed to the further destitution and displacement of ethnic Mexican women and children, especially single women and their families.

Baja California became an area of conquest, migration, and settlement, with strong foreign investment, where approximately fifty thousand banished and repatriated families settled.[59] Guadalupe describes the conditions they found in Pueblo Nuevo: "It was like just this dumpy little dirt town, desert town. . . . There was nothing there except for a casino. . . . It's where Americans used to go in the twenties and thirties during the prohibition. The families basically got stuck there and then had to make the best of a bad situation."[60] During the early twentieth century, Mexicali, like other border towns, was home to numerous saloons and was one of the many places in northern Mexico that sold alcohol to Americans during Prohibition.[61] While white Americans escaped to Mexicali to find liquor and entertainment, banished Mexican Americans found themselves stuck there, unable to return to their native country. Baja California was soon transformed from a remote territory into one of the most successful cotton-producing centers in the border region.[62] This boom coincided with the development of agribusiness in California's Imperial Valley.[63] As planned, banished families contributed to the economic development of Mexicali, as well as that of the Imperial Valley, through their labor.

Even after multiple displacements, and during the Great Depression, Felicitas found ingenious ways to provide shelter and food for her children despite their extreme poverty. In Mexicali, she found a job working in a restaurant that served banished families and American tourists. As Ramona described it, "We arrived in Mexicali emptyhanded. My mom worked as a waitress in Los Angeles, so she asked for a job in a restaurant by the bridge near the border. They paid her with the room, food, and one silver peso per day."[64] Guadalupe added that Felicitas was a "hard worker"; while in the United States, she had worked as a waitress and in a "factory that processed nuts . . . she worked two shifts."[65] After working in Mexico for five years, Felicitas had saved enough money to buy land and build a house in Mexicali. Ramona proudly recounted, "In 1938, my mom bought a lot on the edge of town. We found the deed. She paid one hundred silver pesos. . . . My mom had two adobe rooms built, a kitchen, and a bathroom. Later, she added two rooms."[66] In that humble adobe house, Ramona, as the eldest daughter, helped raise her siblings. Felicitas taught Ramona how to cook on a small wood-burning stove. To help her mom manage home expenses, Ramona would take her siblings and the neighborhood kids "to go to the empty lots on the edge of town to find tumbleweed and bring it back in sacks."[67] Ramona figured that she could save twenty pesos a day by burning tumbleweed instead of wood—a strategy that helped her mother save money to provide for other necessities, including building additional rooms in their house.

Nonetheless, Felicitas could not save enough, and the family's situation deteriorated when she fell ill. A few years after arriving in Mexicali, Felicitas was on mandatory bed rest and unable to work. As an eight-year-old, Ramona had to find food for her family while her mother was recovering at home: "When my mom was sick . . . I had to go ask for food around the neighborhood because my mom had run out of money. So, I went to ask for food, but at that time [Mexicali] was full of repatriated people, they didn't have money, they were poor. I went door to door asking for food and no one could help me. Finally, in one house they gave me old corn tortillas. . . . I remember watching how my siblings ate the hard tortillas, they devoured them—they were hungry. I didn't want to eat; I was not hungry."[68] With the tenacity that defines Ramona, she found a way to provide nourishment for her younger siblings, even if it meant she would skip yet another meal. Ramona matured at a young age; she had to in order to help her mom and her family. In this way she was like other banished children and their descendants, including some introduced in this book: Trinidad Rodríguez, who attempted to emigrate as a teenager; Virginia and Consuelo De Anda, who also rationed their food to survive; and Sara Marie Robles's children, who endured the emotional pain of family separation.[69] The precarity that defined banished families' economic situations was not unusual. Mexican Consul Rafael de la Colina warned that banished Mexicans were "utterly destitute, when they arrive in Mexico," and there were "terrible reports of suffering and death of hundreds by starvation."[70]

Ramona soon found work with a neighbor as a housekeeper and nanny in exchange for food. She recalled: "Our neighbor was a lady whose husband used to cross the border daily to work [in the United States], so he used to buy plenty of food. I used to help her clean the beans and take care of her baby. . . . Whenever she served dinner, her children . . . used to leave food on their plates, and she would give me the leftovers for my siblings. That's how we survived."[71] Even though she was only a child, Ramona made sure her family had enough food while her mother was sick. Children in destitute families, not the government, often shouldered the burden of helping their parents. Ramona began working as a child and never stopped. Even after Felicitas recovered and could work again, Ramona continued contributing to the family's income.

At the age of eleven, Ramona became a farmer of sorts to avoid suffering hunger again. With the help of her siblings, she used their backyard to grow fruits and vegetables, which they then sold to local stores and neighbors. Guadalupe traced her mother's business instincts back to her banishment years, explaining, "In families like my Nana's, who was a single mother, the children look for ways to earn money to help. So, my mom is like, she is *puro* business."[72] While some banished children found jobs herding livestock, shining shoes, and delivering packages, others, like Ramona, found more creative alternatives.[73]

Ramona used the informal market, as she explained: "When my mom bought the lot, there was a grape vine that formed a big arbor and a peach tree. As the peaches fell, new trees were born . . . so we planted nine peach trees. We also planted six quince trees . . . there was a canal in front of our house, so we could water the trees. . . . I used to soften the soil with a shovel to plant beans. Everything I planted grew, the land was very fertile."[74] Ramona and her sister sold the fruits of their labor door to door; they put the peaches "in buckets and sold eight pieces for five cents."[75] To scale up her operation and increase her revenue, Ramona even approached local business owners to sell her harvest.

During the Depression, displaced ethnic Mexicans and Chinese in Mexicali survived by supporting each other in their commercial ventures. Although Chinese people immigrated to Mexico to work in mining, fishing, and agribusinesses, they also opened restaurants and stores.[76] Such Chinese stores thrived in Mexicali's downtown, and it was in these Mexicali stores that the entrepreneurial displaced Chinese and Mexicans joined forces.[77] As Ramona proudly explained: "I used to go to the stores owned by Chinese people. We all became good merchants. I used to sell the grapes for 20 cents . . . depending on the size. . . . I knew how much the Chinese storeowner could earn from each box. So, I used to sell them at a good price. One year I sold twenty boxes. . . . The Chinese man used to speak to me in Chinese and I would respond in Spanish. . . . He used to tell me the numbers [in Spanish], 'tres pesos o cuatro pesos.' Then, I would negotiate the price. We understood each other."[78] Ramona sold her fruit to Chinese store owners, who in turn sold it to local consumers to provide for their own families. Ramona's entrepreneurial skills were born out of necessity, but it was her undeterred nature that helped her, and her family, survive their greatest moment of need.

Felicitas was eventually able to return to the United States when she secured a border-crossing card, but only for short visits to shop in Calexico, California. Restrictions related to the Immigration Act of 1924, along with the requirement for identification papers included in the Passport Act of 1918, further limited movement across the US-Mexico borderlands.[79] Yet some degree of mobility was granted to border residents to address the concerns of local business owners on both sides of the divide. After much debate, the Bureau of Immigration and the US State Department agreed to grant border-crossing cards. Rule 13 of the *Immigration Laws and Rules* provided those living within ten miles of the border with border-crossing cards to travel within a ten-mile radius north or south of the national divide for personal and business matters.[80] Felicitas benefited from this exception and was granted restricted access to the United States. She used the border-crossing card to buy seeds in Calexico for her daughters to plant. Ramona recalled, "My mom brought us things from a seedling store in Calexico. . . . I planted cilantro [and] long green beans, they were huge; with a few, the frying pan will fill up. We planted corn and below it we planted squash, and cucumbers."[81] Felicitas helped Ramona expand her farming from a sales venture to a way of providing food for her family.

Ramona and her siblings' home farming skills transferred to paid positions on both sides of the border. They became seasonal farmworkers, the main job in the Mexicali–Imperial Valley border region. The US-based Colorado River Land Company (CRLC) introduced cotton in Mexicali at the turn of the twentieth century. The CRLC evaded land-reform orders and only sold a few farms to rural Mexicans, but it abided by a 1928 law requiring foreign companies to reserve 50 percent of all jobs for Mexicans.[82] In 1937, under pressure to comply with colonization agreements, CRLC began selling land to local farmers, but it retained control of the land and cotton production.[83] In 1938, Ramona and her sister started working as cotton pickers. As Ramona remembers, "There was a lot of cotton planting. . . . A truck used to drive by recruiting people to pick cotton in Mexicali. So, my sister and I went to pick cotton. When you pick cotton, the cotton bolls are sharp, and if you don't grab it correctly you bleed. We stayed the entire harvesting season. We were hard workers, but you needed to be to survive."[84] Ramona and her sister worked only one season, because it was common to hire women as only part-time or seasonal workers. Full-time employment was reserved for male heads of household and single men, who were presumed to be better suited for manual labor.[85]

Amid the adversity and exploitative labor conditions, Ramona found joy in childhood games. She has happy memories of the hours she spent playing with her siblings and neighbors, most of whom also were banished children. Ramona excitedly recalled: "We used to gather all the children from the neighborhood in the evenings and we would sit them down by the canal banks. . . . They sang a song or recited poetry they learned in school. We had them perform theater. . . . The moms used to sit by the lamppost to watch."[86] Banished children in Pueblo Nuevo made games a neighborhood affair. They took what they learned in school and performed for everyone in the community. Their unity and shared laughter helped them to thrive. Ramona and her friends improvised games and playgrounds. As she described it: "We used to play Tarzan. There was a lot with fig trees, the branches are very flexible. The lot was empty, so it became our ring, we used to jump from branch to branch like Tarzan."[87] The children's imagination helped them escape their harsh reality. Even though banished children in this community had to mature early to help their families, they never stopped playing and finding joy.

As Ramona, her siblings, and their friends grew older, they found happiness in dance. Ramona, a fashionista, enjoyed doing her hair and makeup to go out dancing (Fig. 4.5). She recalled, "There was a dance hall near the town's church . . . my mom took us there every other weekend. My mom was our chaperone. It was fun to go dancing."[88] As historian Vicki L. Ruiz contends, chaperonage was a way for parents to monitor their daughters' activities to protect the family's reputation. In the 1930s and 1940s, on both sides of the US-Mexico divide, behavioral standards governed the conduct of ethnic Mexican daughters.[89] Felicitas strictly enforced chaperonage because, in the absence of a father figure, it was often assumed that daughters raised by a single mother

Figure 4.5 Ramona García, Mexicali, Baja California, Mexico, circa 1946.

might be tempted away from the propriety and righteousness expected
of them. In Pueblo Nuevo's dance hall—where dancers and their chap-
erones came together to enjoy music—banished Mexican American
adolescents not only enjoyed themselves, but also found romance and
love. Guadalupe explained, "Repatriates met there, and [many] ended
up marrying each other."[90] Ramona affirmed, "I married a repatriate,
and two of my sisters also married repatriates."[91]

CREATING A DISPOSABLE WORKFORCE

During the late 1930s and early 1940s, there were numerous shifts in the labor force for California agricultural and canning industries due to immigration restrictions, the Depression, and agribusiness interests. When Felicitas and her then husband were legally admitted to the United States in 1922, it was likely to fill post–World War I labor shortages because they were exempted from newly established immigration regulations under the 1917 Immigration Act.[92] That moment in the early 1920s marked a period of ideological flux, as narratives welcoming Mexicans to the United States as desirable workers overlapped with nativist cries for Mexicans to be banished on LPC charges. After all, 1922 was the year when both Trinidad Rodríguez was banished from the United States and Felicitas Castro was legally admitted into the United States to work. That ethnic Mexicans were simultaneously welcomed and vilified gestures toward the contradictions that characterized the decision-making of immigration officers, who at their own discretion, and based on their own assumptions, admitted and removed them.

Similar pressures in the early 1920s recruited Filipinos to work in fisheries, canneries, and agriculture to replace Chinese and Japanese workers who had been barred by the Asian exclusion laws.[93] The Immigration Act of 1917 made an exception to Asian exclusion by allowing Filipinos to migrate to the mainland as US nationals (because the Philippines was a US colony).[94] Exemptions under the 1917 Immigration Act for Mexicans and Filipinos made them the principal California workforce in canneries and agriculture by the early 1930s.[95] The 1917 Immigration Act transformed Mexican and Filipino immigration, but it was also used for their removal. Increased pressures by restrictionists during the Depression led to Mexican banishments and Filipino repatriations; in both cases, the LPC clause of the 1917 law was used as grounds for their exclusion, a change that reduced the workforce in canneries and agriculture.

During the mid-1930s, following the exclusion of Chinese, Japanese, and Mexicans, Filipinos also came to be seen as "undesirables" who were taking agricultural and canning jobs away from deserving white Americans during the Depression, and both Mexicans and Filipinos were removed through what was described as repatriation campaigns. In 1935, following the Tydings-McDuffie Act that would grant independence to the Philippines from the United States in ten years, Representative Richard Welch of Texas introduced the Filipino Repatriation Act.[96] Notably, the Tydings-McDuffie Act reclassified the legal status of Filipinos from US nationals to unauthorized immigrants, effectively rendering them excludable. From 1935 to 1940, Congress approved and extended the Repatriation Act three times and allocated a total of $250,000 for the project, which removed approximately 2,064 Filipinos. INS Commissioner Cahill proudly referred to the Repatriation Act as "my brainchild" and claimed that he suggested the idea to Welch. Most of the Filipino expulsions happened in California, where Cahill supervised both the Mexican and Filipino so-called repatriation projects.[97] Like Mexicans, the more than 150,000 "repatriated" Filipinos were virtually unable to return to the United States because the act had a quota restriction of only fifty immigrants per year.[98]

Meanwhile, anti-Filipino violence increased, pushing many out of cannery and agricultural jobs. On the night of Sunday, June 18, 1939, two hundred white men gathered at a California cannery and demanded that "they discharge the Filipinos and put no more to work."[99] Then a few of the men proceeded to the camp located behind the cannery, searching for Filipinos. The majority of the Filipino workers "took to the brush" to hide, but "in one cabin they found Quiton [a Filipino man]. . . . One of the white men assaulted him while the others stood in the doorway."[100] The report of the attack stated that it was likely that "no jury will convict these men," and conveyed concern that "the cannery will have difficulty in securing Filipinos when they open for the canning season."[101] Similar anti-Filipino attacks occurred throughout California, "with white mobs using dynamite, bombs, and guns to intimidate Filipinas / os across the state."[102] The racist attacks pushed many Filipinos to find other jobs or leave the state altogether.[103] The "repatriation" of Filipinos and the violence against them that ensued—combined with World War II recruitment, the prospects of Japanese incarceration, and the exodus of rural workers from California who moved to industrial jobs in urban areas—created labor shortages in agriculture and canneries.[104]

The labor decline reversed abruptly when destitute white migrants escaping the severe Dust Bowl drought of the Midwest and Southern Plains arrived in California to work in agriculture. It is estimated that California's population increased by 1,500,000 in the 1930s. The main population growth took place between 1935 and 1939, when approximately 400,000 white migrants arrived.[105] The Farm Security Administration reported that 75 percent of the migrants arriving in California came from four states: Oklahoma (42 percent), Texas (16 percent), Arkansas (11 percent), and Missouri (7 percent).[106] California agriculture had relied on marginalized Native American, Chinese, Japanese, Hindustani, Filipino, and Mexican workers since the nineteenth century. Their working-class status, legal vulnerability, and race had subjected them to exploitation for agricultural profits, with growers popularizing the myth that workers of color who were deemed foreigners did not want or deserve fair wages and labor protections afforded by US laws and American standards of living.[107] Agriculturalists thus grew accustomed to cheap and readily available labor, a combination that allowed them to depress wages. But when racial immigration exclusions and mass removals depleted this labor force and replaced it with white American workers, racial biases entitled them to stronger labor protections, relief aid, and federal assistance, which produced higher costs for agribusiness and the state.[108] Imperial Valley grower Martin Wahl complained that in previous years growers had paid "$6.50 per acre for thinning lettuce and sugar beets and weeding carrots," but in 1941, they were "reconciled to paying $10 or better" for the same job.[109] To regain a cheap and readily available workforce, California agribusiness lobbied Congress to import Mexican workers.

While labor scarcity had existed in California during the late 1930s and early 1940s, growers exaggerated the need for a new influx of workers to regain control of wages. After all, a ready supply of fungible workers would drive down labor costs. Newspapers helped by widely overstressing the need for labor. For instance, California's Imperial Valley, according to local news reports, was having its "most severe labor shortage in the history of [the] agricultural industry."[110] Major agricultural leaders voiced the urgent need to turn to "Mexican labor from south of the international line" to "import it into the valley."[111] Some officials, however, opposed the importation of Mexican labor. In 1941, the Board of Supervisors of the County of Los Angeles sent a petition to the Committee on Immigration and Naturalization objecting to the proposal that it "permit entry, under bond, of 30,000 Mexican nationals for common labor."[112] Nonetheless, growers' interests prevailed, as Representative Samuel Dickstein of New York reported to Congress in 1940: "During seasonal employment of farm hands in the West . . . [growers] bring in a lot of peon cheap labor. Instead of giving this employment to people in this country at American wages, they bring in these peons from Mexico at 15 cents or 20 cents a day to go out in the fields and do this work."[113] Growers used *enganchistas* (recruiters), an established, if unofficial, way to import Mexican workers.[114]

From 1939 to 1942, before the start of the Bracero Program (1942–1964), Mexicans who lived in border towns, including banished Mexican Americans, were recruited to work seasonally in California's agriculture and canning industries. In a practice reminiscent of the recruitment of Mexican agricultural workers during World War I, US growers signed agreements with the US government that outlined the conditions for importing laborers and returning them to Mexico. Employers arranged the legal admission processes, transportation, housing, and meals for recruited agricultural workers.[115] Ethnic Mexicans living in border towns formed an on-demand, cheap, and disposable workforce that did not initially require the formal transnational labor agreement implemented in the Bracero Program that followed.

Banished US-citizen youth who lived in border towns like Mexicali, where Ramona lived, were easily recruited because they could legally enter the United States using their birth certificates or baptismal records (Figs. 4.6a,b). Additionally, many had farming experience like Ramona, her sisters, and her friends did. Furthermore, growers could manipulate wages because Mexican and Mexican American workers were often unaware of US labor rights. Mexican American youth were also likely to return to Mexico at the end of each season due to their young age, family ties, and the proximity of Mexicali to the Imperial Valley. Recruitment tactics replicated the Department of Labor's practices from the 1920s. George P. Clements, manager of the Agricultural Department of Los Angeles Chamber of Commerce, argued in favor of a proposed a plan to import Mexican workers in 1926: "We cannot

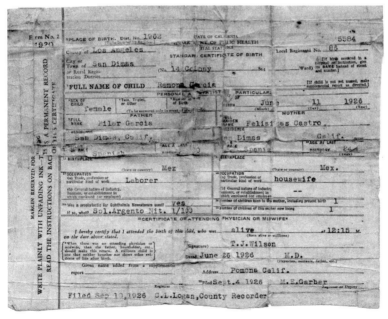

Figure 4.6a Ramona García's birth certificate (*front*), 1926.

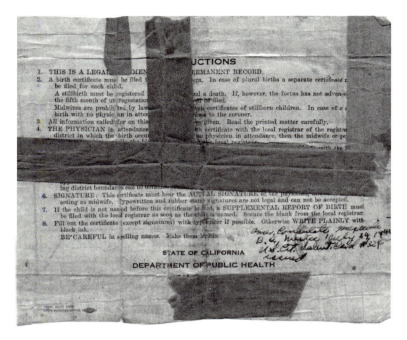

Figure 4.6b Ramona García's birth certificate (*back*) with a 1944 US-citizen
dentity note.

get along without the Mexican laborer. . . . The question is entirely
economic. . . . To get him we must offer just inducements and guarantee
him security. . . . Then return him to his home, a living advertisement
to others, that the supply may not fail us."[116] Clements envisioned a
migration regime in which US business interests could churn through a
large supply of distinctly impermanent Mexican workers.

It was through this process that Ramona, her sisters, and her
friends—all banished Mexican Americans living in Mexicali—became
seasonal farmworkers in California's Imperial Valley in 1941. She explained how she and her peers began working in the fields:

> We started going to the carrot fields once we were a bit older. . . .
> I finished sixth grade, and I used to cry because I wanted to continue

going to school, we really liked to study. But I knew I would not be able to continue my studies because my mom had no money to send us to middle school . . . or high school. . . . There were two girls who started first grade with my sister and me, their dad worked in the fields [in the United States]. After we finished [elementary] school . . . we began working with them in the fields. We used our birth certificate to cross the border. . . . It was falling apart because I used it so often to enter and exit the country. . . . We used to cross at dawn, very early in the morning, my mom used to walk us to the border sometimes. They used to let us enter the US because they needed workers during the Second World War. There was a lot of field work in the Imperial Valley. . . . We used to go to the fields in the Valley, in Calexico, but there were fields all throughout the Valley.[117]

Ramona's friends' father served as the "living advertisement" that Clements had devised in his agricultural-labor importation project. Ramona and her friends grew up listening to the man's stories of working in the United States and witnessed the fruits of his higher salary. Thus, when continuing their education was no longer an option, Ramona, her sister, and her friends became seasonal agricultural workers themselves. Socioeconomic and racial hierarchies pushed all ethnic Mexicans to the bottom, regardless of legal status. In the shadow of such continued transnational marginalization in the United States, then in Mexico, and then again in the United States, banished Mexican Americans found themselves dealing with impermanent legality in a new form. Unlike other Mexican American agricultural workers who lived and worked in the United States, banished Mexican Americans not only experienced labor exploitation; they were also continually displaced when labor needs increased and decreased. They were allowed to return to their native country only to meet labor needs, then were removed again when no longer needed. Their baptismal records and birth certificates—documents that were supposed to verify their claims to the United States—became a hollow symbol of the protections that were promised by US citizenship but were never guaranteed to Mexican Americans, and other marginalized citizens.

During World War II, especially after the United States joined the war in 1941, both US citizens and immigrants entering and leaving the country were closely regulated. In 1941, Congress authorized the US president to "impose new restrictions and prohibitions upon the departure of persons from and their entry into the United States when the United States is at war."[118] That same year, President Roosevelt used an executive order to establish a wartime passport-permit system. All US citizens were required to obtain passports, and immigrants had to secure border-crossing cards approved by the secretary of state or a consular officer.[119] The new measures required authorization for all US departures and arrivals, both to prevent eligible US citizens from emigrating to evade military service and to avert the immigration of potential war enemies.[120]

Banished Mexican Americans who were recruited to work as seasonal farmworkers were also required to follow the new guidelines. Ramona remembers going through this process when the immigration inspector at her usual port of entry told her, "'You must go to the American consulate because you will no longer be able to enter with your [birth certificate].' . . . There was an American consulate in Mexicali. . . . So, we went to the consulate, and they gave us small cards. We began using those cards to cross. When they gave us the cards, they asked us for our address, names, and place of birth."[121] Ramona, her sisters, and friends had consular-approved US-citizen identity cards adhered to the back of their baptismal records and birth certificates to use as entry/exit border permits (Figs. 4.6b and 4.7a,b). A stamp and handwritten note dated July 24, 1944, on the back of Ramona's birth certificate confirms that the US consulate in Mexicali issued her a US-citizen identity card (number 321). The following year, in 1945, Esthela and Natalia, Ramona's sisters, also obtained US-citizen identity cards (numbers 323 and 673), but theirs were typed instead of handwritten notes, indicating a more formalized process of identification.

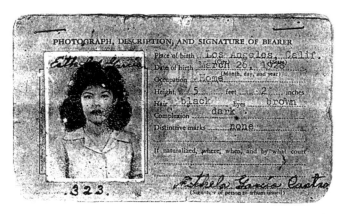

Figure 4.7a The US-citizen identity card for Esthela García (Ramona's sister), no. 323 (*front*), 1944.

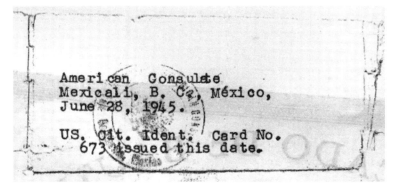

Figure 4.7b The US-citizen identity card for Natalia García (Ramona's sister), no. 673 (*back*), 1945.

Esthela's US-citizen identification (number 323) provides a visual record for the front of the card, which carefully listed identity markers including place and date of birth, occupation, height, hair and eye color, distinctive marks, and naturalization information if applicable. This meant that banished Mexican Americans became more closely regulated, because they were now registered with the US consulate.[122]

But this regulation was intended to facilitate their recruitment as workers, not their inclusion as US citizens. While immigrants received border-crossing cards, US citizens who resided in border towns were assigned citizen identity cards in lieu of passports. This created confusion, since immigration officers sometimes referred to citizen identity cards as "border-crossing permits."[123] This practice reinforced the liminality of US citizens banished to Mexico and then recruited as temporary workers. When the officers confused citizen identity cards with "border-crossing permits," the legality of ethnic Mexicans' US citizenship was thrown into question because their identities were read as "not American." Ethnic Mexican US citizens could never be "American" enough in the eyes of immigration officers, who coded them as Mexican immigrants rather than US citizens. In this process of ascribing an in-between legal status—desirable in their capacity as exploitable workers but never quite enough to escape being marked as "other" or "outsider"—US officials reaffirmed their condition of impermanent legality.

During the same period that Imperial Valley growers recruited ethnic Mexicans from Mexicali, California canneries engaged in similar recruitment practices. Ramona, her sisters, and their friends transitioned from their daily border crossings to longer stays to process tomatoes and apricots for the Thornton Cannery Company. Ramona pointed to the irony of being recruited for these jobs: "Americans from the canneries, with their interpreters, went to recruit door to door in the Mexicali neighborhood where I was raised. They first kicked us out and then went to look for us."[124] Her indignation stems from the continual displacement, exploitation, and abuse to which she, and others in her community, were subjected from US immigration and labor policies. Cannery owners and growers specifically sought out ethnic Mexicans from border towns so that they could work around significant labor-organizing victories that were affecting their profits. During the 1930s and early 1940s, as Mexicans, Filipinos, and other immigrant workers formed labor alliances throughout California to demand better wages, employers often responded by recruiting low-wage, temporary workers from Mexico to break strikes.[125] Contracting workers—in particular, women—from different border regions in Mexico destabilized those organizing efforts and kept wages low. Vicki L. Ruiz found that in 1938, women comprised 72.7 percent of the entire labor pool for the canning industry, because employers could pay women less than men. Mexican women received the lowest wages among all California food-processing operatives.[126] The practice of contracting ethnic Mexicans for cyclical agricultural and canning labor not only characterized all Mexicans across legal statuses as a racialized class of disposable workers, but also consigned women—because they were women—to the lowest-paid positions.

Despite these conditions, banished Mexican Americans who worked seasonally in the United States bonded together, forged friendships, and found love. In 1942, Ramona met Arturo Espinoza while harvesting carrots in Calexico. In November 1937, at the end of the third period of removals, Arturo's mother and her children were also banished from the United States, and they settled in Mexicali. Ramona and Arturo had a lot in common; both were US citizens of Mexican descent who had been banished as children during the Depression, and both were later recruited from Mexicali to work in California. Ramona recounted that she met Arturo after "he arrived from Tijuana. . . . He worked in San Diego, where they made ships for the war. When he returned to Mexicali, he began working in the fields, too, and we met there while picking carrots."[127] Arturo first returned to the United States after his banishment when he was recruited from Mexicali to perform wartime labor in San Diego. When he returned to Mexicali, he joined other ethnic Mexicans as a transnational farmworker in the Imperial Valley.

The labor of banished Mexican Americans and Mexicans with experience in the United States helped to develop the economies of

Mexicali during the 1930s and the Imperial Valley in the 1940s. During the interwar period, Mexicali became a major producer and exporter of cotton, which was in high demand during the Great Wars, and the Mexican government benefited from the taxation of cotton during its boom.[128] On the US side of the border, the Imperial Valley transformed into one of the most important agricultural regions in the country. During World War II, the crop values in the Imperial Valley surged from 41 million dollars in 1938 to 64 million dollars in 1945.[29]

Ramona and Arturo dated for five years while they continued working transnationally in California, and in 1948, they got married in Mexico. A year later, they finally permanently resettled in their native country in a humble home in Cypress, California. Arturo continued working in agriculture, and Ramona raised their children. In 1962, Ramona and Arturo opened immigration petitions for their mothers, who were still living in Mexico. Ramona explained that her mom underwent immigration petitions twice because Felicitas had been legally admitted to the United States in 1922, prior to the Espinoza family's banishment. Ramona and Arturo spent the rest of their lives in Southern California, where their children and grandchildren were born and raised. Though seasonal employment was designed to be temporary, moving from one job to another allowed some banished Mexican Americans to return permanently to their native country. Nonetheless, their banishment and relegation to performing cheap labor cemented the sociopolitical imaginary of Mexican illegality that has dispossessed ethnic Mexicans of political and economic power. The banishment of Mexican Americans threw their families into a cycle of continual displacement, dispossession, and marginalization that limited their long-term economic opportunities in the United States and Mexico. Moreover, the reductive portrayal of Mexican Americans as low-skilled, disposable "immigrant" workers in the United States denied this community of birthright US citizens any claim to full political belonging.

THE "WOULD HAVE" GENERATION

Banishment deprived a generation of Mexican Americans from securing opportunities and stability in their native country. The Espinoza family faced hunger and homelessness in Mexico. Ramona and her siblings were unable to continue their education after finishing elementary school because their destitution forced them to start working as children—an experience many banished Mexican Americans share.[130] After Guadalupe's father died, she and her mother became "roommates," as they affectionately call each other, and Ramona began sharing more banishment memories with Guadalupe (Fig. 4.8). Reflecting on her mother's life, Guadalupe aptly concluded: "My mother's generation is *los hubieran* (the 'would haves'). I think, *sí, le desgraciaron la vida* (they ruined her life), because she survived in Mexicali, but *la vida no se trata de sobrevivir* (life is not about surviving)."[131] Banished people were left to fend for themselves, even when the United States and Mexico both had assistance programs for the needy. Guadalupe added, "My mother *would have* gotten an education. . . . One day, I took my mom to the neighborhood where she was born. . . . And then my mom said, 'I *would have* gone to this school.' She *would have* ended up . . . at Garfield High School. . . . She *would have* become a doctor because she really liked school . . . but my Nana [Felicitas] needed her to work."[132] Ramona affirmed, "I wanted to be a doctor. . . . Sara and I were the only two students who earned scholarships. . . . One time she went to her ranch and came back with a medicine book that explained how to deliver babies. I wanted to study that [obstetrics], my friend and me knew the entire book by heart. But my mom did not have money for me to go to [Mexico City] to study."[133] Banishment ruined the dreams of young Mexican Americans, who—in part because both the United States and Mexico kept Mexican Americans from receiving aid—had to forgo education and other means of personal development in order to help their families survive. As the Espinoza family's history demonstrates, during the greatest economic recession in modern history, both

Figure 4.8 Ramona Espinoza (*left*) and María Guadalupe Espinoza (*right*), Anaheim, California, 2017.

the US and Mexican governments disregarded the needs of banished people even as they continued to benefit from their labor.

Survivors and their descendants still feel the prolonged effects of banishment, which include not only economic and political disenfranchisement, but also emotional instability. As Guadalupe, Ramona's daughter, reflected, "They did this to my Nana [Felicitas], the adults in the story. And the children, the American-born children with American constitutional rights . . . suffered . . . all of the deprivations. But their children and their grandchildren, we are also *afectados*, survivors. . . . It's a cascading effect . . . it's still there, this wound."[134] Ramona's grandson Arturo added his take on the organized abandonment of banished Mexican families by both the United States and Mexico: "My grandmother's repatriation impacted me by not having an established family, you neglect your children, and then they neglect their children . . . no one is stable. Everybody's mad maybe, angry, resentful."[135] In the effort to survive amid extreme poverty, banished families traded emotional stability for economic stability. As a result, multiple subsequent generations now bear the prolonged emotional consequences of the wounds of banishment. These effects expanded to the political and economic realms as well. Ramona explained, "They sent children out even when they were born here, so there are no votes [representing us]. . . . When we returned to the [United States], my husband and I had to start from zero, even though we were born here. There is no progress, the new generations can't progress."[136]

Ramona's observation about the inability to progress underscores the ways in which banishment, and the meanings of illegality that accompanied it, haunted banished Mexican families across several generations. For example, banishment disrupted Mexican Americans' citizenship rights by removing a significant number of citizens who were eligible to vote. This disruption also interrupted the right to derivative citizenship, as the other families in this study experienced. Entangled in a cycle of continual displacement and dispossession—as they relocated from the United States to Mexico, internally within Mexico, and from Mexico to the United States—banished families also often found themselves caught in a spiral of downward social mobility. In the 1930s, they were forced to leave their lives and possessions behind and found themselves in dire economic straits when they arrived in Mexico. When they returned to the United States to fill the demand for cheap labor, they experienced further downward social mobility as temporary low-wage workers. Even when Mexican Americans like Ramona and Arturo defied their banishment by resettling back in their native country, the conditions had already been set for their economic and social stagnation. Banished Mexican Americans, their children, and their grandchildren are still enduring the emotional effects of banishment as well as its prolonged consequences of political, economic, and ethnic disempowerment. But as we will see in Chapter 5, Ramona and other banished survivors have not only broken their silence by sharing their stories; they have also begun to challenge their imposed illegality by demanding redress.

CHAPTER FIVE

THE APOLOGY ACT AND REDRESS RECOMMENDATIONS

The end of the American Civil War marked the beginning of a formal US model for reparations, a process used to repair a legal injury carried out by the state at any level of government. On January 16, 1865, Union General William T. Sherman issued Special Field Order no. 15, a short-lived but radical promise to redistribute some 400,000 acres of confiscated Confederate land to resettle thousands of newly emancipated Black people in the US South.[1] Specifically, Sherman's order promised forty acres of land to formerly enslaved Black people living along the coasts of South Carolina, Georgia, and Florida. Sherman later ordered the Army to loan mules to the newly settled Black farmers; together, these orders became the basis of the US government's briefly offered and largely unrealized promise of "forty acres and a mule" as reparations for the legal injustices of chattel slavery.[2] Later that year, President Andrew Johnson revoked General Sherman's special field order, rescinded all promises of property to formerly enslaved people in the South, and returned most property to the Confederate planters who had previously owned it.[3] While General Sherman's promise is now understood to be one of the first attempts at reparations by the United States, President Johnson's reversal—which dispossessed tens of thousands of Black landholders in the South and left them with little option but to become sharecroppers—aptly symbolizes the US government's long-standing lack of commitment to correcting injustices that it has committed against historically marginalized communities.

A new chapter in the history of US reparations demands is now being written by banished Mexican Americans, their children, and their grandchildren, who are still suffering the prolonged consequences of banishment. The mass expulsion of mixed-status Mexican families during the interwar period interrupted their derivative citizenship rights, deprived them of transgenerational wealth, reduced their upward mobility, and debilitated their mass political power in the United States, with ripple effects across three generations. In this chapter, I present a small sample of the wide variety of recommendations for redress, given the multiplicity of banishment experiences and the distinct ways that banishment affected different families across generations, and contend that a singular, one-size-fits-all proposal for redress cannot possibly respond to the many kinds of injustices that banishment has dealt to mixed-status Mexican families. I also offer an overview and analysis of various state and national legislative proposals that have called for reparations for the coerced removals of Mexican Americans and legally admitted Mexican immigrants during the Great Depression. Though these various efforts have attempted to provide reparations to so-called repatriated Mexican Americans directly, none have fully addressed the needs of banished women and their descendants, who continue to experience the long-term social, economic, and legal consequences of banishment. Notably, none of the reparation proposals address the harms endured by Mexican immigrants who were expelled without due process even when they were long-term residents of the United States. If we continue to follow contemporary reparations discourse, which exclusively considers the direct targets of past injuries—and only when those targets were US citizens or legally admitted immigrants—then we will make the mistake of ignoring the many legal and social injustices that have occurred across multiple generations of mixed-status Mexican families.

The mainstream discourse around reparations for historical injustices is already very limited in scale and scope. Indeed, it is not uncommon for politicians and the public to argue that historical injustices committed against minoritized communities are best forgotten. But their investment in maintaining a positive public opinion about the government only helps to erase the lived experiences of marginalized communities.[4] Official apologies for acts of violent injustice are often suppressed out of political fears that deep probes and inquiry would expose the unjust and inhumane acts carried out by the government. As legal scholar Emma Coleman Jordan argues, the significance of reparations, regardless of its potential drawbacks, lies in the process of "verification and acknowledgment" of a history that has often been erased from the official record.[5] That is why first-person accounts of banishment and its devastating, prolonged effects—accounts like those shared by the families in this book—compel us to consider restitution specifically and reparations more broadly.

In the spirit of reimagining what is possible, a transformative model of reparations might productively expand the scale and scope of reparations discourse. In thinking through reparations for formerly enslaved Black people, Jordan presents an integrated, transformative model for reparations that requires advocacy in three main arenas: the political, the legal, and the intellectual. In the political arena, activism and advocacy apply political pressure on legislators to provide reparations and formal apologies. The legal arena allows for class-action lawsuits to provide financial compensation for material losses and other harms. And the intellectual arena consists of producing counternarratives that document the history of past injustices and integrating these histories into academic curricula.

Reparations for Mexican American banishment, in particular, must be reframed, because existing reparation efforts in all three arenas have focused too narrowly on the immediate effects of these unjust removals, rather than their prolonged consequences. As I have argued throughout this book, banishment resulted in an imposition of *transgenerational illegality* on the banished families themselves as well as on their descendants. Because these notions of presumptive illegality and conditional legality have continued to haunt these family members in distinct ways—often rendering them particularly vulnerable to various modes of dispossession, displacement, and premature death—a truly comprehensive approach to reparations for banishment must also address how these harms have taken place across a large geographic area and over generations. Based on their lived experiences, the recommendations of the Rodríguez, De Anda, Robles, and Espinoza families—and other banished mixed-status Mexican families that have had similar experiences—offer a starting point for imagining this more complete approach to reparations for Mexican American banishment.

RECOMMENDATIONS FOR REPARATIONS

The suggested reparations included here come directly from families affected by banishment, whose experiences demonstrate that the mass removals influenced mixed-status Mexican families and their descendants in complex, nuanced, and uneven ways. They cover a wide scope to address the impact of the state-imposed transgenerational illegality on banished Mexican Americans, their children, and their grandchildren. Mexican American women and their families remained in banishment for different periods and endured diverse devastating prolonged effects across three generations. The recommended reparations outlined here vary based on the time it took each banished matriarch to resettle back in the United States because some of their recommendations are informed by the time they spent in banishment. Ramona Espinoza was banished in 1932 and unable to return to her native country for sixteen years—a significant length of time, but a shorter period in comparison to the other banished women in this book. Virginia and Consuelo De Anda returned to the United States after twenty-one and twenty-three years, respectively. Sara Marie Robles came back after thirty-three years, and Trinidad Rodríguez returned, briefly before her death, after forty-seven years.

Banished Mexican American women and children were rendered "excludable" from their own native country. In the process of orchestrating their removals, US officials disregarded their US citizenship, underscoring the ways in which Mexican Americans' legal claims to belonging in the United States have always been mediated by a particular condition of legal impermanence that relies on various assumptions about ethnicity, class status, age, and gender. But this conditional legality and presumptive illegality extended far beyond the lives of the banished women and children. In fact, officials who carried out these banishments juridically and discursively imposed an illegalized status onto not only the Mexican American women and children themselves, but also subsequent generations of their families. I describe the result of this unjust imposition—which spans geographies and generations— as transgenerational illegality. In the long shadow of banishment, the legal, social, and bureaucratic barriers that delayed resettlement for some banished women, including Sara Marie and Trinidad, meant that their children and even their grandchildren were born in Mexico. In these cases, the second and third generations of their families encountered additional legal barriers to accessing US citizenship. The banishment of mixed-status Mexican families also meant that upon their return to the United States, banished women and their direct descendants faced significantly diminished legal rights. Yet despite all of the ways that banishment has made their lives and livelihoods more challenging, they continue to fight the imposition of transgenerational illegality and its effects on their families.

Returned banished women and their families proposed recommendations for reparations that include financial renumeration and formal recognition of the harms of banishment from the United States and Mexico. Their recommendations—which include various forms of political, legal, and intellectual redress—highlight the diversity, unevenness, and heterogeneity of banishment experiences, which have been shaped by the particular experiences endured by each banished woman in her resettlement process. Some families advocated for a formal national apology and a national holiday as an act of remembrance. Others championed incorporating banishment and repatriation history in the K–12 curriculum. Yet another group supported the creation of a legal path to citizenship for descendants of US citizens who have been unable to secure derivative citizenship through their banished mothers. The suggestions here are just starting points toward relevant legislative actions for redress that could answer the needs of affected families. Banished mixed-status families and their descendants remain resilient, and their continued resistance should inspire politicians to act.

The recommendations for reparations from resettled banished women and their families in this book also reflect the multigenerational legacies of banishment. In the case of the Espinoza family (whose story appears in Chapter 4), Ramona Espinoza recommended *both* a formal apology and financial reparations for what her family experienced during and after their banishment. Ramona was banished from Los Angeles in 1932, at the age of six. Her family was first sent to Sinaloa, Mexico, and then moved to Mexicali, Baja California, where she lived until her eventual resettlement in the United States. The Espinozas suffered poverty, hunger, and homelessness when they arrived in Mexico. They tried to return to the United States multiple times, but border patrol agents—operating on presumptive notions of illegality connected to their ethnic Mexican identity rather than their actual legal status as US citizens—turned them away at the border. In 1941, during World War II, sixteen-year-old Ramona was finally able to use her birth certificate to return to the United States. She entered her native country with a group of seasonal farm laborers to work in the agricultural fields in California's Imperial Valley. There she met other banished Mexican Americans, including her future husband, who were also working seasonally in the fields of Calexico, California. In 1943, the Thornton Canning Company recruited Ramona and other ethnic Mexicans, including banished Mexican Americans, living in Mexican border towns to labor and live as seasonal workers in Sacramento, California. Thus, after her banishment, Ramona returned to the United States only to fill wartime labor shortages in the agriculture and food-processing industries. In 1932, despite her US citizenship, US officials racialized her as a deportable Mexican immigrant, then, in the 1940s, US employers recruited her back as a temporary, disposable worker. It was not until 1948 that Ramona resettled permanently in the United States as a twenty-two-year-old married woman.

Members of the Espinoza family recommend that the Mexican and US governments take responsibility for their roles in banishing Mexican Americans. Ramona explained, "When we were repatriated, Mexico did not do anything to help. They should do something."[6] Though Ramona believes that the Mexican government should also enact reparations, her recommendations mainly centered on actions the US government should take. She emphasized that banishment had hampered the economic prospects of expelled Mexican Americans, and suggested that the US government "should give them money for the mistake, it was a mistake they made."[7] She also spoke of the life-threating consequences that some banished people suffered because of that mistake: "Well, look, not everyone came back [to the United States], people died. People were sick and they still sent them [to Mexico]. It is inhumane. . . . They are responsible for those fatalities. There were many who did not die due to sickness, but because of other situations as well. It almost happened to us, we almost died in the desert. . . . Others died of hunger. . . . We did not have a house when we arrived [to Mexico]. We arrived emptyhanded. . . . We all have the right to receive money, and they should apologize."[8] Ramona's daughter, Guadalupe Espinoza, who was present during my interview with Ramona, added: "But it should be a national [apology,] mom," to which Ramona agreed.[9] As we will see later in this chapter, California has formally apologized for its role in the coerced removals of Mexican Americans. Aware of this state apology, both Guadalupe and Ramona want the federal government to follow California's lead by officially apologizing to banished mixed-status Mexican families expelled from states across the country.

Ramona's suggestions for both financial reparations and a formal federal apology are based on the severe hardships that she, her family members, and other banished Mexican Americans experienced during and following their relocation to Mexico. As Guadalupe further emphasized, "The government stepped in and *les desgraciaron la vida* [they ruined their lives], the way I see it. . . . My mom always told us . . . if you say I'm sorry and you don't fix [the problem] . . . that's not enough."[10] The Espinozas recommend reparations based in the long-term economic consequences that banishment has had across generations of their family—and other banished families who lived in their Mexicali neighborhood—in terms of decreasing the potential for upward socioeconomic mobility and a better quality of life. Sometimes, as in the case of the De Anda family's children, banishment even led to death, underscoring how their displacement limited their life chances. As such, the Espinozas consider a federal apology paired with financial restitution to be an important (even if not wholly sufficient) step toward repairing the prolonged damages of banishment.

Other families, however, including the De Anda family (whose story is featured in Chapter 2) and the Robles family (see their story in Chapter 3), do not see financial redress as the most effective form of reparation. Due to their particular experiences of family separation, the Robles family, like the De Andas, do not see value in monetary reparation. As Sara Marie said, "What for now? When I needed it, they didn't help me."[11] Sara Veronica, Sara Marie's granddaughter, added, "I think money [as reparation] is dumb. You cannot put a price tag for what people went through mentally or emotionally."[12] Chabelo, Sara Marie's son, shared the same sentiment: "Money cannot pay for having to grow up without my mother."[13] As the second-youngest child in his family, Chabelo was the last one to make the trip north to reunite with his mother, his father, and his siblings, who had already established themselves in the United States. The Robles family urgently needed financial and legal reinstitution during Sara Marie's resettlement process. At this point, however, they see official recognition as more meaningful than financial restitution.

Like the Espinoza family, the Robles family also wants a national apology and formal recognition for the displacement that erased thousands of Mexican Americans from the United States. Sara Marie Robles was banished as a child and unable to return to the United States for thirty-three years. When she did return, Sara Marie worked and saved money to open family-based immigration petitions over a twelve-year period, because she was unaware of her children's right to derivative citizenship. Her immigration-petition process separated Sara Marie from her children, who had to learn to function as a transnational family and endure the devastating pain of family separation. While transnational families are not uncommon among immigrant communities, in the case of banished US citizens, they were pushed into an immigrant transnational family experience largely due to the circumstances of their banishment and return to the United States.[14]

Commenting on the idea of a formal apology from the United States, Sara Veronica referenced the redress granted to survivors of Japanese American incarceration during World War II: "It would be great to have an apology letter like the one they gave to Japanese people from World War II, like something that you can hold on to, you know."[15] A personalized letter—even if that only means having your name printed on a standard apology letter—offers a unique kind of personal recognition. It would be tangible proof of the past and the prolonged injustices banishment caused. In addition to an apology letter, Sara Veronica proposed a national holiday to commemorate this chapter in US history. For her, a national holiday can bring awareness about banishment. She explained: "I think it's about *knowing*. Knowing the stories and understanding this history. The US remembers all these wars and they remember Pearl Harbor. . . . Well, just remember us and remember that the government fucked up and they were supposed to protect their citizens and they let them go."[16]

Sara Veronica's description of the US government's actions mirrors the sense of betrayal that other families conveyed when describing their own banishment. While Sara Veronica criticizes the US government for "letting" its own citizens "go," other families described their banishment as being "kicked out." They point to a wound that has not been given the care and opportunity to heal. The personal and community acknowledgment that would accompany formal apologies could support this healing.[17] A formal federal apology paired with a national holiday would acknowledge and disseminate the history of banishment that the Robles family, like many other families, has preserved through their shared family stories. A national commemoration would not only restore an erased part of our national memory; it would also allow for some of the prolonged, devastating effects on these families to be addressed. Commemorating injustices requires inquiring into the past to heal the present. After all, "to commemorate is to seek historical closure."[18]

The families in this book also want to share what happened to banished Mexican Americans with the mainstream public by incorporating its history into the K–12 curricula nationwide. They understand that the project of reparations must be grounded in knowledge production, or what Jordan calls the intellectual arena. As Ramona's daughter Guadalupe explained when she recommended including banishment experiences in the history books or the curriculum: "I feel like as important as it is to make sure that it doesn't happen again"—the history must "not [be] forgotten. . . . Let people know."[19] The De Anda family agrees with this recommendation. The De Anda sisters' grandchildren, like many extended members of banished families, are not very familiar with their family's banishment history; in fact, they learned about it only very recently. Given the shame and pain associated with the removals, some of the children and grandchildren of banished people learn about this history only decades later, if at all. Thus, the De Andas want the story to be documented, incorporated, and made accessible through the K–12 public educational system across the nation. Joe Yáñez, Virginia's son, explained his reasoning:

> I don't think money is the answer. If I could have anything I wanted, I would put this in the history books. That will be it. No money. Yeah, my mom would probably love that, but I don't think it is a matter of money, nor do I think that money is the issue. I think it is education. I think that the Japanese were fortunate because they got the money and that was fine, but they got the publicity also. And of course, we treated the Indians and the African Americans poorly also, but I think we still have the Chinese who were treated poorly, and I think their story still needs to be told. So, we are only one chapter. This is only one chapter in the history of America, but it's a missing chapter. So, if given a choice, I would say give us a couple of pages in the history books. So that kids in the United States, at least you plant the idea in their heads; they know that bad things have happened. A lot of times, when you know that bad things have happened, you don't repeat them again, so that will be it.[20]

For Joe, monetary compensation is not as important as sharing this history so that it will never be repeated. His daughter Marisa shares this sentiment, asserting that "there is no amount of money that would fix it."[21] While Joe acknowledged that his mother would probably enjoy financial restitution, he considers education a more valuable form of reparation.

Although scholars have documented the mass removals of Mexican immigrants and to a certain extent that of Mexican Americans, most K–12 students and the mainstream public are still largely unfamiliar with this history. As Joe noted, the system of chattel slavery and its abuses of Black people, the project of westward expansion and the impact of settler colonialism on Native peoples, and draconian anti-Asian policies like the Chinese Exclusion Acts and Japanese incarceration have received some attention in K–12 curricula, even if just a few paragraphs. Until very recently, however, the history of banished mixed-status Mexican families was completely missing from K–12 curricula. As of this writing, reparations in the intellectual arena have been approved in Illinois and California. In 2010, the Illinois state legislature enacted Public Act 096–0629, which mandates that public schools teach the history of unjustly removed Mexican Americans during the Great Depression as a requirement for eighth-grade graduation.[22] And in 2015, the California state legislature enacted Assembly Bill 146, recommending that public schools teach this history.[23] Joe's recommendation is more ambitious, in that he wants it added to the curricula at the national level. After all, mixed-status Mexican families were not only banished from Illinois and California; banishment was an orchestrated effort to remove ethnic Mexicans from places across the country. Students throughout the United States could benefit from learning about this past injustice.

The banished families I interviewed also voiced deep frustration about the various forms of legal dispossession and political marginalization they have endured, and the continued legal struggles they face, which have motivated some recommendations for legal redress. For example, members of the Rodríguez family (whose story appears in Chapter 1) are still contesting the transgenerational illegality that has haunted the family since Trinidad's banishment. Trinidad Rodríguez's removal and her denied resettlement attempts meant that neither her children nor her grandchildren have access to US citizenship. Jesús, Trinidad's grandson, arrived in his grandmother's native country as an unauthorized immigrant, while Refugio, Trinidad's son, has been granted only a temporary tourist visa, even when his mother was a US citizen. The xenophobic policies that banished Trinidad have created ripple effects two generations later, because some of her grandchildren live under constant risk of deportation. Undeterred, Refugio and his family are contesting their state-imposed illegality by working with an immigration attorney to establish a legal claim to derivative citizenship. Sadly, as noted earlier, their efforts have been complicated by the fact that Trinidad's death certificate and other identity documents processed by Mexican officials while she was in banishment are riddled with clerical mistakes. Though Trinidad spent her life attempting to return to the United States to reclaim her citizenship and open immigration cases for her two children and husband, she passed away before she could reach that goal. Now Refugio has taken on this arduous immigration-petition process, in the context of a US immigration system that continues to disadvantage working-class people attempting to secure their rightful legal status.

The Rodríguez family recommends legal integration as a fundamental component of redress for families like theirs. In particular, Jesús urges the federal government to create a path to legalization for direct descendants of banished US citizens, as a way to undo their inherited transgenerational illegality:

> I would ask the United States government not to have repatriated my grandmother [to Mexico] because of all the damage that not being been born here has caused us. If my great-grandmother was a citizen of the United States and my grandmother was too, it is unjust for us to be living here as undocumented immigrants. We have faced many difficulties, such as family separation. And, for example, I want to study but I face more difficulties because I do not have my papers, my citizenship. . . . It is more difficult because I cannot receive all the benefits given to students here, like financial aid and those types of things.[24]

Jesús highlights his family's established US citizenship roots, given that his grandmother and great-grandmother were Mexican Americans. Jesús's inherited transgenerational illegality—all stemming from Trinidad's unjust banishment decades earlier—meant that he has been denied access to higher education, financial aid, and potential upward mobility in the United States.

Conscious of the racialized construction of inadmissibility and deportability that has long been used to remove ethnic Mexicans,

members of the Rodríguez family narrate themselves through the language of good moral character. Carmela, Refugio's wife, also recommended a path to legalization for her family and that of other descendants of banished US citizens by insisting they are worthy of legal
inclusion: "We are not asking the government for public assistance, we
do not depend on them. We do not come from delinquent people.
We are all hard workers . . . but they still see us as a public charge
when all my family is composed of hard-working people."[25] Indeed, as
the research in this book has demonstrated, the "likely to become a
public charge" (LPC) clause of the 1917 Immigration Act established a
basic premise that played a central role in the banishment drives during
the interwar period. Carmela's reasoning—common among many immigrants today—counters nativist arguments that immigrants live off
the dole of the American government. Inherent criminality and dependence on public assistance, a rhetoric that ran rampant during the turn
of the twentieth century, is now cemented in legal and public percep-
tions of marginalized immigrants.[26]

Some families articulated critiques of banishment—and of the
various forms of displacement, dispossession, and marginalization that
their families faced in its shadow—that could not always fall into neat,
legible forms of redress. For example, the De Anda sisters' only wish
is that their government had protected their civil and legal right to live
and grow up in the United States. In contrast to Joe's more elaborate
recommendation of incorporating the history of Mexican American
banishment in educational curricula, his mother, Virginia, simply
wishes that it had never happened: "I would have asked that they never
forced us to leave [the United States]. That is the only thing that I would
ask for. . . . Not to have sent us to Mexico."[27] Consuelo echoed her
sister's sentiment: "I did not want to be over there because it was not
the same as here. The way we lived over there [in Mexico], it was not
the same."[28] The De Anda sisters lament their banishment, which displaced them from everything they knew and had enjoyed in their na-

tive country. They were banished from the economically stable life their family had built in the United States and forced into extreme poverty when they first arrived in Mexico. The malnutrition they endured in Mexico proved deadly for seven of their nine siblings who passed away soon after they were born. The De Anda sisters reaffirm the ways in which banishment resulted in economic marginalization that resulted in devastating loss.

When asked for reparations recommendations for the Mexican government, Virginia further emphasized the transnational displacement she experienced: "The Mexican government could not do anything for its citizens. If it did not do anything to help its citizens, it would do much less for foreigners!"[29] Some banished Mexican Americans who were denied civil rights protections by their native country's government encountered further marginalization once in Mexico. Virginia believes that the Mexican government will be even less willing than the United States to approve reparations because banished Mexican Americans were not Mexican citizens. Even so, the mass removal raids were a transnational effort, and both governments should offer redress for their roles in uprooting a Mexican American generation.

Collectively, the Rodríguez, De Anda, Robles, and Espinoza families recommended that reparations for banishment be more expansive, in both scale and scope. They prioritize reparations that seek national recognition on the part of the US government, an acknowledgment of their suffering in Mexico, and a reminder of their protracted struggles to return to the United States. Their broad approach to reparations also calls on the US government to take responsibility for the immediate and prolonged effects of banishment, with financial compensation, educational opportunities, commemoration, and a path to US citizenship for those who have been harmed. Some of these measures have already been implemented, but by only a few state and local governments in the United States.

SYMBOLIC VERSUS MATERIAL REPARATIONS

A series of reparation proposals have been drafted at different levels of government, but only a few have been authorized, mainly as symbolic gestures. In the early 2000s, California State Senator Joseph Dunn was shocked to learn about the history of the coerced removals of Mexican Americans during the Great Depression.[30] Determined to take political action, he organized a series of town hall meetings with returned banished Mexican Americans and their families, in which the De Anda and Espinoza families participated.[31] Informed and inspired by their resilience, Senator Dunn proposed bills for an official state apology and reparations for damages. From 2003 to 2017, Dunn and his colleagues in the California legislature proposed several reparation bills. The ten proposed resolutions and bills focus on five key areas: (1) extending the statute of limitations for banished survivors to file lawsuits (SB 933 and SB 37); (2) creating fact-finding commissions at the state and federal levels (SJR 21, SB 427, SB 645, and HR 5161); (3) a formal state apology (SB 670); (4) revising California's K–12 social science curricula to include the history of Mexican repatriation (AB 146, SB 552, and CFT's Resolution 34–04); and (5) establishing a state reparations fund (SB 552). Of the ten propositions, the state apology and the extension of the statute of limitations for expelled ethnic Mexicans initially received the most support.

, On February 22, 2005, Dunn first proposed California Senate Bill 670 (SB 670), Apology Act for the 1930s Mexican Repatriation Program, to "express the apology of the State of California to those individuals who were illegally deported and coerced into emigrating to Mexico . . . between the years of 1929 and 1944."[32] The bill also required the installation of a plaque commemorating banished people at a public landmark in Los Angeles. California Governor Arnold Schwarzenegger signed the Apology Act into law on October 7, 2005. More than six years later, Supervisor Gloria Molina, a longtime Chicana community activist, recommended that the Los Angeles

County Board of Supervisors join the state legislature's efforts by issuing a formal apology for the county's participation in the repatriation and banishment raids. Supervisor Molina explained that, regrettably, the Los Angeles County Board of Supervisors had participated in the efforts to separate "United States citizens and legal residents . . . from their families and country," which caused them to be "deprived of their livelihood and United States Constitutional rights, and many were never reunited with their families."[33] As historian Monica Muñoz Martinez reminds us, historical markers can shift the public historical landscape and popular historical narrative in locations where largely forgotten injustices have taken place.[34] To this end, the "repatriation apologies" and commemorative plaque offer an important public reminder of the untold lessons of the past.

The public commemoration of the "Mexican repatriation program" that included the banishment of Mexican Americans has continued in recent years. On September 28, 2024, California Governor Gavin Newsom signed into law SB 537, which was introduced by Senate Majority Leader Lena Gonzalez and Senator Josh Becker.[35] This law authorizes a nonprofit organization representing ethnic Mexicans to begin negotiations to propose, construct, and conserve a memorial for Mexican Americans and Mexican immigrants who were forcibly removed from the United States during the Great Depression. The memorial will be constructed in a public space in the City or County of Los Angeles. The author's office reported that "despite California issuing a formal apology in 2005 and requiring the SBE [State Board of Education] to consider including related content in the next revision of the History-Social Science Framework, the forced and unconstitutional deportation during the Mexican Repatriation Program of the 1930s remains a shamefully ignored period in California and United States history."[36] This second public landmark will expand the commemoration of the mass removals of mixed-status Mexican families in hopes of bringing broader attention to this dark but important chapter in United States history.

Formal apologies, though symbolic in nature, are significant in that they recognize past injustices and provide the type of official acknowledgment that some banished Mexican Americans and their descendants have been asking for. On February 26, 2012, during the unveiling of the commemorative monument at LA Plaza de Cultura y Artes, Virginia and Consuelo De Anda were among the banished Mexican Americans present to accept the state apology. Reflecting on the significance of this commemoration, Virginia noted how the inscribed apology plaque acknowledged, in both English and Spanish, "all the suffering we have endured."[37] The bilingual inscription on the plaque speaks to banished US citizens who were unable to return to their native country until decades later and remained monolingual Spanish speakers (Fig. 5.1). It also allows Spanish speakers visiting the site to

Figure 5.1 Commemorative Plaque, "Forced Removal of Mexican Americans During the Great Depression," LA Plaza de Cultura y Artes, Los Angeles, California, February 26, 2012.

learn this history. Two photographs of the De Anda sisters at the event capture them contemplating the commemorative plaque and show Virginia running her fingers across its surface (Figs. 5.2a,b). Virginia's gesture demonstrates the importance of having tangible proof of past injustices; the plaque is an official record of the hidden histories that Virginia and her family lived through. This was the first time the De Anda sisters saw their history acknowledged in a well-known, frequently visited public space. Now they hope others will also learn about the history of banished Mexican Americans as they walk through this popular destination and contemplate the significance of the events that led to the commemorative plaque. The second plaque authorized by SB 537 in 2024 contributes to this effort: both landmarks will become part of a public history project that attempts to teach general audiences about this forgotten history.

Another California reparation bill, SB 933, gathered support in 2003, but was ultimately vetoed. SB 933 sought to extend the statute of limitations for legal redress. In the legal arena, a statute of limitations sets a time limit for when people can take legal action for restitution of any

Figure 5.2a The De Anda sisters accepting the formal apology for their 1929 banishment, LA Plaza de Cultura y Artes, Los Angeles, California, 2012.

Figure 5.2b The De Anda sisters, Consuelo (*left*) and Virginia (*right*), pose in front of the commemorative plaque, LA Plaza de Cultura y Artes, Los Angeles, California, 2012.

protected legal claim. In the case of banishment, survivors could sue for personal losses such as property and other goods, and for denial of derivative citizenship, except that the statute of limitations to file such lawsuits has long expired. This bill sought to extend the existing statutes of limitations for legal action against (1) injury to real property, which has only a three-year window for legal action from the date a cause of action occurred; (2) personal injury, which has only a two-year statute of limitations; and (3) imprisonment, because some ethnic Mexicans were arrested prior to removal, and there is only a one-year window to file suit under current law.[38] Potential beneficiaries were defined as "victims [of] unconstitutional, wrongful, or coerced repatriation," including a "US citizen or legal resident of Mexican descent induced to emigrate from California during the period of 1929 to 1944 by any local or state government authority or anyone acting under the color of that authority, to violate the California Constitutional or property rights of that person."[39] SB 933 would have allowed banished survivors and their heirs to take legal action under any of the three legal areas by creating a two-year window to file claims on or before December 31, 2006.[40]

After SB 933 was introduced in 2003, the Mexican American Legal Defense and Education Fund (MALDEF) and the law firm Kiesel, Boucher & Larson jointly filed a class-action lawsuit in the Superior Court of Los Angeles County. MALDEF attorneys filed the lawsuit— *Emilia Castañeda v. the State of California, County of Los Angeles, and Los Angeles Chamber of Commerce*—on behalf of Emilia Castañeda, who was just one of approximately 400,000 ethnic Mexicans expelled from California between 1929 and 1944.[41] In September 2003, the California Assembly and the Senate passed SB 933 with an overwhelming majority.[42] The weight of this bill was its attempt to assign responsibility to the California government for banishing US citizens and legal residents of Mexican descent and for their lost property. Despite strong support from both houses, Governor Gray Davis vetoed it. The veto forced MALDEF to withdraw the lawsuit, which had sought both monetary reparations for property losses and a state legal apology from California, to avoid an unfavorable ruling. Avoiding a negative holding in court was crucial so that a new class-action lawsuit could be filed if the statute of limitations was eventually extended.[43]

In spelling out the coerciveness of banishment and the racist motives behind it, SB 933 stated, "People of Mexican descent were an easy target for America's economic problems and racist tendencies. The rights guaranteed by the US Constitution were abandoned in the drive to send them South of the border."[44] With the overwhelmingly supportive vote, both the California Senate and Assembly officially recognized the legal injustice of banishment. Governor Davis did not disagree with the legal arguments and claims to legal injury that Senator Dunn presented in this bill. In fact, Davis had signed bills that extended the statute of limitations, including one in 2002 that approved a three-year window so that Mexican citizens who participated in the Bracero Program could take legal action for missing wages.[45] Despite the strong recent precedent on extension of limitations, Governor Davis vetoed SB 933 based on a procedural disagreement: that "private litigation can be inefficient and expensive."[46] This places the burden on banished mixed-status families so the state could avoid the cost of legal reparations. In lieu of SB 933, Davis recommended that the legislature create a reparations fund with an expedited administrative procedure for processing claims. This suggestion was modeled on the fund used to compensate victims of the Cypress Freeway collapse in 1990.[47] Davis assured the public that this reparations fund "would be quicker and less expensive for both taxpayers and plaintiffs."[48]

Fact-finding commissions would, by necessity, establish the nature of the mass removals of mixed-status families at the state and federal levels. They would have to explore the impact of those experiences, interview people, locate potentially concealed governmental documents, examine the damages of coerced removal, and make recommendations for reparation. Political acknowledgment of this shameful history could, in turn, be the catalyst needed to pass new and pending bills at both the state and national levels. Senator Dunn recognized this point when he introduced Senate Bill 427 in 2003 calling for a fact-finding commission on Mexican repatriation and banishment in the state of California. Dunn, in a likely attempt to maximize the chance for a reparations bill to be enacted, introduced SB 427 on February 20, 2003, and SB 933 a day later. SB 427 described "unconstitutional deportation"—or, as I refer to it in this book, *banishment*—as the process in which "[immigration] raids indiscriminately targeted persons of Mexican descent, with authorities and others characterizing these persons as 'illegal aliens' even when they were citizens or permanent legal residents."[49] The legal classification of all ethnic Mexicans as unauthorized immigrants created a state-imposed condition of illegality that has been passed down over generations, as some of the stories in this book attest.

But a political acknowledgment of repatriation and banishment was derailed in California when Governor Schwarzenegger vetoed SB 427 on September 29, 2004, and warned against the creation of bureaucratic boxes in the legislature. While he did not explain what constitutes one, he did classify the fact-finding commission as an "unnecessary new box."[50] The veto language instead suggested that "the Legislature and the Administration can create commissions to advise them without the need for legislation."[51] But no resources were secured to provide the findings and recommendations that SB 427's fact-finding commission had proposed. The inability of the Senate to find those resources without legislation prompted a new bill, which Dunn introduced on February 22, 2005. This bill, SB 645, was a revised version of SB 427 and called once more for the establishment of a fact-finding commission on "Mexican repatriations and unconstitutional deportations" during the Great Depression.[52] Despite significant support from the legislature, Governor Schwarzenegger vetoed SB 645 and offered the following reasoning in his veto message: "This bill is substantially similar to Senate Bill 427 that I vetoed last year."[53] The governor restated that a new commission was not necessary, but he failed to establish specific guidelines for alternative existing resources. Both California Senate Bill 427 (2003) and Senate Bill 645 (2005) are very similar and have one major objective: to validate the mass removals of ethnic Mexicans and put the banishment of US citizens on the political official record. These bills are, however, currently inactive and marked as non-urgent. Moreover, the multiple vetoes of bills that attempted to create fact-finding commissions to expand the statute of limitations for banished families to have financial claims for property losses effectively halted any additional advancements on the legal arena for reparations in California.

Other states in the midwestern region of the United States have also taken political action to make reparations for having removed Mexicans and Mexican Americans en masse during the Great Depression.

In 2004, Michigan introduced a resolution to create a commission to investigate the mass removals of Mexican Americans and Mexican immigrants legally residing in that state.[54] But the Michigan legislature did not gather enough support to approve the commission. Six years later, Illinois—another midwestern state that participated in the mass removals—took political action and won. Starting in 2010, Illinois public schools have had to teach the history of Mexican American removals as an eighth-grade graduation requirement.[55] Despite such efforts to mandate teaching about the mass ethnic Mexican expulsions in public classrooms, it remains a largely unknown history because it is currently taught in public schools in only two states, California and Illinois.

Nonetheless, reparation efforts at the state level encouraged representatives to act at the national level. For instance, in 2017, Representatives Hilda L. Solis and Lucille Roybal-Allard, both Democratic Congresswomen from California, introduced a bill to create a fact-finding commission on the 1929 to 1941 expulsions of Mexican Americans from the United States to Mexico.[56] The commission would investigate, report its findings, and make recommendations for legislative action. Yet neither this bill, nor two others introduced on this matter, in 2006 and 2016, were ever brought to a vote. While these bills provide important political recognition, the lack of federal reparations means that only a small number of banished mixed-status families and their communities have benefited from selective educational initiatives, two public landmarks, and a formal state apology.

In August 2003, California State Senators Joseph Dunn, Gil Cedillo, Martha Escutia, and Gloria Romero, along with California State Assembly Member Fabian Núñez, wrote and introduced California State Senate Joint Resolution (SJR) 21, which requested that Congress establish a fact-finding commission to "determine whether the federal government committed a wrong against those American citizens and permanent-resident aliens of Mexican descent who were deported or coerced to emigrate during the 1930s and to recommend appropriate remedies."[57] If it had passed, copies of SJR 21 would have been distributed by the US secretary of state to the governor of California, the president and vice president of the United States, the Speaker of the House of Representatives, the Senate majority leader, and each California state senator and representative, in the hopes that at least one of these entities would then take political action at the federal level to establish a federal fact-finding commission. Notably, the language of SJR 21 underlined the complicity of the federal government in the mass banishment of mixed-status families: "Local authorities, with the knowledge and assistance of the federal government, instituted programs to facilitate the wrongful deportation of persons of Mexican descent and secured transportation arrangements with railroads, ships, and airlines to effectuate the wholesale removal of persons of Mexican descent to the interior of Mexico."[58] A federal fact-finding commission could investigate the level of involvement of the federal government in the banishment of Mexican Americans and thus determine responsibility and suggest recommendations for adequate reparations for the damages at the federal level.

On April 6, 2006, Representative Hilda L. Solis of California introduced House Bill (HR) 5161 in an affirmative response to SJR 21.[59] The commission proposed by HR 5161 would seek to investigate and determine the federal government's responsibility in the forced and coerced removals of Mexican nationals and US citizens of Mexican descent and to investigate "the impact of such removal on those individuals, their families, and the Mexican-American community in the United States and to recommend appropriate remedies."[60] This bill marked an important advance in reparation attempts made in the political arena because it proposed investigating the effects on not only those who had been removed, but their families as well. All members of the commission would be required to have expertise on human rights, civil rights, immigration, labor, business, or other pertinent issues.[61] They would have to adequately prepare, investigate, report findings, and provide recommendations for legislative action.

While the establishment of fact-finding commissions remains unresolved, California senators have begun legislative efforts to establish a state reparations fund, which former governors Davis and Schwarzenegger both suggested alongside their vetoes of SB 933 (2003) and SB 37 (2004). Both governors argued that such a fund would be more effective than individual or class-action lawsuits in addressing the injury of banishment. After Senator Dunn retired, in March 2007, Senator Gil Cedillo took the lead in proposing SB 552, which would establish such a reparations fund. Within three months, the bill was sent to the Senate floor for a vote and on June 4, 2007, it passed with twenty-four votes in favor and fourteen against, but it never made it out of Assembly Committee hearings. Thus, the bill died because it never progressed past this point in the legislative process.

In lieu of legislative action, primary and secondary public-education advocates have contributed to redress efforts in the intellectual arena. K–12 educational curricula is in large part dictated and funded by the state government. Accordingly, advocates have pushed the California legislature to revise the social science curriculum to include the history of Mexican American banishment and Mexican repatriation. Christine Valenciana, education scholar and daughter of banished Mexican American Emilia Castañeda, has been at the forefront of California's efforts to include the history of banished Mexican Americans in public-education curricula. As Valenciana has argued, "unconstitutional deportation and Mexican repatriation" continues to be an example of intolerance, and this history must be reflected in social science textbooks adopted by local and state boards of education in California.[62] To fill the void in the current curriculum, Valenciana created a social science guide for teachers that incorporates oral histories of repatriation and "unconstitutional deportations." She explains that assignments included in this teachers' guide would satisfy reading, critical discussion, and other language arts activities requirements, all of which are related to state content-area standards.[63]

These curricular recommendations have been supported publicly by the California Federation of Teachers (CFT), a labor union representing teachers and other school employees throughout the state. In 2004, four hundred members attended the CFT convention in University City, California, where they advocated for the adoption of social science curricula in California in order to help this little-known history of the mass removals of ethnic Mexicans become public knowledge.[64] The CFT also took further steps in supporting Valenciana's efforts in the political arena when it proposed resolution 34.04, "Unknown History: Deportation of Mexican Americans," which supports reparations and bills such as SB 933.[65] To aid Valenciana's efforts, the CFT also promoted, in that same resolution, distributing information on this history to influential organizations working in education and labor across the United States, including the American Federation of Teachers (AFT) and the American Federation of Labor and Congress of Industrial Organizations (AFL-CIO). CFT members supported the comprehensive resolution and passed it quickly with a significant majority of votes.[66]

Despite the passage of the CFT resolution, little political action was taken up on reparations for more than a decade; since then, policymakers have introduced a number of bills that advocate for redress for ethnic Mexicans who were coerced to leave the United States en masse. In 2014, a Montebello Unified School District elementary school teacher, Leslie Hiatts, collaborated with student teacher Ana Ramos to implement lesson plans on the history of these mass removals for their fifth-grade class. The history lesson both shocked and resonated with the students, many of whom lived in mixed-status households and in fear of having their loved ones deported. Inspired to act, the students, who were guided by Hiatts and Ramos, began a campaign to implement this history in classrooms across California. They shared their proposal with their local state representative, Assemblywoman Cristina Garcia, who encouraged them to enter her "There Ought to Be a Law" contest, and they won.[67] On March 25, 2015, California State Assembly

Member Cristina Garcia introduced Assembly Bill (AB) 146, asking the State Board of Education to consider inclusion of "repatriation" history in the next revision of the history–social science framework and related materials.[68] A few months later, on October 1, 2015, California Governor Jerry Brown signed AB 146 into law, which required the State Board of Education to consider including content on the mass ethnic Mexican removals from the United States in the next revision of the history and social science framework.[69] This and past bills are important political strides that could lead to a broader scope for reparations.

Notably, these bills usually temporally limit the discussion of mass expulsions to the decade of the 1930s or from 1929 to 1944, ignoring those removed during the first phase of banishment in the 1920s. The reasons for this historical oversight in the legislation is twofold. First, this earlier period of banishment remains an even less-known chapter in US history. Second, most of the exclusions in the 1920s primarily involved Mexican nationals. Yet, this first period of removals also included US citizens, as the case of the Rodríguez family in Chapter 1 shows. Moreover, though they may not have been US citizens, removed Mexican nationals also have a claim to legal restitution because their removal often violated due-process protections. Officers were aware that due process could possibly be more costly than keeping Mexicans on relief rolls.[70] As a result, local and federal government officials expelled Mexicans—who, local officials claimed, wanted to return to Mexico voluntarily—without a rightful public hearing and without formal deportation proceedings. According to journalist Carey McWilliams, this happened when county employees, namely social workers, "betrayed Mexicans by telling officials that they 'wanted' to return home."[71] In short, officials documented these removals as "voluntary" departures, an administrative maneuver that sidestepped the need for formal deportation proceedings. Now, decades later, this administrative classification has denied, and continues to deny, expelled Mexican citizens the right to reparations.

A BATTLE AGAINST TIME

Drawn from their lived experiences, the recommendations of the Ro-dríguez, De Anda, Robles, and Espinoza families offer a starting point for imagining a more complete approach to reparations for ethnic Mexican banishment in the political, legal, and intellectual arenas. This comprehensive approach to reparations must expand its scale and scope to address how these harms have taken place across geographies and generations. Banished ethnic Mexicans and their descendants have an urgent and valid need for restitution and have offered suggestions that are relevant to their own experiences. Their voices are crucial at a time when political momentum for restitution has slowed, though efforts resurfaced again in September 2024 with the approval of California SB 537. Through the various efforts to obtain redress during the last two decades, some progress has been made—but only at the local and state levels. As the legal fights to pass formal reparations legislation have shown, banished Mexican Americans and their families must first win a battle against time before they can win federal and legal redress from those involved in their coerced removal.

At the state and federal levels, battles for reparations continue to fail, in part due to the political climate and resurgent xenophobic discourses that continue to racially construct Mexicans, regardless of legal status, as alleged problems who should be blamed for the social, economic, and political ills of the nation. As Guadalupe, Ramona's daughter, contends: "I do believe that it's not enough to just say that this happened to us and that it's in the books, history books or in the schoolbooks or we now know what happened to us and now we're healing. It's not enough because of the type of society it is. They don't respect us. They didn't re-spect us back then and they don't respect us now. And the only way they respect you is if you win in court because it's a litigious society."[72] Ethnic Mexicans in the United States continue to negotiate the particular state of conditional belonging that I have referred to as impermanent legality that insists on rendering them unworthy of legal and social recognition and inclusion.

Without new laws or waivers of the statute of limitations on claiming such reparations, little can be done to repair the legal injuries of banishment. Critics of such waivers believe that the United States should not be held accountable for unjust acts of the distant past. This issue was addressed in *United States v. Kubrick* (1979), in which the Supreme Court provided the following reasoning on statutes of limitations in their holding: "Statutes of limitations . . . [afford] plaintiffs what the legislature deems a reasonable time to present their claims, they protect defendants and the courts from having to deal with cases in which the search for truth may be seriously impaired by the loss of evidence, whether by death or disappearance of witnesses, fading memories, disappearance of documents, or otherwise."[73] While this holding validates the utility of a statute of limitations in a general sense, in the case of banishment, Mexican Americans and their families could not access US courts from abroad. This is why banished ethnic Mexican and their descendants are now requesting an extension of the statute of limitations for claiming legal action. Without such an extension, the banished Mexican American generation will pass away without access to material redress. Immediate action is urgently needed. While the United States has ostensibly "moved on" from the post–World War I recession and Great Depression, banished US citizens and their descendants—like the Rodríguez, De Anda, Robles, and Espinoza families introduced in this book—are still suffering from the transgenerational illegality they inherited, which continues to haunt their lives and livelihoods.

EPILOGUE

This book tells the story of a collective search for belonging among banished Mexican American women and their families who managed to resettle in the United States decades after their expulsion. Through the original oral histories and personal collections from members of the Rodríguez, De Anda, Robles, and Espinoza families—as well as archival sources from Mexico and the United States—it has traced the struggles of mixed-status Mexican families to claim their right to belong not only in their own native country but also in that of their ancestors. In turn, each of these banished families found ways to contest, resist, and refuse the meanings of illegality imposed on them in various historical contexts and on both sides of the US-Mexico border.

In the early twentieth century, from 1921 to 1944, US officials and other stakeholders regularly mobilized legal and policy discourse to connect notions of racialized illegality to Mexican American women and children as well as the generations of their family that followed. This transgenerational illegality continues to haunt—legally, socially, culturally, and economically—US returnees and their descendants. Banished mixed-status families' lived experiences attest to the processes under which legacies of coverture doctrine and the likely to become public charge (LPC) clause of the 1917 Immigration Act gave way to transgenerational illegality and the related condition of impermanent legality, which have shaped their lives, livelihoods, and even life chances. Their experiences collectively challenge and complicate common ideas of citizenship and US-Mexico immigration as a linear south-to-north migration process. As the narrators in this book explain, individuals and families have worked together—and continue to work together—to contest the transgenerational illegality they have inherited and to make direct claims to US citizenship through their ancestors. Their oral histories provide a lens for understanding the legacies of banishment across generations that only they can provide. Combined, the personal family collections, transnational archival sources, and individual as well as transgenerational familial oral histories helped me to rethink and rewrite the history of repatriation as a process of banishment that disproportionately targeted US-citizen women and children of Mexican descent in mixed-status families.

There are still so many more histories—in photos, and letters, and scrapbooks, and the voices of countless families—to which we must continue to attune our ears. It is through these stories that we may begin to understand parts of this history that remain too little known even as their legacies are felt to this day. Consider that as early as the 1930s, coerced removal campaigns also began to target other ethnic and racial groups marked as "undesirable" in both the United States and Mexico. The mass coerced removals that largely targeted Mexican immigrants and Mexican Americans in fact catalyzed efforts to remove other marginalized ethnic groups—namely, Filipinos who were considered US nationals—during the Great Depression. When the United States expanded its so-called repatriation campaign by extending Asian exclusion with the passage of the 1935 Filipino Repatriation Act, it marked the first time that US nationals were classified as deportable and inadmissible. In an echo of the unofficial process of ethnic Mexican banishment, the Filipino Repatriation Act of 1935 offered free one-way transportation assistance to single adults residing in the continental

United States who "voluntarily" wished to return to the Philippines.[1] Approximately 2,064 Filipinos were relocated with government-paid transportation under the stipulation that they could never return to the United States.[2]

In California, the State Emergency Relief Administration (SERA) that covered transportation expenses for removed ethnic Mexicans did the same for US-citizen children of Filipino parents and US-citizen women married to Filipino nationals. As in the cases of banished Mexican Americans, the banished US-citizen wives and children of repatriated Filipinos experienced transnational marginalization in the United States and the Philippines. Worried that those families would become public charges, Philippine government officials threatened deportation but eventually allowed them to remain in the Philippines. The Filipino Repatriation Act expired in 1940, by which time the 1934 Tydings-McDuffie Act (known officially as the Philippine Independence Act) had established a path for the Philippines to become independent by 1946.[3] Notably, the pathway to independence for the Philippines also provided a way for the United States to reclassify Filipinos from US nationals to excludable immigrants. Both mass removals—of ethnic Mexicans and of Filipinos—not only aimed to remove working-class families en masse from the United States, but also disguised the banishment of US-citizen wives and children, which was actually driven by nativism, behind the pretext of humanitarian concern for destitute people of color during the interwar period.

The exclusion of other ethnic groups was delayed in part because policymakers could not agree on the appropriate immigration policies to retrench a newly developing racial hierarchy as the United States emerged as a world power. In 1929, as state and federal policymakers debated immigration restrictions that would target Mexicans, opponents of anti-Mexican exclusionary policies lauded the value of Mexican labor to the US economy. In racially infused and gender-charged conversations, policymakers and other stakeholders argued about which ethnic and racial minorities constituted a more suitable source of cheap and disposable labor, and thus deserved to be exempt from US immigration restrictions. In April 1929, George P. Clements, manager of the Agricultural Department of the Los Angeles Chamber of Commerce, wrote to California State Assembly Member Isaac Jones to oppose the Mexican immigration restrictions that Assembly Joint Resolution No. 11 proposed to the US Congress. Clements argued:

> We believe accumulated facts show the need of casual labor to the agricultural districts of California, a labor which cannot be supplied from any other quarter except Mexico unless we invite the negro of Porto Rico—a citizen of the United States who in coming becomes a part of us rather than an alien whom we are not able to deport. . . . If we are not making wise use of these people [Mexicans] it is our own fault, and legislation should be directed towards their economic service rather than their exclusion. . . . The serious aspect, as I see it, is that we are confronted with an influx from the Philippine Islands of a type of labor which is not only unfitted but enters into direct competition with the female labor of the country. We are informed that in California alone this invasion already amounts to above 80,000 of single Filipinos, lacking our standards of morals and lending to mixed racial marriage. Here, it seems to me, we are confronted with a real biological problem worthy of consideration.[4]

The racial and gendered calculus in Clements's letter underscores the political reality that maintaining white racial dominance in the United States figured prominently in the policy debates surrounding Mexican immigration restrictions. Despite their long presence and growing numbers in the United States, ethnic Mexicans were racialized as deportable "outsiders" whose excludability made them an ideal source of cheap, disposable, and temporary "casual labor." Clements argued that Puerto Rican workers were not an ideal substitute for Mexican labor because, as US citizens, they could not be deported en masse and would likely establish a permanent presence. Unlike ethnic Mexicans who could be removed to Mexico even if they were US citizens, Puerto Ricans, because they were from a (then) colony of the United States, could not be removed when their labor was no longer needed.

Clements also claimed that Puerto Ricans' African roots would contribute to the "negro problem" in the United States. This is not to say that Mexicans do not have strong and marked Black ancestry as well. But Mexicans posed less of a racial threat to the United States because they intermarried with white women in much smaller numbers at the time, largely because Mexican women were not affected by immigration exclusion laws. In his "Mexican Immigration and Its Bearing on California's Agricultural Report," Clements claimed that "the Mexican is never a biological problem. He rarely marries out of his own people. A Mexican man never marries a white woman."[5] While Mexican Americans—who represented an undesirable nonwhite segment of the American population—were often referred as a "biological problem," Mexican immigrants were not always understood as such. Compared to Filipino, Puerto Rican, and Black men, Mexican immigrant men would not "brown," or otherwise allegedly contaminate, the notions of white purity and femininity that policymakers in the United States were invested in protecting.

In 1929, Clements noted in an alarmist and xenophobic tone that the more than eighty thousand single Filipinos in California had already constituted an "invasion." His observation suggested his concern not that the number of Filipinos exceeded that of ethnic Mexicans in California, but that they were single men who were likely to marry white women. Mexicans, regardless of legal status, were segregated into Mexican barrios where Mexican women lived as well.[6] Additionally, Mexicans living in California could, in a matter of days, cross the US-Mexico border to marry and then come back to work in the United States. This was not feasible for Filipinos, Puerto Ricans, and diasporic Black communities, given the geographical distance between California and their places of origin. Thus, these debates did not consider Mexican immigrants to be part of either the "embarrassing negro problem" or the "biological problem" to which Filipinos, Puerto Ricans, and Blacks allegedly contributed.[7] The new emerging racial hierarchy informed by eugenic ideals insisted on maintaining a legally white nation that would admit people of color only as temporary, disposable workers who could be excluded as necessary.

During the same period, in Mexico, a similar type of banishment—that is, one fueled by xenophobic political discourses that depicted destitute people, regardless of their legal status, as social and economic burdens—was taking place. For example, in 1930, Mexican officials banished Mexican-citizen Rosa Murillo de Chan, her Mexican-citizen children, and her Chinese husband from their home in Sinaloa, Mexico, to Guangdong Province in China.[8] Much like anti-Mexican discourse in the United States, anti-Chinese propaganda in Mexico characterized Chinese immigrants as undesirable, their Mexican wives as so-called race traitors, and their biracial Mexican children as "abominations." Anti-Chinese sentiment facilitated the mass expulsion of an estimated two thousand Chinese Mexicans.[9] Mixed-status Mexican and Filipino families banished from the United States and mixed-status Chinese Mexican families expelled from Mexico during the years leading to and shortly following the Great Depression were all recast as outsiders in their home countries, rendered excludable regardless of any legal and political claims to belonging they had, and targeted for removal with no regard for their civil rights. Exclusionary US laws have been as fluid as the border itself, influencing policies in other countries as well.

As the California case demonstrates, US policymakers, businessmen, and other stakeholders considered Mexican immigrants to be preferable to Filipinos, Puerto Ricans, and Blacks precisely because Mexican immigrants did not have legal claims to US citizenship in the same ways that other minoritized groups did. The extension of meanings of illegality onto banished Mexican Americans marks both their distinctly racialized vulnerability to being rendered as excludable "foreigners" and nativist desires to preserve the "white racial purity" of the United States. Once dominant mainstream discourses had solidified ethnic Mexicans' racial status as "immigrants," they were welcomed back into the United States to fill the demand for cheap, disposable labor.

As the mass removals during the early twentieth century demonstrate, working-class people of color often feel the brunt of criminal and immigration laws that are changed to be "more effective," which in practice means "less humane."[10] In the case of early twentieth-century banishment, ethnic Mexicans became economic scapegoats, cast as burdens on US society during the interwar period. Officials used this racialized discourse to justify the coerced mass banishments of ethnic Mexicans—all in the name of protecting jobs for white Americans to facilitate national economic recovery in the United States. This process created a new racial hierarchy that intended to erase Mexicans from the US national polity and include them only as temporary and disposable workers. To facilitate this, officials targeted Mexican American women and children for banishment in order to remove entire mixed-status Mexican families, stop ethnic Mexican women from reproducing US citizens, and disrupt the right to derivative citizenship for direct descendants of banished Mexican American women.

Over time, the discursive construction of ethnic Mexicans as foreign workers, as well as persistent mass deportations and restrictive immigration laws, have normalized this view of mixed-status Mexican families as removable. As of 2022, there were approximately 11 million unauthorized immigrants living in the United States.[11] Most of them—some 8.8 million people—live in mixed-status families, usually immigrant parents with US-citizen children.[12] Unauthorized immigrant parents are often ineligible to adjust their immigration status or have to wait over two decades to do so (all while risking deportation). In 1960, the US Congress amended Section 245(a) of the Immigration and Nationality Act (INA), limiting the eligibility for adjustment of status to applicants who were "inspected and admitted or paroled" into the United States.[13] As such, immigrant parents who entered the United States without inspection became ineligible for status adjustment even if they had US-citizen children, a relationship that established strong ties to the United States with certain humanitarian protections from deportation. This change in the naturalization law made illegality permanent for many immigrant parents in mixed-status families, making the possibility of family separation through deportation a threat that will continue indefinitely. And although a US-citizen child can still petition for their eligible immigrant parents' lawful permanent resident status, which creates a path to US citizenship, the child must be at least twenty-one years of age to begin that process.

Family separation also remains a threat for mixed-status marriages in the United Sates. There are currently approximately 726,000 unauthorized immigrants married to US citizens, and most of these immigrant spouses have lived in the country for at least ten years.[14] To adjust their status, the unauthorized spouse could leave the country, then apply for an immigrant visa at a US consulate in their native country to be legally admitted into the United States, which then makes them eligible for immigration adjustment through marriage per INA 245(a) regulations.[15] This process increases the risk of separation for mixed-status families, primarily because there is no guarantee that a visa will be granted after they leave the United States. Moreover, leaving the United States places the unauthorized spouse at risk of triggering a three- or ten-year reentry bar: in other words, a requirement that the person remain in their native country for three or ten years before they return.[16] Thus, couples in this situation are advised to file a provisional waiver to avoid the immigration bar, which can be a long and costly process. Some mixed-status couples have opted not to pursue an immigration adjustment process for fear of family separation. The immigration bar then serves as a punishment for having violated immigration law by entering the United States without inspection, even when immigration law is not criminal law, and punishment is permissible only under criminal law.

In June 2024, President Joe Biden addressed this issue by introducing the Keeping Families Together initiative that extends a "parole in place" process to unauthorized spouses of US citizens who entered the country without inspection. This means that the unauthorized spouse no longer has to leave the United States to apply for an immigrant visa abroad, which eliminates the risk that they will be denied reentry. To qualify for the parole-in-place exception, the mixed-status couple must have legally married prior to June 17, 2024, and the unauthorized spouse must have been continuously in the country since June 17, 2014. It is estimated that 455,000 unauthorized spouses of US citizens could benefit from the extension of the parole-in-place immigration rule.[17] This program was short-lived. On November 7, 2024, after the US presidential election but before president-elect Trump's inauguration, a federal court in Texas issued a declaratory judgment and permanent injunction against the Keeping Families Together initiative, which made it unlawful. On November 13, 2024, the US Citizenship and Immigration Services (USCIS) ceased processing and accepting applications under this program.[18] Now, unauthorized spouses who entered the country without inspection again face complicated legal hurdles to adjust their status.

Family separation is a fear that all mixed-status families live with, including unauthorized parents of US-citizen children. Under the second Trump presidential term, the threat of family separation looms larger than it did during his first term. In October 2024, Tom Homan—who began his career as a border patrolman and worked his way up to acting director of Immigration and Customs Enforcement (ICE) during the first year and a half of the first Trump administration—shared his views of Trump's revived mass deportation plan during an interview. When asked if there is a way to prevent separating families under a mass deportation during Trump's second presidential term, Homan answered without hesitation, "Of course there is. Families can be deported together."[19] Homan's proposal to deport families wholesale is a punitive and inhumane approach to deportations. The Immigration and Nationality Act of 1965 repealed the national origins quotas that had been in effect since the 1920s. The 1965 legislation implemented a preference system based on an immigrant's family relationship with

US citizens or lawful permanent residents, a process that favored family unification over national origin.[20] But ethnic Mexican mixed-status families have never fully benefited from policies that aim to keep families together in the United States. Homan's proposed plan to deport entire mixed-status families mirrors the tactics that government officials used to banish mixed-status Mexican families during the interwar period.

Two months into Trump's second presidential term, at the time of this writing, the past-present parallels are even more apparent. For instance, among its many immigration directives, the Trump administration is encouraging agents in US Immigration and Customs Enforcement (ICE), the Border Patrol, and the Coast Guard to use "common sense to do their jobs effectively."[21] This approach grants wide discretion to immigration enforcement agents when deciding who they deem inadmissible and deportable. The commonsense method runs the risk of encouraging officers to use their own racial, classed, and gendered assumptions—not legal statute—to enforce immigration law. In line with the reduction of immigrant protections, Trump also lifted the "sensitive location" enforcement policy to allow immigration searches to be conducted in schools, churches, and hospitals as was done during the mass removals of the interwar period.[22]

Such an approach creates widespread fear to coerce immigrants and mixed-status families to leave the country—a strategy that was officially implemented on March 10, 2025, when the secretary of Homeland Security, Kristi Noem, announced a new attempt at mass removals advertised as a "self-deportation" campaign. The project consists of a series of "hyper-targeted ads" that will run on radio, television, and digital broadcasting, circulate in social media, and be sent through text messages.[23] The ad will air in multiple countries and in diverse regions in the United States as part of "a larger $200 million domestic and international ad campaign encouraging illegal aliens to 'Stay Out and Leave Now.'"[24] The hyper-targeted marketing approach reveals that the Trump administration is taking aim at a particular group for mass removal, making this a potential racial or ethnic exclusion project that comes complete with a US Customs and Border Protection (CBP) app that, as Noem explained, "gives aliens the option to leave now and self-deport, so they may still have the opportunity to return legally in the future and live the American dream. If they don't, we will find them, we will deport them, and they will never return."[25] Banished mixed-status Mexican families were also promised that they could return a year after their expulsion, once the economy in the United States stabilized, which proved to be false as attested by the banished families in this book. In fact, banished US citizens of Mexican descent faced multiple obstacles that delayed resettlement for decades.

Promoted as economic efforts that will save US taxpayer funds, both banishment drives, and the "self-deportation" campaign, operate at the expense of working-class mixed-status families. The economic motivations for the "self-deportation" project echo "repatriation" discourses that present the mass removals as voluntary and benevolent efforts. The Department of Homeland Security claimed that "Self-deportation is the safest option for illegal aliens, while preserving law enforcement resources. Not only is it safer, but it also saves U.S. taxpayer dollars and valuable Customs and Border Protection (CBP) and Immigration and Customs Enforcement (ICE) resources to focus on dangerous criminal aliens."[26] If this renewed effort for mass removals is carried out without contestation, it will inevitably create new generations of mixed-status families that will inherit an imposed transgenerational illegality while it continues to criminalize immigrants. The specifics for the "self-deportation" campaign are still unknown, but the app asks migrants if they have "enough money to depart the United States" and whether they have "a valid, unexpired passport from your original country of citizenship."[27] It is unclear if the United States plans to pay for the one-way transportation expenses for this campaign, but the questions in the app hint at approaches recycled from the mass removals during the interwar period.

As the participating banished families in this book proved, their banishment resulted in violations of civil and human rights and prolonged consequences across three generations. Nonetheless, almost identical removal approaches were used on other racialized groups in the United States and Mexico during the 1930s. Now, we once again face the threat of the replication of banishment through the removals of mixed-status families. Working-class mixed-status families could again be targeted for banishment based on racialized notions of US citizenship, economic scapegoating, and attempts to maintain white supremacy. Today, however, we could learn from past injustices and insist on upholding the rights of people across ethnic, class, gender, and racial lines.

As the official apologies, proposed reparations legislation, and commemorative plaque at LA Plaza de Cultura y Artes in Los Angeles attest, mass removals during the early twentieth century have since been recognized as having violated the human and civil rights of the mixed-status families who were removed.[28] The current threat is that immigrants and entire mixed-status families will once again be expelled through a "self-deportation" campaign that employs similar tactics to those used during the interwar period, tactics that will likely have the same dire consequences. While the families in this book have shown that return migration was not eliminated during the mass removals, their return to the United States was significantly delayed and had transgenerational repercussions. Let the acknowledgment of this history, which was so important to the families in this book and to so many banished women and children like them, not remain a symbolic act, but serve as a reminder to enforce the civil and human rights of immigrants and US citizens in mixed-status families.

Notes

Acknowledgments

Credits

Index

NOTES

INTRODUCTION

1 LA Plaza de Cultura y Artes is a Mexican American museum and cultural center, owned by Los Angeles County, that opened its doors to the public in April 2011. The term *ethnic Mexicans* is used in this book to refer to both Mexican immigrants and Mexican Americans in the United States. I differentiate the legal status of the communities examined in this book by applying the term *Mexican Americans* when discussing US citizens of Mexican descent and *Mexicans* or *Mexican immigrants* when referring to non-US-citizens.

2 "Bosses Drive On Mexican Workers: Deport 1,300 Workers from Los Angeles," *Daily Worker* (New York, NY), September 5, 1931; "Starving Mexican Workers Terrorized by Deportation," *Daily Worker* (New York, NY), August 22, 1931; "1,500 Mexicans Sent Home," *Evening Star* (Washington, DC), July 8, 1932.

3 "Bosses Drive On Mexican Workers." The terms *repatriation, voluntary deportation,* and *deportation* were used interchangeably in newspaper and governmental files to describe the mass removals, effectively obscuring the legal status of those removed and their right to remain in the United States.

4 "Bosses Drive On Mexican Workers."

5 For examples of US citizens and legally admitted ethnic Mexicans removed in similar raids, see Abraham Hoffman, *Unwanted Mexican Americans in the Great Depression: Repatriation Pressures, 1929–1939* (Tucson: University of Arizona Press, 1974), 60–61; and Francisco E. Balderrama and Raymond Rodríguez, *Decade of Betrayal: Mexican Repatriation in the 1930s,* rev. ed. (Albuquerque: University of New Mexico Press, 2006), 149–151, 73–74.

6 The term *mixed-status* is used here to refer to families composed of members with diverse legal statuses. For the families discussed in this book, they were mainly composed of US-citizen women and children whose husbands and fathers were Mexican immigrants. In other cases, the children were US citizens, and the parents were Mexicans legally admitted to the United States as temporary workers. While the term mixed-status was not commonly used during the period discussed in this book, it is the most concise and effective way to describe the diverse legal statuses of the families I write about. For an examination of the development of the term mixed-status families, see Michael Fix and Wendy Zimmermann, "All Under One Roof: Mixed-Status Families in an Era of Reform," *International Migration Review* 35, no. 2 (2001): 397–419.

7 "Mexicans Return to Their Home Land," *Coolidge Examiner* (Coolidge, AZ), June 26, 1931.

8 "Los Angeles Spends $180,000 to Repatriate 13,000 Mexicans: Charity Organizations Find It Difficult, However, to Convince Indigents," *Evening Star* (Washington, DC), April 22, 1934.

9 Historians have established that family reunification is an important factor for emigration and returned migration. See Dino Cinel, *From Italy to San Francisco: The Immigrant Experience* (Stanford: Stanford University Press, 1982), 168; and George J. Sánchez, *Becoming Mexican American: Ethnicity, Culture and Identity in Chicano Los Angeles, 1900–1945* (New York: Oxford University Press, 1993), 135.

10 "11 mexicanos presos en un aparatoso raid a la Placita," *La Opinión* (Los Angeles, CA), February 27, 1931.

11 Fernando Saúl Alanís Enciso, "La labor consular mexicana en Estados Unidos: El caso de Eduardo Ruiz (1921)," *Secuencia: Revista de Historia y Ciencias Sociales* 52 (2002): 48–49.

12 Hoffman, *Unwanted Mexican Americans,* esp. chap. 4.

13 Patricia Morgan, "Shame of a Nation: A Documented Story of Police-State Terror Against Mexican-Americans in the USA," p. 16, box 27, folder 9, "Race: Anti-Mexican-Americans," American Civil Liberties Union of Southern California Records (Collection 900), Special Collections, Charles E. Young Research Library, University of California, Los Angeles.

14 On this topic refer to Fernando Saúl Alanís Enciso, *They Should Stay There: The Story of Mexican Migration and Repatriation During the Great Depression* (Chapel Hill: University of North Carolina Press, 2017), 34–35; Balderrama and Rodríguez, *Decade of Betrayal,* 120–125; Cybelle Fox, *Three Worlds of Relief: Race, Immigration, and the American Welfare State from the Progressive Era to the New Deal* (Princeton: Princeton University Press, 2012), 167, 181.

15 Balderrama and Rodríguez, *Decade of Betrayal,* 149–151.

16 Ian Haney López, *White by Law: The Legal Construction of Race* (New York: New York University Press, 2006), 20–21, 27–30; Mae M. Ngai, *Impossible Subjects: Illegal Aliens and the Making of Modern America* (Princeton: Princeton University Press, 2004), 50–55.

17 Mercedes Carreras de Velasco, *Los Mexicanos que devolvió la crisis, 1929–1932* (Tlatelolco, Mexico: Secretaría de Relaciones Exteriores, 1974), 41, 57.

18 Kevin R. Johnson, "The Forgotten 'Repatriation' of Persons of Mexican Ancestry and Lessons for the 'War on Terror,'" *Pace Law Review* 26, no. 1 (2005): 9–10.

19 Ana Raquel Minian, *Undocumented Lives: The Untold Story of Mexican Migration* (Cambridge: Harvard University Press, 2018); Natalia Molina, *How Race Is Made in America: Immigration, Citizenship, and the Historical Power of Racial Scripts* (Berkeley: University of California Press, 2014); Ngai, *Impossible Subjects.*

20 Ngai, *Impossible Subjects,* 3–5, 56–58.

21 Notable historical studies on Mexican repatriation campaigns include Alanís Enciso, *They Should Stay There;* Fernando Saúl Alanís Enciso, *Voces de la repatriación: La sociedad mexicana y la repatriación de mexicanos de Estados Unidos, 1930–1933* (Zamora: El Colegio de Michoacán, 2015); Balderrama and Rodríguez, *Decade of Betrayal;* Carreras de Velasco, *Los Mexicanos que devolvió la crisis;* Camille Guerin-Gonzales, *Mexican Workers and American Dreams: Immigration, Repatriation, and California Farm Labor, 1900–1939* (New Brunswick: Rutgers University Press, 1996); and Hoffman, *Unwanted Mexican Americans.*

22 Martha Gardner, *The Qualities of a Citizen: Women, Immigration, and Citizenship, 1870–1965* (Princeton: Princeton University Press, 2005), 3, 158–159; Jessica R. Pliley, *Policing Sexuality: The Mann Act and the Making of the FBI* (Cambridge: Harvard University Press, 2014), 34–35; Marylynn Salmon, *Women and the Law of Property in Early America* (Chapel Hill: University of North Carolina Press, 1986), 41.

23 Only seven years later, the Chinese Exclusion Act of 1882 restricted the immigration of all Chinese laborers, both women and men, to the United States. For more on the Chinese Exclusion Act and the Page Act, see Mae Ngai, *The Chinese Question: The Gold Rushes and Global Politics* (New York: W. W. Norton, 2021), 15–20; Elliott Young, *Alien Nation: Chinese Migration in the Americas from the Coolie Era through World War II* (Chapel Hill: University of North Carolina Press, 2014), 98–103, 130.

24 For more on immigration laws aiming at the exclusion of working-class women, see Fox, *Three Worlds of Relief;* Gardner, *Qualities of a Citizen;* Kelly Lytle Hernández, *Migra! A History of the U.S. Border Patrol* (Berkeley: University of California Press, 2010); Natalia Molina, "Constructing Mexicans as Deportable Immigrants: Race, Disease, and the Meaning of 'Public Charge,'" *Identities: Global Studies in Culture and Power* 17, no. 6 (2010); and Vicki L. Ruiz, *From Out of the Shadows: Mexican Women in Twentieth-Century America* (New York: Oxford University Press, 2008), esp. chap. 1.

25 Repatriated Alien Records, US Department of Labor, Immigration and Naturalization Services, October 6, 1939, RG 85, box 455, US National Archives and Records Administration, Washington, DC.

26 Repatriated Alien Records, US Department of Labor, Immigration and Naturalization Services, October 6, 1939.

27 US Congress, House of Representatives, *Hearings on Reynolds-Starnes and Kerr-Coolidge Bills,* 74th Cong., 2nd sess., May 8, 1936 (Washington, DC: US Government Printing Office, 1936), 6981–6984.

28 Nancy Cott, *Public Vows: A History of Marriage and the Nation* (Cambridge: Harvard University Press, 2000), 157; Gardner, *Qualities of a Citizen,* 14; Robert G. McCloskey, ed., *The Works of James Wilson* (Cambridge: Harvard University Press, 1976), 600–601.

29 Lee J. Alston and Joseph P. Ferrie, *Southern Paternalism and the American Welfare State: Economics, Politics, and Institutions in the South, 1865–1965* (Cambridge: Harvard University Press, 1999); Roy Lubove, *The Struggle for Social Security, 1900–1935* (Cambridge: Harvard University Press, 1968).

30 Evelyn Nakano Glenn, *Unequal Freedom: How Race and Gender Shaped American Citizenship and Labor* (Cambridge: Harvard University Press, 2002), 100–101, 212–213.

31 Theda Skocpol, *Protecting Soldiers and Mothers: The Political Origins of Social Policy in the United States* (Cambridge: Harvard University Press, 1992), 34.

32 Eileen Boris, "Labor's Welfare State: Defining Workers, Constructing Citizens," in *The Cambridge History of Law in America,* vol. 3, ed. Michael Grossberg and Christopher Tomlins (Cambridge: Cambridge University Press, 2008), 319–358; Robert H. Bremner, *From the Depths: The Discovery of Poverty in the United States* (New York: New York University Press, 1956).

33 For a detailed discussion of repatriations during the nineteenth century and the quoted estimates, see José Angel Hernández, *Mexican American Colonization During the Nineteenth Century: A History of the U.S.–Mexico Borderlands* (Cambridge: Cambridge University Press, 2012), 122, 137–138.

34 Francisco F. De la Maza, "Decreto de 19 de agosto de 1848: para que las familias mexicanas que se encuentran en los Estados Unidos puedan emigrar a su patria," in *Código de Colonización y Terrenos Baldíos de la República Mexicana, formado por Francisco F. De la Maza y Publicado Según el Acuerdo del Presidente de la República, Por Conducta de la Secretaría de Estado y del Despacho de Fomento, Años de 1451 a 1892* (Mexico City: Oficina Tipográfica de la Secretaría de Fomento, 1893), 407–412.

35 Laura Gómez, *Manifest Destinies: The Making of the Mexican American Race* (New York: New York University Press, 2007), 118; Oscar J. Martínez, "On the Size of the Chicano Population: New Estimates, 1850–1900," *Aztlán* 6, no. 1 (Spring 1975): 44–45, 56.

36 David Gutiérrez, *Walls and Mirrors: Mexican Americans, Mexican Immigrants, and the Politics of Ethnicity* (Berkeley: University of California Press, 1995), 72–74; Michael Innis Jiménez, *Steel Barrio: The Great Mexican Migration to South Chicago, 1915–1940* (New York: New York University Press, 2013), 143.

37 Erika Lee, *America for Americans: A History of Xenophobia in the United States* (New York: Basic Books, 2019), 163.

38 Matt Garcia, *A World of Its Own: Race, Labor, and Citrus in the Making of Greater Los Angeles, 1900–1970* (Chapel Hill: University of North Carolina Press, 2001), 107; Monica Perales, *Smeltertown: Making and Remembering a Southwest Border Community* (Chapel Hill: University of North Carolina Press, 2010), 217.

39 For "usurping American jobs," see Daughters of the American Revolution, "Reynolds Assails Cost of Aliens," *Evening Star* (Washington, DC), April 24, 1936; for "unworthy burdens," see Vicki L. Ruiz, *Cannery Women, Cannery Lives: Mexican Women, Unionization, and the California Food Processing Industry, 1930–1950* (Albuquerque: University of New Mexico Press, 1987), 8.

40 Marin Dies, "The Immigration Crisis," *Saturday Evening Post,* April 20, 1935; "Back Where They Came From," *New Masses,* April 18, 1939; Balderrama and Rodríguez, *Decade of Betrayal,* 69.

41 On March 2, 1917, President Woodrow Wilson signed into law the Jones Act, which granted US citizenship to Puerto Ricans, a retroactive benefit that extended back to October 18, 1898, when Puerto Rico first became a colony of the United States. See Jorell A. Meléndez Badillo, *Puerto Rico: A National History* (Princeton: Princeton University Press, 2024), 121; Lorrin Thomas, *Puerto Rican Citizen: History and Political Identity in Twentieth-Century New York City* (Chicago: University of Chicago Press, 2010), 6, 8, 36. On removals due to political subversion claims, see Elizabeth E. Sine, *Rebel Imaginaries: Labor, Culture, and Politics in Depression-Era California* (Durham: Duke University Press, 2021), 83.

42 Hoffman, *Unwanted Mexican Americans,* 86.

43 Lytle Hernández, *Migra!,* 70–82.

44 *Mexicans in California,* Report of Governor C. C. Young's Mexican Fact-Finding Committee (1930; San Francisco: R. and E. Research Associates, 1970), 30.

45 David Lavender, *California: Land of New Beginnings* (Lincoln: University of Nebraska Press, 1972), 313, 346, 372; Sánchez, *Becoming Mexican American,* 67–68, 71.

46 Hoffman, *Unwanted Mexican Americans,* 45.

47 Alanís Enciso, *Voces de la repatriación,* 73–75; Hoffman, *Unwanted Mexican Americans,* 42–43.

48 Gordon L. McDonough to Los Angeles Board of Supervisors, "Report of Repatriation," November 21, 1938, in Los Angeles County Board of Supervisors Minutes, 244:33, as cited in Balderrama and Rodríguez, *Decade of Betrayal,* 132.

49 The names "Transportation Section" and "Deportation Section" were used interchangeably. The Department of Charities oversaw the county hospital, and together they removed those on medical assistance. See Natalia Molina, *Fit to Be Citizens? Public Health and Race in Los Angeles, 1879–1939* (Berkeley: University of California Press, 2006), 136–137.

50 Report to the Los Angeles County Board of Supervisors from the Superintendent of Charities, August 7, 1933, p. 4, box 64, 14 a, bb, aaa (1), John Anson Ford Collection, Huntington Library, San Marino, CA, as cited in Molina, *Fit to Be Citizens?,* 136, 237n98.

51 Gómez, *Manifest Destinies*; Clare Sheridan, "'Another White Race:' Mexican Americans and the Paradox of Whiteness in Jury Selection," *Law and History Review* 21, no. 1 (Spring 2003).

52 The Knights of Columbus, "Fifth Annual Report of the Mexican Welfare Committee of the Colorado State Council," May 28, 1928, box 16, Carey McWilliams Papers (collection 1243), UCLA Library Special Collections, Charles E. Young Research Library, University of California, Los Angeles.

53 For the history of how these three categories were created, see Adam Goodman, *The Deportation Machine: America's Long History of Expelling Immigrants* (Princeton: Princeton University Press, 2020), esp. chaps. 1 and 2.

54 Robert N. McLean, "Goodbye, Vicente!," *The Survey,* May 1, 1931, 183.

55 US Department of Labor, Bureau of Immigration, *Annual Report of the Commissioner General of Immigration* (1932), p. 72, RG 85, US National Archives and Records Administration, Washington, DC.

56 Associated Press, "60,000 Mexicans Go Home Since Jan 1: Exodus from Southern California Called Greatest Since Huguenot Hegira in 16th Century," *Evening Star* (Washington, DC), June 19, 1931.

57 Associated Press, "60,000 Mexicans Go Home."

58 US Department of Labor, Bureau of Immigration, *Annual Report of the Commissioner General of Immigration* (1932), p. 72.

59 Hoffman, *Unwanted Mexican Americans,* 125.

60 McLean, "Goodbye, Vicente!," 196.

61 McLean, "Goodbye, Vicente!," 195.

62 "More Emigrants," *Waterbury Democrat* (Waterbury, CT), March 27, 1931.

63 McLean, "Goodbye, Vicente!," 196.

64 Cott, *Public Vows,* 164; Gardner, *Qualities of a Citizen,* 150, 156, 172.

65 McLean, "Goodbye, Vicente!," 195.

66 McLean, "Goodbye, Vicente!," 195.

67 Guerin-Gonzales, *Mexican Workers and American Dreams,* 109.

68 Hoffman, *Unwanted Mexican Americans,* 151.

69 Balderrama and Rodríguez, *Decade of Betrayal,* 67.

70 Transcript, testimony before Executive Session of the House Immigration Committee, January 15, 1930, file 55688 / 876-1, entry 9, US Immigration and Naturalization Service, RG 85, US National Archives and Records Administration, Washington, DC, as cited in Ngai, *Impossible Subjects,* 56.

71 Ngai, *Impossible Subjects,* 68–69. On this topic, see also Hidetaka Hirota, *Expelling the Poor: Atlantic Seaboard States and the Nineteenth-Century Origins of American Immigration Policy* (New York: Oxford University Press, 2017), 211; Lytle Hernández, *Migra!,* 48–51; Ivón Padilla-Rodríguez, "'A Violation of the Most Elementary Human Rights of Children': The Rise of Migrant Youth Detention and Family Separation in the American West," in *The North American West in the Twenty-First Century,* ed. Brenden W. Rensink (Lincoln: University of Nebraska Press, 2022), 206–207.

72 R. Reynolds McKay, "Texas Mexican Repatriation During the Great Depression" (PhD diss., University of Oklahoma at Norman, 1982), 98–119, 125.

73 During the Great Depression, the Children's Bureau was charged with providing information on families' needs. See Fox, *Three Worlds of Relief,* 163–164.

74 Jane Perry Clark, "Aliens in the Deportation Dragnet," *Current History* 36, no. 1 (April 1932): 29.

75 US National Commission on Law and Observance, *Report on the Enforcement of the Deportation Laws of the United States* (Washington, DC:

Government Printing Office, 1931), as cited in Julia Rose Kraut, *Threat of Dissent: A History of Ideological Exclusion and Deportation in the United States* (Cambridge: Harvard University Press, 2023), 93.

76 Roger Daniels, *Coming to America: A History of Immigration and Ethnicity in American Life,* 2nd ed. (New York: HarperCollins, 2002), 296–300; Gardner, *Qualities of a Citizen,* 194.

77 Daniel Kanstroom, *Deportation Nation: Outsiders in American History* (Cambridge: Harvard University Press, 2007), 214.

78 Hoffman, *Unwanted Mexican Americans,* 2–3.

79 This transnational agreement on transportation expenses is discussed by Immigration and Naturalization Service District directors from across the United States, and the letters are housed in the National Archives and Records Administration in Washington, DC. For one notable example from the last period of removals, see Fred J. Schlotfeldt, Immigration District Director in Chicago, Illinois to I. F. Wixon, Deputy Commissioner, January 19, 1938, RG 85, file 55957 / 456, "Repatriation of Mexican Nationals," US National Archives and Records Administration, Washington, DC.

80 General Consul of México, "Informe Especial," no. 71, January 27, 1932, 29.

81 Jeffrey Marcos Garcílazo, *Traqueros: Mexican Railroad Workers in the United States, 1870–1930* (Denton: University of North Texas Press, 2012), 38–39, 138.

82 Balderrama and Rodríguez, *Decade of Betrayal,* 67, 122.

83 Committee Report on "The Mexican Problem," p. 1, Cleofas Calleros Papers (MS 231), C. L. Sonnichsen Special Collections Department, University of Texas at El Paso Library.

84 Carey McWilliams, "The Los Angeles Archipelago," *Science & Society* 10, no. 1 (1946): 44; Norman D. Humphrey, "Mexican Repatriation from Michigan Public Assistance in Historical Perspective," *Social Service Review* 15, no. 3 (1941): 498.

85 Verónica Castillo-Muñoz, *The Other California: Land, Identity, and Politics on the Mexican Borderlands* (Oakland: University of California Press, 2017), 58.

86 For a discussion of the first period of removals, see Alanís Enciso, "La labor consular"; Fernando Saúl Alanís Enciso, "No cuenten conmigo: La política de repatriación del gobierno mexicano y sus nacionales en Estados Unidos, 1910–1928," *Mexican Studies / Esudios Mexicanos* 19, no. 2 (2003): 401–431; Lawrence A. Cardoso, "La repatriación de braceros en la época de

Obregón: 1920–1923," *Historia Mexicana* 26, no. 4 (1977): 576–595; Mireya Loza, "'Let Them Bring Their Families': The Experiences of the First Mexican Guest Workers, 1917–1922," *Journal of American History* 109, no. 2 (September 1, 2022): 320.

87 For the recruitment of entire Mexican families during the first Bracero Program, see Fernando Saúl Alanís Enciso, *El primer programa bracero y el gobierno de México, 1917–1918* (San Luis Potosí: El Colegio de San Luis, 1999), 28–31; Loza, "Let Them Bring Their Families," 313–315.

88 The second period has received significant attention from scholars. See Gabriela F. Arredondo, *Mexican Chicago: Race, Identity, and Nation, 1916–1939* (Urbana: University of Illinois Press, 2008), esp. chap. 3; Francisco E. Balderrama, *In Defense of La Raza: The Los Angeles Mexican Consulate and the Mexican Community, 1929–1936* (Tucson: University of Arizona Press, 1982); Carreras de Velasco, *Los Mexicanos que devolvió la crisis;* Manuel G. Gonzales, *Mexicanos: A History of Mexicans in the United States,* 2nd ed. (Bloomington: Indiana University Press, 2009); Abraham Hoffman, "Stimulus to Repatriation: The 1931 Federal Deportation Drive and the Los Angeles Mexican Community," *Pacific Historical Review* 42, no. 2 (1973): 205–219; Enda Ewing Kelley, "The Mexicans Go Home," *Southwest Review* 17, no. 3 (1932): 303–311; Sánchez, *Becoming Mexican American,* esp. chap. 10.

89 Lawrence A. Cardoso, *Mexican Emigration to the United States, 1897–1931: Socio-Economic Patterns* (Tucson: University of Arizona Press, 1980), 150.

90 Fox, *Three Worlds of Relief,* 218.

91 For a discussion on the third period of removals, see Alanís Enciso, *They Should Stay There,* esp. chaps. 3 and 4; Balderrama and Rodríguez, *Decade of Betrayal;* Hoffman, *Unwanted Mexican Americans;* Sánchez, *Becoming Mexican American,* esp. chap. 10.

92 Balderrama and Rodríguez, *Decade of Betrayal,* 179.

93 Alanís Enciso, *They Should Stay There,* 70.

94 Balderrama and Rodríguez, *Decade of Betrayal,* 159–185; Carreras de Velasco, *Los Mexicanos que devolvió la crisis,* 19.

95 Balderrama and Rodríguez, *Decade of Betrayal,* 183; Hoffman, *Unwanted Mexican Americans,* 155.

96 Statement of Ernesto Galarza, chief of the Division of Labor and Social Information of the Pan-American Union, before the Select Committee of the US House of Representatives to Investigate the Interstate Migration of Destitute Citizens (Tolan Committee), *Resolutions to Inquire into the Migration of Destitute Citizens, to Study, Survey, and Investigate the Social and*

Economic Needs and the Movement of Indigent Persons Across State Lines, 76th Cong., 3rd sess., pt. 10, Washington Hearings, December 11, 1940, and February 26, 1941 (Washington: Government Printing Office, 1941), 3884; Hoffman, *Unwanted Mexican Americans,* 154–156.

97 Memorandum for Edward J. Shaughnessy, US Deputy Commissioner of Immigration and Naturalization regarding April 14, 1939 Department of State conference on Mexican immigration, May 4, 1939, RG 85, file 55739 / 858, "Repatriation of Mexican Nationals," US National Archives and Records Administration, Washington, DC.

98 Wm. A. Whalen, San Antonio, Texas District Director to INS Commissioner in Washington, DC, April 11, 1939, Repatriated Alien Records, US Department of Labor, Immigration and Naturalization Services, RG 85, file 2014 / 130, pt. 6, US National Archives and Records Administration, Washington, DC.

99 The fourth period remains understudied as compared to the first three periods. Some historians who have written about the fourth period, a least a portion of it, include Alanís Enciso, *They Should Stay There,* esp. chaps. 5, 7 and 8; Balderrama and Rodríguez, *Decade of Betrayal*; Hoffman, *Unwanted Mexican Americans.*

100 Removal lists ranging from May 19, 1939, to October 25, 1940, Repatriated Alien Records, US Department of Labor, Immigration and Naturalization Services, RG 85, file 2000/301-D, box 455, US National Archives and Records Administration, Washington, DC.

101 Castillo-Muñoz, *Other California,* 62–63.

102 Zaragosa Vargas, *Proletarians of the North: A History of Mexican Industrial Workers in Detroit and the Midwest, 1917–1933* (Berkeley: University of California Press, 1999), 182–183, 185–186.

103 Balderrama and Rodríguez, *Decade of Betrayal,* 173.

104 Vargas, *Proletarians of the North,* 182–183, 185–186.

105 Mexican repatriation report, folder "Sleepy Lagoon," Ronald W. Lopez Papers, Chicano Studies Research Institute, University of California, Los Angeles.

106 General Consul of México, "Informe Especial," 25.

107 General Consul of México, "Informe Especial," 25. For more on the history of Mexican mutual-aid societies in the US-Mexico borderlands during the 1920s and 1930s, see Geraldo L. Cadava, *Standing on Common Ground: The Making of a Sunbelt Borderland* (Cambridge: Harvard University Press, 2013), 46, 71.

108   The Bracero Program—officially named the Mexican Farm Labor Program—was a joint wartime emergency labor agreement that the US and Mexico established on August 4, 1942, and extended until December 31, 1964. This labor program granted an estimated 4.6 to 5.2 million contracts, primarily to men, to work in agriculture and railroads. For the history and effects of the Bracero Program, see Kitty Calavita, *Inside the State: The Bracero Program, Immigration, and the INS* (New Orleans: Quid Pro Books, 2010); Lori A. Flores, *Grounds for Dreaming: Mexican Americans, Mexican Immigrants, and the California Farmworker Movement* (New Haven: Yale University Press, 2016); Ernesto Galarza, *Merchants of Labor: The Mexican Bracero Story; An Account of the Managed Migration of Mexican Farm Workers in California, 1942–1960* (San Jose: Rosicrucian Press, 1964); Mireya Loza, *Defiant Braceros: How Migrant Workers Fought for Racial, Sexual, and Political Freedom* (Chapel Hill: University of North Carolina Press, 2016); Alicia Schmidt Camacho, *Migrant Imaginaries: Latino Cultural Politics in the U.S.-Mexico Borderlands* (New York: New York University Press, 2008).

109   Juan Ramon García, *Operation Wetback: The Mass Deportation of Mexican Undocumented Workers in 1954* (Westport: Greenwood, 1980); Kelly Lytle Hernández, "The Crimes and Consequences of Illegal Immigration: A Cross-Border Examination of Operation Wetback, 1943 to 1954," *Western Historical Quarterly* 37, no. 4 (2006): 421–444.

110   The term *survivor* is used here to center narrators' use of the term *sobreviviente* when referring to their banished relatives who persevered during their removals and in their efforts to resettle in the United States. *Survivor* is also used to avoid victimization. Additionally, *survivor* alludes to banished US citizens who are still alive, given that they belong to a generation of elders who are passing away.

111   Mireya Loza, "From Ephemeral to Enduring: The Politics of Recording and Exhibiting Bracero Memory," *Public Historian* 38, no. 2 (2016): 29–30.

112   For an analysis of transgenerational and family-based approaches to oral history methodology, see Marla A. Ramírez, "Gendered Banishment: Rewriting Mexican Repatriation Through a Transgenerational Oral History Methodology," *Latino Studies* 20, no. 3 (2022): 306–333.

113   Vicki L. Ruiz, "Situating Stories: The Surprising Consequences of Oral History," *Oral History Review* 25, no. 1/2 (1998): 72.

114   National Endowment for the Humanities, "Vicki Lynn Ruiz: National Humanities Medal 2014," https://www.neh.gov/about/awards/national -humanities-medals/vicki-lynn-ruiz.

115   Eddy Francisco Alvarez Jr., "Finding Sequins in the Rubble: The Journeys of Two Latina Migrant Lesbians in Los Angeles," *Journal of Lesbian Studies* 24, no. 2 (2020): 81; Lynn Abrams, *Oral History Theory,* 2nd ed. (New York: Routledge, 2010), 23, 81; Alessandro Portelli, *The Battle of Valle Giulia: Oral History and the Art of Dialogue* (Madison: University of Wisconsin Press, 1997), 44–45.

116   Alessandro Portelli, *The Order Has Been Carried Out: History, Memory, and Meaning of Nazi Massacre in Rome* (New York: Palgrave Macmillan, 2003), 14.

117   Horacio N. Roque Ramírez, "A Living Archive of Desire: Teresita La Campesina and the Embodiment of Queer Latino Community Histories," in *Archive Stories: Facts, Fictions, and the Writing of History,* ed. Antoinette Burton (Durham: Duke University Press, 2005), 119.

118   For a detailed examination of how the hidden histories of banished US-citizen women have been unearthed using oral history methodology and private collections, see Ramírez, "Gendered Banishment."

119   Monica Muñoz Martinez, *The Injustice Never Leaves You: Anti-Mexican Violence in Texas* (Cambridge: Harvard University Press, 2018), 294.

I. THE RODRÍGUEZ FAMILY: TRANSGENERATIONAL ILLEGALITY

1   Jesús Molina, interview conducted in English by author. Digital audio recording, March 22, 2012, Rosemead, CA, in author's possession.

2   Jesús Molina interview.

3   Jesús Molina interview.

4   Leisy Abrego, *Sacrificing Families: Navigating Laws, Labor, and Love Across Borders* (Stanford: Stanford University Press, 2014), 7; Mae M. Ngai, *Impossible Subjects: Illegal Aliens and the Making of Modern America* (Princeton: Princeton University Press, 2004), 57–58.

5   Refugio Molina, interview conducted in Spanish and translated to English by author. Digital audio recording, February 12, 2012, Rosemead, CA, in author's possession.

6   For more on how US citizenship was constructed across racial, gendered, and class lines, refer to Candice Lewis Bredbenner, *A Nationality of Her Own: Women, Marriage, and the Law of Citizenship* (Berkeley: University of California Press, 1998); Laura E. Gómez, *Manifest Destinies: The Making of the Mexican American Race* (New York: New York University Press, 2007); Daniel

Kanstroom, *Deportation Nation: Outsiders in American History* (Cambridge: Harvard University Press, 2007); Natalia Molina, *How Race Is Made in America: Immigration, Citizenship, and the Historical Power of Racial Scripts* (Berkeley: University of California Press, 2014); Ngai, *Impossible Subjects.*

7   Naturalization Act of 1790, 1 Stat. 103 (1790).

8   Naturalization Law of 1802, 2 Stat. 153 (1802).

9   The 1798 Alien and Sedition Acts—a set of four laws including the Naturalization Act of 1798—attempted to deter electoral power by extending the five-year residence requirement for naturalization to fourteen years. Alien Act of 1798, 1 Stat. 570 (1798); Alien Enemies Act of 1798, 1 Stat. 577 (1798); Sedition Act of 1798, 1 Stat. 596 (1798); the Naturalization Act of 1798, 1 Stat. 566 (1798). The voting base for Thomas Jefferson and his party was largely composed of immigrants, so the 1798 Alien and Sedition Acts were an attempt to diminish support for the Democratic-Republicans, the political opponents of the Federalists. Shortly after, the Naturalization Law of 1802 replaced the Naturalization Act of 1798, which maintained the "free white person" naturalization requirement but reduced the residence requirement from fourteen back to five years. The five-year residence is still the prerequisite today. Marla A. Ramírez, "The Making of Mexican Illegality: Immigration Exclusions Based on Race, Class Status, and Gender," *Journal of New Political Science* 40, no. 2 (2018): 4.

10   Michael G. McFarland, "Derivative Citizenship: Its History, Constitutional Foundation, and Constitutional Limitations," *New York University Annual Survey of American Law* 63, no. 3 (2008): 478–481.

11   Immigration Act of 1882, ch. 376, § 2, 22 Stat. 214–215 (1882).

12   Immigration Act of 1891, ch. 551, 26 Stat. 1084–1087 (1891).

13   Natalia Molina, "Constructing Mexicans as Deportable Immigrants: Race, Disease, and the Meaning of 'Public Charge,'" *Identities: Global Studies in Culture and Power* 17, no. 6 (2010): 641–666.

14   Naturalization Act of 1855, ch. 71, 10 Stat. 604.

15   Leti Volpp, "Divesting Citizenship: On Asian American History and the Loss of Citizenship Through Marriage," *UCLA Law Review* 53, no. 405 (2005): 420.

16   Gómez, *Manifest Destinies,* 118; Clare Sheridan, "'Another White Race': Mexican Americans and the Paradox of Whiteness in Jury Selection," *Law and History Review* 21, no. 1 (Spring 2003): 133–135.

17   Mexicans have Black, Asian, and Indigenous roots, but mainly their indigeneity was contested in citizenship cases. Tomás Almaguer, *Racial Fault*

Lines: The Historical Origins of White Supremacy in California (Berkeley: University of California Press, 1994), 55; Ian Haney López, *White by Law: The Legal Construction of Race,* 10th ed. (New York: New York University Press, 2006), 43–44.

18 The Bancroft Treaty also determined that naturalized US citizens would not automatically lose their American citizenship if they temporarily resided in Mexico. Martha Menchaca, *Naturalizing Mexican Immigrants: A Texas History* (Austin: University of Texas Press, 2011), 155.

19 Martha Menchaca, "Chicano Indianism: A Historical Account of Racial Repression in the United States," *American Ethnologist* 20, no. 3 (1993): 152–155, 593.

20 Gabriela F. Arredondo, *Mexican Chicago: Race, Identity, and Nation, 1916–39* (Chicago: University of Illinois Press, 2008), 22–23; Abraham Hoffman, *Unwanted Mexican Americans in the Great Depression: Repatriation Pressures, 1929–1939* (Tucson: University of Arizona Press, 1974), 11–12.

21 Cindy I-Fen Cheng, *Citizens of Asian America: Democracy and Race During the Cold War* (New York: New York University Press, 2013), 25, 175; Ngai, *Impossible Subjects,* 52–53.

22 US Department of Labor, Bureau of Immigration, *Annual Report of the Commissioner General of Immigration to the Secretary of Commerce and Labor for the Fiscal Year Ended June 30, 1920* (Washington, DC: Government Printing Office, 1920), file 9275615, Harvard Law School Library, Historical & Special Collections, Cambridge, MA; Fernando Saúl Alanís Enciso, *El primer programa bracero y el gobierno de México, 1917–1918* (San Luis Potosí: El Colegio de San Luis, 1999), 15.

23 Louis Bloch, "Facts About Mexican Immigration Before and Since the Quota Restriction Laws," *Journal of the American Statistical Association* 24, no. 165 (1929): 56; Cybelle Fox, *Three Worlds of Relief: Race, Immigration, and the American Welfare State from the Progressive Era to the New Deal* (Princeton: Princeton University Press, 2012), 75.

24 US Department of Labor, Bureau of Immigration, *Annual Report of the Commissioner General of Immigration to the Secretary of Commerce and Labor for the Fiscal Year Ended June 30, 1912* (Washington, DC: Government Printing Office, 1913), file 215 / 2500, Harvard Law School Library, Historical & Special Collections, Cambridge, MA; *Annual Report of the Commissioner General of Immigration,* June 30, 1920, file 9275615.

25 Wilson T. Longmore and Homer L. Hitt, "A Demographic Analysis of First and Second Generation Mexican Population of the United States: 1930," *Southwestern Social Science Quarterly* 24, no. 2 (1943): 142–143.

26 Matt Garcia, *A World of Its Own: Race, Labor, and Citrus in the Making of Greater Los Angeles, 1900–1970* (Chapel Hill: University of North Carolina Press, 2001), 57–58; Longmore and Hitt, "Demographic Analysis," 146.

27 Sonia Hernández, *Working Women into the Borderlands* (College Station: Texas A&M University Press, 2014), 108–109; Mireya Loza, "'Let Them Bring Their Families': The Experiences of the First Mexican Guest Workers, 1917–1922," *Journal of American History* 109, no. 2 (September 1, 2022): 317–318; Vicki L. Ruiz, *Cannery Women, Cannery Lives: Mexican Women, Unionization, and the California Food Processing Industry, 1930–1950* (Albuquerque: University of New Mexico Press, 1987), 28–29.

28 Census figures serve as a reference for population count, but ethnic Mexicans were undercounted because they either did not participate in the surveys or were classified as "other races." Lawrence A. Cardoso, *Mexican Emigration to the United States, 1897–1931: Socio-economic Patterns* (Tucson: University of Arizona Press, 1980), 52–53.

29 Garcia, *World of Its Own,* 89–92.

30 Garcia, *World of Its Own,* 88.

31 Immigration Act of 1917, Pub. L. no. 64–301, 39 Stat. 874 (1917).

32 Ngai, *Impossible Subjects,* 50, 60.

33 Mercedes Carreras de Velasco, *Los Mexicanos que devolvió la crisis, 1929–1932* (Tlatelolco, Mexico: Secretaría de Relaciones Exteriores, 1974), 46.

34 Garcia, *World of Its Own,* 33; Richard Hofstadter, *Social Darwinism in American Social Thought* (Boston: Beacon Press, 1944), 161.

35 Harry H. Laughlin, House of Representatives, Committee on Immigration and Naturalization, *Immigration from Countries of Western Hemisphere,* 70th Cong., 1st sess., 1928, Hearing no. 70.1.5, 711, 712, quoted in Garcia, *World of Its Own,* 91.

36 Katherine Benton-Cohen, "Other Immigrants: Mexicans and the Dillingham Commission of 1907–1911," *Journal of American Ethnic History* 30, no. 2 (2011): 33–57.

37 Committee Report on "The Mexican Problem," p. 2, Cleofas Calleros Papers (MS 231), C. L. Sonnichsen Special Collections Department, University of Texas at El Paso Library.

38 Arthur G. Arnoll to George P. Clements, February 25, 1931, box 80, George Pigeon Clements Papers, 1825–1945, UCLA Library Special Collections, Charles E. Young Research Library, University of California, Los Angeles.

39 For a full discussion on public and media constructions of immigration and citizenship, see Leo R. Chavez, *The Latino Threat: Constructing*

Immigrants, Citizens, and the Nation (Stanford: Stanford University Press, 2008), 21–43, 132–151.

40 George J. Sánchez, *Becoming Mexican American: Ethnicity, Culture and Identity in Chicano Los Angeles, 1900–1945* (New York: Oxford University Press, 1993), 211–212.

41 Molina, "Constructing Mexicans as Deportable Immigrants"; Natalia Molina, *Fit to Be Citizens? Public Health and Race in Los Angeles, 1879–1939* (Berkeley: University of California Press, 2006), 120–130, 136–141.

42 The Immigration Act of 1917 authorized two distinct removal regulations. Section 19 stated that an immigrant could be removed within five years after entry if they became LPC based on conditions that arose before their arrival. Section 23 authorized the removal of immigrants who became LPC within three years of their arrival due to conditions that occurred after their entry. The latter was used for the mass removals during the interwar period. Immigration Act of 1917, Pub. L. no. 64–301, 39 Stat. 874, 892 (1917).

43 Benny J. Andrés Jr., "Invisible Borders: Repatriation and Colonization of Mexican Migrant Workers Along the California Borderlands During the 1930s," *California History* 88, no. 4 (2011): 11.

44 For more on mutual aid societies founded in the early 1900s, see Albert Camarillo, *Chicanos in California: A History of Mexican Americans in California* (San Francisco: Boyd and Fraser Publishing Company, 1984), 37.

45 Jesús Molina interview.

46 Refugio Molina interview.

47 Carmela Ruano, interview conducted in Spanish and translated to English by author. Digital audio recorder, February 12, 2012, Rosemead, CA, in author's possession.

48 Carmela Ruano interview.

49 Francisco E. Balderrama and Raymond Rodríguez, *Decade of Betrayal: Mexican Repatriation in the 1930s,* rev. ed. (Albuquerque: University of New Mexico Press, 2006), 75.

50 Los Angeles Consul Rafael de la Colina to the Secretaría de Relaciones Exteriores, October 20, 1930, box 4, file 357, record 5, Archivo de documentos de Secretaría de Relaciones Exteriores (ASRE), Archivo Histórico Genaro Estrada, Ciudad de México, México.

51 Balderrama and Rodríguez, *Decade of Betrayal,* 136; Hoffman, *Unwanted Mexican Americans,* 149.

52 Balderrama and Rodríguez, *Decade of Betrayal,* 136.

53 Ann S. Blum, *Domestic Economies: Family, Work, and Welfare in Mexico City, 1884–1943* (Lincoln: University of Nebraska Press, 2009), xvi.

54 Blum, *Domestic Economies*, xxii, 46–47.

55 Jesús Molina interview.

56 "A Bill to Provide for the Suspension of Immigration of Aliens into the United States (H.R. 109)," 73rd Cong., 1st sess., *Congressional Record* (March 9, 1933); "Suspension for a Period of 10 Years of Immigration of All Aliens," September 7, 1934, file 55876 / 53, US Immigration and Naturalization Service, RG 85, US National Archives and Records Administration, Washington, DC.

57 73rd Cong. Rec. 5076–5077 (1934) (statement of Rep. Blanton).

58 Refugio Hernández, interview by Rosy Chivardi (no. 1098), November 12, 2005, Institute of Oral History, University of Texas at El Paso.

59 Refugio Hernández, interview by Rosy Chivardi.

60 Vicki L. Ruiz, *From Out of the Shadows: Mexican Women in Twentieth-Century America* (New York: Oxford University Press, 2008), 11.

61 Carmela Ruano interview.

62 Carmela Ruano interview.

63 Committee Report on "The Mexican Problem."

64 George L. Coleman, "Mexican Border Conditions Report," addressed to the Commissioner General of Immigration and Naturalization and referred to MacCormack, September 16, 1933, RG 85, file 55877 / 443, US National Archives and Records Administration, Washington, DC.

65 Coleman, "Mexican Border Conditions Report."

66 Ana Raquel Minian, *Undocumented Lives: The Untold Story of Mexican Migration* (Cambridge: Harvard University Press, 2018), 54.

67 Yanek Mieczkowski, *Gerald Ford and the Challenges of the 1970s* (Lexington: University of Kentucky Press, 2005), 4.

68 Thomas Borstelmann, *The 1970s: A New Global History from Civil Rights to Economic Inequality* (Princeton: Princeton University Press, 2012), 61.

69 Bill Clark, State of Texas House of Representatives, Austin, Texas, Position on Immigration, box 13, folder 5, Ruben Bonilla Collection, 1973–1984, General Counsel (1981–1984), LULAC Archives, Benson Library, University of Texas at Austin; as cited in Minian, *Undocumented Lives*, 55.

70 Richard L. Strout, "U.S.-Mexico Alien Problem Increases," *Christian Science Monitor*, December 14, 1976, 3.

71 Carmela Ruano interview.

72 Ruiz, *From Out of the Shadows;* Denise A. Segura, "Working at Motherhood: Chicana and Mexicana Immigrant Mothers and Employment," in *Mothering: Ideology, Experience and Agency*, ed. Evelyn Nakano Glenn, Grace Chang, and Linda Rennie Forcey (New York: McGraw Hill Higher Education, 2009), 211–233; Patricia Zavella, *I'm Neither Here nor There: Mexicans'*

Quotidian Struggles with Migration and Poverty (Durham: Duke University Press, 2011).

73   Carmela Ruano interview.

74   Refugio Molina interview; Carmela Ruano interview.

75   Jesús Molina interview.

76   Segura, "Working at Motherhood," 264–268.

77   Carmela Ruano interview.

78   Chavez, Latino Threat; Sara Veronica Hinojos, "Lupe Vélez and Her Spicy Visual 'Accent' in English-language Print Media," Latino Studies 17 (2019): 338–361; Jonathan Xavier Inda, Targeting Immigrants: Government, Technology, and Ethics (Malden: Blackwell, 2006).

79   Pierrette Hondagneu-Sotelo and Ernestine Avila, "'I'm Here, but I'm There': The Meanings of Latina Transnational Motherhood," Gender and Society 11, no. 5 (1997); Alexandra Minna Stern, "Responsible Mothers and Normal Children: Eugenics, Nationalism, and Welfare in Post-revolutionary Mexico, 1920–1940," Journal of Historical Sociology 12 no. 4 (1999): 371–372.

80   Carmela Ruano interview.

81   Carmela Ruano interview.

82   Gardner, Qualities of a Citizen, 172–174.

83   Nationality Act of 1940 (H.R. 9980; Pub. L. 76-853; 54 Stat. 1137), 201(g).

84   INS Interpretations § 301.1(b)(5)(iii–iv).

85   INS Interpretations § 301.1(b)(5)(iii–iv).

86   Jesús Molina interview.

2. THE DE ANDA FAMILY: CULTURAL LIMINALITY

1   David G. Gutiérrez, Walls and Mirrors: Mexican Americans, Mexican Immigrants, and the Politics of Ethnicity (Berkeley: University of California Press, 1995), 76–77; Monica Perales, Smeltertown: Making and Remembering a Southwest Border Community (Chapel Hill: University of North Carolina Press, 2010), 190–191; Vicki L. Ruiz, From Out of the Shadows: Mexican Women in Twentieth-Century America (New York: Oxford University Press, 2008), 33–34; George J. Sánchez, "'Go After the Women': Americanization and the Mexican Immigrant Woman, 1915–1929," in Unequal Sisters: A Multicultural Reader in U.S. Women's History, 2nd ed., ed. Vicki L. Ruiz and Ellen Carol Dubois (New York: Routledge, 1994), 286–287.

2   Jackson K. Putnam, "The Persistence of Progressivism in the 1920's: The Case of California," Pacific Historical Review 35, no. 4 (1966): 396.

3 Joe William Yáñez, interview conducted in English by author. Digital audio recording, May 20, 2012, Santa Ana, CA, in author's possession.

4 Virginia (Yáñez) De Anda, interview conducted in Spanish and translated to English by author. Digital audio recording, March 3, 2012, Hemet, CA, in author's possession.

5 See Camille Guerin-Gonzales, *Mexican Workers and American Dreams: Immigration, Repatriation, and California Farm Labor, 1900–1939* (New Brunswick: Rutgers University Press, 1996), 2, 26–27; Jose Hernández Alvarez, "A Demographic Profile of the Mexican Immigration to the United States, 1910–1950," *Journal of Inter-American Studies* 8, no. 3 (1966): 472.

6 Mario T. García, *Desert Immigrants: The Mexicans of El Paso, 1880–1920* (New Haven: Yale University Press, 1981), 49; Lori A. Flores, *Grounds for Dreaming: Mexican Americans, Mexican Immigrants, and the California Farmworker Movement* (New Haven: Yale University Press, 2016), 42; George J. Sánchez, *Becoming Mexican American: Ethnicity, Culture, and Identity in Chicano Los Angeles, 1900–1945* (New York: Oxford University Press, 1993), 41, 55.

7 Zaragosa Vargas, *Proletarians of the North: A History of Mexican Industrial Workers in Detroit and the Midwest, 1917–1933* (Berkeley: University of California Press, 1993), 90; Julia G. Young, *Mexican Exodus: Emigrants, Exiles, and Refugees of the Cristero War* (New York: Oxford University Press, 2015), 34–36.

8 Notable studies include Guerin-Gonzales, *Mexican Workers and American Dreams;* Hernández Alvarez, "A Demographic Profile," 472; Mae M. Ngai, *Impossible Subjects: Illegal Aliens and the Making of Modern America* (Princeton: Princeton University Press, 2004), 52; Mark Reisler, *By the Sweat of Their Brow: Mexican Immigrant Labor in the United States, 1900–1940* (Westport: Greenwood Press, 1976), 14–17, 41–42, 55–58; and Richard Romo, "Responses to Mexican Immigration, 1910–1930," *Aztlan* 6, no. 2 (1975): 173.

9 Cleofas Calleros, interview transcript, pp. 3–4, interview by Oscar J. Martínez (interview no. 157), September 14, 1972, Institute of Oral History, University of Texas at El Paso; Flores, *Grounds for Dreaming,* 42.

10 Lawrence A. Cardoso, *Mexican Emigration to the United States, 1897–1931* (Tucson: University of Arizona Press, 1980), 13–16; Sánchez, *Becoming Mexican American,* 39, 45.

11 For a map illustrating the Mexican National Railway lines and passenger stops, see Gustave Niox, "Map of the Mexican National Railway Showing the Lines Granted by the Mexican Government to the Mexican National Construction Company (Palmer-Sullivan Concession)," Library of Congress Geography and Map Division, Washington, DC, http://hdl.loc.gov/loc.gmd/g4411p.cws00188.

12 Cleofas Calleros, interview transcript, 2.

13 Supervising Inspector F. W. Berkshire, Immigration Service, El Paso, Texas, to Commissioner-General of Immigration, June 30, 1910, file 52546 / 31B, Immigration and Naturalization Service (INS), RG 85, US National Archives and Records Administration, Washington, DC, as cited in Sánchez, *Becoming Mexican American,* 40.

14 Cindy I-Fen Cheng, *Citizens of Asian America: Democracy and Race during the Cold War* (New York: New York University Press, 2013), 25, 69, 174; Flores, *Grounds for Dreaming,* 21–22; Natalia Molina, *How Race Is Made in America: Immigration, Citizenship, and the Historical Power of Racial Scripts* (Berkeley: University of California Press, 2014), 72–76; Ngai, *Impossible Subjects,* 39, 205–206; Sánchez, "'Go After the Women,'" 287.

15 The 1907 law repealed the Immigration Act of 1903, but retained most of the exclusions outlined in this law. Immigration Act of 1903, Pub. L. no. 57–1012, 32 Stat. 1213 (1903).

16 Immigration Act of 1907, Pub. L. no. 59–1134, § 2, 34 Stat. 898, 899 (1907).

17 Supervising Inspector F. W. Berkshire to Commissioner-General of Immigration, June 30, 1910.

18 Starting in 1921, after the United States lifted the Mexican exemption to the 1917 Immigration Act, unauthorized crossings increased for a number of likely reasons: many working-class Mexicans could not afford the new head tax; some were unable to pass the literacy test; women traveling alone and those without funds or who had no relatives in the United States were excluded on LPC grounds; and the medical examinations were often humiliating. See García, *Desert Immigrants,* 49; Sánchez, *Becoming Mexican American,* 41, 55; and Alexandra Minna Stern, "Buildings, Boundaries, and Blood: Medicalization and Nation-Building on the U.S.-Mexico Border, 1910–1930," *Hispanic American Historical Review* 79, no. 1 (1999): 41–81.

19 F. W. Berkshire, Supervising Inspector, to the Commissioner-General of Immigration, November 1, 1909, file 52546 / 31, Immigration and Naturalization Service (INS), RG 85, US National Archives and Records Administration, Washington, DC, as cited in Sánchez, *Becoming Mexican American,* 52.

20 Cleofas Calleros, interview transcript, 9.

21 Virginia De Anda interview.

22 Joe William Yáñez interview.

23 Immigration officers often interpreted federal immigration law at their individual discretion, which tended to be informed by stereotypical assumptions of the immigrants' perceived class, race, and gender. See Kelly Lytle

Hernández, *Migra! A History of the U.S. Border Patrol* (Berkeley: University of California Press, 2010), 47; and S. Deborah Kang, *The INS on the Line: Making Immigration Law on the US-Mexico Border, 1917–1954* (New York: Oxford University Press, 2017), 20.

24 Natalia Molina, *Fit to Be Citizens? Public Health and Race in Los Angeles, 1879–1939* (Berkeley: University of California Press, 2006), 94, 1280; Sánchez, *Becoming Mexican American*, 55–56; John Mckiernan-González, *Fevered Measures: Public Health and Race at the Texas-Mexico Border, 1848–1942* (Durham: Duke University Press, 2012), 232–233; Stern, "Buildings, Boundaries, and Blood," 45–46.

25 Anna Pegler-Gordon, *In Sight of America: Photography and the Development of U.S. Immigration Policy* (Berkeley: University of California Press, 2009), 176, 193.

26 Immigration Act of 1924, ch. 190, 43 Stat. 153. Subsequent immigration laws maintained the practice of visual record-keeping. The Immigration Act of 1924 (also known as the National Origins Act of 1924) did not place quota restrictions on Mexican immigrants, but it required Mexicans to submit photographs to fulfill new visa requirements. Then, in 1928, a US Department of Labor order required all immigrants to carry identification cards. See U.S. Dept. of Labor, Order no. 106 (July 1, 1928).

27 Pegler-Gordon, *In Sight of America*, 10.

28 For studies on the convergence of US immigration policy and racial formation, see Kitty Calavita, *Inside the State: The Bracero Program, Immigration, and the I.N.S.* (New York: Routledge, 1992); Laura Gómez, *Manifest Destinies: The Making of the Mexican American Race* (New York: New York University Press, 2007); Ian Haney López, *White by Law: The Legal Construction of Race* (New York: New York University Press, 1996); and Pegler-Gordon, *In Sight of America*.

29 Coco Fusco, "Racial Time, Racial Marks, Racial Metaphors," in *Only Skin Deep: Changing Visions of the American Self*, ed. Coco Fusco and Brian Wallis (New York: International Center of Photography, 2003), 16.

30 Pegler-Gordon, *In Sight of America*, 207.

31 Pegler-Gordon, *In Sight of America*, 12.

32 California agriculture study (1920–1930, no exact date provided), Collection 1243, box 1, folder 2–3, Carey McWilliams Collection, UCLA Library Special Collections, Charles E. Young Research Library, University of California, Los Angeles.

33 Clifford Alan Perkins, *Border Patrol: With the U.S. Immigration Service on the Mexican Boundary, 1910–1954* (El Paso: Texas Western Press, 1978), 54.

34   Field Notes of Mexican Labor in the US, series-A, set-I, June 18, 1928, BANC MSS 84 / 38 c, carton 10, folder 4, Paul Schuster Taylor Papers, Bancroft Library, University of California, Berkeley.

35   Biographical sketch of Mexican immigrant workers in Arizona (1927): José, Banc Film 2322, box 2568, folder 1:2, notes gathered for Manuel Gamio's book *Mexican Immigrants to the United States* and related material, 1926–1928, Manuel Gamio Papers, Bancroft Library, University of California, Berkeley. Pseudonyms have been used to keep the identity of participants confidential, as requested by Gamio's notes on this collection.

36   Biographical sketch (1927): Carlos, Banc Film 2322, box 2568, folder 1:3, Manuel Gamio Papers, Bancroft Library, University of California, Berkeley. Pseudonyms used to protect confidentiality.

37   For the transportation of Mexican workers from El Paso, TX, to locations throughout the Southwest and Midwest to fill employment needs in railroad, agriculture, and mining, see Cardoso, *Mexican Emigration,* 26–27; García, *Desert Immigrants,* 37–38, 40; Guerin-Gonzales, *Mexican Workers,* 37–38, 54, 58–59; Ruiz, *From Out of the Shadows,* 22–24; Sánchez, *Becoming Mexican American,* 39–42.

38   Virginia De Anda interview.

39   Cleofas Calleros, interview transcript, 3.

40   US Congress, Senate, Dillingham Commission, *Immigrants in Industries: Japanese and Other Immigrant Races in the Pacific Coast and Rocky Mountain States,* vol. 3, pts. 1–4, as cited in García, *Desert Immigrants,* 38.

41   Judith Fincher Laird, "Argentine, Kansas: The Evolution of a Mexican American Community, 1905–1940" (PhD diss., The University of Kansas, 1975), 121.

42   García, *Desert Immigrants,* 38–39; Jeffrey Marcos Garcílazo, *Traqueros: Mexican Railroad Workers in the United States, 1870–1930* (Denton: University of North Texas Press, 2012), 111–113; Ruiz, *From Out of the Shadows,* 22.

43   Cleofas Calleros, interview transcript, 4.

44   Biographical sketch of Mexican immigrant workers in Texas (1928), Banc Film 2322, box 2568, folder 1:8, notes gathered for Manuel Gamio's book *Mexican Immigrants to the United States* and related material, 1926–1928, Manuel Gamio Papers, Bancroft Library, University of California, Berkeley. Names are kept confidential as requested by Gamio's notes on this collection.

45   Cleofas Calleros, interview transcript, 5; Garcílazo, *Traqueros,* 192, 208–212; Ruiz, *From Out of the Shadows,* 23.

46 Garcílazo, *Traqueros*, 208–212, 217–218, 222–223; Sonia Hernández, *Working Women into the Borderlands* (College Station: Texas A&M University Press, 2014), 110.

47 Richard J. Orsi, *Sunset Limited: The Southern Pacific Railroad and the Development of the American West, 1850–1930* (Berkeley: University of California Press, 2005), 329–330; Leonard M. Davis, *The Story of Roseville, California: Milestones and Memories, 1850–2000* (Roseville: Roseville Arts Center, 2002); Leonard "Duke" Davis, "History of Roseville," City of Roseville, CA, 2009, https://www.roseville.ca.us/cms/One.aspx?portalId=7964922&pageId=11247017#panel-0.

48 Reports on test trips by the Pacific Fruit Express Company (July 1919), MS 49, legal box, folder 20, Inventory of the Pacific Fruit Express Company Collection, 1906–1989, California State Railroad Museum Library, Sacramento, CA.

49 Joe William Yáñez interview.

50 Flores, *Grounds for Dreaming*, 16–17.

51 Davis, "History of Roseville."

52 Joe William Yáñez interview.

53 Virginia De Anda interview.

54 Janis Wilton, "Imagining Family Memories: My Mum, Her Photographs, Our Memories," in *Oral History and Photography*, ed. Alexander Freund and Alistair Thomson (New York: Palgrave Macmillan, 2011), 61–95; James C. Curtis, "Documenting Photography as Texts," *American Quarterly* 40, no. 2 (June 1988): 246; Alexander Freund and Alistair Thomson, "Introduction: Oral History and Photography," in *Oral History and Photography*, ed. Alexander Freund and Alistair Thomson (New York: Palgrave Macmillan, 2011), 3–5, 13, 18; Paul Thompson, *The Voice of the Past: Oral History*, 3rd ed. (New York: Oxford University Press, 2000), 6.

55 Freund and Thomson, "Introduction," 13.

56 For reform movements during the Progressive Era, see Paul Boyer, *Urban Masses and the Moral Order in America, 1820–1920* (Cambridge: Harvard University Press, 1978); Richard Hofstadter, *The Age of Reform: From Bryan to FDR* (New York: Vintage, 1955); and Peggy Pascoe, *Relations of Rescue: The Search for Female Moral Authority in the American West, 1874–1939* (New York: Oxford University Press, 1990).

57 Diane Claire Wood, "Immigrant Mothers, Female Reformers, and Women Teachers: The California Home Teacher Act of 1915" (PhD diss., Stanford University, 1996), 23, 87.

58 A diverse ethnic and racial immigrant population was recruited to California. Additionally, during the Dust Bowl, white migrants also made California their home (see Chapter 4). Thus Americanization programs were quickly institutionalized in the state to address the diverse migrant populations. Here my focus is on the Americanization experiences of ethnic Mexican communities.

59 Perales, *Smeltertown*, 190, 192–194; Ruiz, *From Out of the Shadows*, 34, 38; Sánchez, "'Go After the Women,'" 286–288.

60 The typical California progressive leader was male, young, midwestern, of northern European ancestry, Protestant, and formally educated. Wood, "Immigrant Mothers," 18.

61 Division of Immigration and Housing, *Directory of Immigrant Serving Agencies: Prepared by the Committee of Immigrant Serving Agencies of the Family Welfare Council*, p. 8, collection 1243, box 16, folder 8, "Minorities: Misc.," Carey McWilliams Collection, UCLA Library Special Collections, Charles E. Young Research Library, University of California, Los Angeles.

62 Division of Immigration and Housing, *Directory of Immigrant Serving Agencies*, 8.

63 The first five leaders and their roles were as follows: (1) Sacramento-based Simon J. Lubin, president (1913–1923); (2) the Archbishop of San Francisco, Rt. Reverend Edward Joseph Hanna, vice president (1913–1923) and president (1923–1927); (3) San Francisco-based Paul Scharrenberg, secretary (1913–1923); (4) Mary Simons Gibson from Los Angeles, commissioner (1913–1922); and (5) Pasadena-based Dr. James Harvey McBride, commissioner (1915–1927). Economists Carleton H. Parker and George L. Bell served as executive directors. State funds were allocated for the commission every two years; additionally, the legislature allocated $60,000 for work done from 1915 to 1917. Christina A. Ziegler-McPherson, *Americanization in the States: Immigrant Social Welfare Policy, Citizenship, and National Identity in the United States, 1908–1929* (Gainesville: University of Florida Press, 2009), 40.

64 Spencer Olin, *California's Prodigal Sons: Hiram Johnson and Progressives, 1911–1917* (Berkeley: University of California Press, 1968), 76–80; Sánchez, "'Go After the Women,'" 288; Ziegler-McPherson, *Americanization in the States*, 39–40, 74.

65 California Commission of Immigration and Housing (CCIH), *Report on Fresno's Immigration Problem: With Particular Reference to Educational Facilities and Requirements* (March 1918), p. 18, collection 1243, box 16, folder 8: "Minorities: Misc.," Carey McWilliams Collection, UCLA Library Special Collections, Charles E. Young Research Library, University of California, Los Angeles.

66 Division of Immigration and Housing, *Directory of Immigrant Serving Agencies*, 8.

67 For a detailed discussion of the treatment of immigrants by social settlements, see Allen F. Davis, *Spearheads for Reform: The Social Settlements and the Progressive Movement, 1890–1914* (New York: Oxford University Press, 1967), 84–102; John Higham, *Strangers in the Land: Patterns of American Nativism, 1860–1925*, 2nd ed. (New York: Atheneum, 1963), 116–123; and Sánchez, "'Go After the Women,'" 288.

68 California Commission of Immigration and Housing (CCIH), "Advisory Pamphlet on Camp Sanitation and Housing," rev. 1919 (San Francisco: California State Printing Office, 1919), 5–8.

69 CCIH, "Advisory Pamphlet," 5.

70 CCIH, "Advisory Pamphlet," 6.

71 CCIH, "Advisory Pamphlet," 5.

72 California Commission of Immigration and Housing (CCIH), *Second Annual Report, January 2, 1916* (San Francisco: California State Printing Office, 1916), 151.

73 Wood, "Immigrant Mothers, Female Reformers, and Women Teachers," 28–29. See also David G. Herman, "Neighbors on the Golden Mountain: The Americanization of Immigrants in California. Public Instruction as an Agency of Ethnic Assimilation, 1850–1933" (PhD diss., University of California, Berkeley, 1981), 351–352.

74 Pearl Idelia Ellis, *Americanization Through Homemaking* (Los Angeles: Wetzel, 1929), 31.

75 CCIH, *Second Annual Report*, 139.

76 California Home Teacher Act of 1915, no. 1617b, ch. 37, 1915 Cal. Stat. 66. Reprinted in CCIH, *Second Annual Report*, 150.

77 CCIH, *Second Annual Report*, 152–153.

78 CCIH, *Second Annual Report*, 150.

79 CCIH, *Second Annual Report*, 152.

80 Sánchez, "'Go After the Women,'" 287–288.

81 Alfred Eugene White, "The Apperceptive Mass of Foreigners as Applied to Americanization, the Mexican Group" (master's thesis, University of California, Berkeley, 1923), 34–35.

82 Perales, *Smeltertown*, 187; Ruiz, *From Out of the Shadows*, 63–65; Sánchez, "'Go After the Women,'" 284.

83 For an examination of what Vicki L. Ruiz has called cultural coalescence, see Ruiz, *From Out of the Shadows*, 50.

84 Virginia De Anda interview.

85 García, *Desert Immigrants,* 202; Manuel Gamio, *Mexican Immigration to the United States* (Chicago: University of Chicago Press, 1930), 76–83; Ruiz, *From Out of the Shadows,* 36, 48.

86 For the Los Angeles Section of the National Council of Jewish Women's health camp, see collection 1243, box 11, folder 2, Carey McWilliams Collection, UCLA Library Special Collections, Charles E. Young Research Library, University of California, Los Angeles. For the Diocesan Council of the Catholic Women and the Catholic Daughters of America in Denver Colorado's free clinic, see Knights of Columbus, *Fifth Annual Report of the Mexican Welfare Committee of the Colorado State Council* (May 28, 1928), collection 1243, box 16, folder "Mexicans-Anthropological," Carey McWilliams Collection, UCLA Library Special Collections, Charles E. Young Research Library, University of California, Los Angeles.

87 Perales, *Smeltertown,* 187.

88 Consuelo De Anda, interview conducted in Spanish and translated to English by author. Digital audio recording, March 3, 2012, Hemet, California, in author's possession.

89 Ellis, *Americanization Through Homemaking,* 19–21.

90 CCIH, *Second Annual Report,* 160–196.

91 Bogardus Armour, "Child in the Rio Grande Valley," *Mission Times* (Mission, TX), January 30, 1933.

92 Armour, "Child in the Rio Grande Valley."

93 Mexican parents' legal victory in the *Mendez v. Westminster* (1947) case in California helped pave the way to school desegregations at the national level through the *Brown v. Board of Education* (1954). See Charles Wollenberg, "*Mendez v. Westminster:* Race, Nationality and Segregation in California Schools," *California Historical Quarterly* 53, no. 4 (Winter 1974): 317–332.

94 Virginia De Anda interview.

95 CCIH, *Second Annual Report,* 196.

96 "Old McDonald Had a Farm," Traditional Ballad Index, http://www.fresnostate.edu/folklore/ballads/R457.html.

97 María Herrera-Sobek, "Danger! Children at Play: Patriarchal Ideology and the Construction of Gender in Spanish Language Hispanic / Chicano Children's Songs and Games," in *Chicana Changing Traditions,* ed. Norma E. Cantú and Olga Nájera-Ramírez (Chicago: University of Illinois Press, 2002), 81–83.

98 Janett Barragán Miranda, "Mexican-Origin Newsmakers: Utilizing Health in *La Opinión* Microfilm for Data Collecting and Methodology,"

Latino Studies 20 (2022): 346–347; Vicki L. Ruiz, "'Star Struck': Accultura-tion, Adolescence, and Mexican American Women, 1920–1940," in *Small Worlds: Children and Adolescents in America*, ed. Elliot West and Paula Petrik (Lawrence: University of Kansas Press, 1992), 61–80; Roberto R. Treviño, "Prensa y Patria: The Spanish-Language Press and the Biculturation of the Tejano Middle Class, 1920–1940," *Western Historical Quarterly* 22, no. 4 (1991): 460.

99 Virginia De Anda interview; Consuelo De Anda interview.

100 Virginia De Anda interview.

101 For the natural processes of Americanization, see Perales, *Smeltertown*, 186–187; and Ruiz, *From Out of the Shadows*, 52–53.

102 Sánchez, *Becoming Mexican American*, 106.

103 Sánchez, "'Go After the Women,'" 294.

104 California Commission of Immigration and Housing (CCIH), *Annual Report of the California Commission of Immigration and Housing, January 1927* (San Francisco: California State Printing Office, 1927), 8.

105 Francisco E. Balderrama and Raymond Rodríguez, *Decade of Betrayal: Mexican Repatriation in the 1930s*, rev. ed. (Albuquerque: University of New Mexico Press, 2006), 67.

106 N. T. N. Robinson, "The Alien Deportation Controversy in Congress," *Congressional Digest: Informative, Balanced, Impartial Pros & Cons Since 1921*, November 1935, 120.

107 Catherine S. Ramírez, *Assimilation: An Alternative History* (Berkeley: University of California Press, 2020), 89.

108 Virginia De Anda interview.

109 Consul General Luis Lupián to Secretaría de Relaciones Exteriores, May 20, 1931, Legajo 329, Expediente 3, Archivo de documentos de Secretaría de Relaciones Exteriores (ASRE), Archivo Histórico Genaro Estrada, Ciudad de México, México; *Los Angeles Times*, January 10, 1931. Both sources are cited in Balderrama and Rodríguez, *Decade of Betrayal*, 121.

110 Benny J. Andrés Jr., "'I Am Almost More at Home with Brown Faces Than with White:' An Americanization Teacher in Imperial Valley, California, 1923–1924," *Historical Society of Southern California* 93, no. 1 (Spring 2011): 73; Perales, *Smeltertown*, 217.

111 Sánchez, *Becoming Mexican American*, 211.

112 Committee Report on "The Mexican Problems," Cleofas Calleros Papers (MS 231), C. L. Sonnichsen Special Collections Department, University of Texas at El Paso Library.

113   General Consul of México, "Informe especial sobre las condiciones de los mexicanos en el Distrito Consular de Los Angeles," no. 71 (January 27, 1932), 24–30; Sánchez, *Becoming Mexican American,* 211.

114   General Consul of México, "Informe especial sobre las condiciones de los mexicanos en el Distrito Consular de San Bernardino," no. 69 (January 1, 1932), 6–8.

115   General Consul of México, "Informe especial," no. 69, 6.

116   General Consul of México, "Informe especial," no. 69, 7.

117   General Consul of México, "Informe especial," no. 69, 7.

118   On long-established US residence among those removed, see Gabriela F. Arredondo, *Mexican Chicago: Race, Identity, and Nation, 1916–39* (Chicago: University of Illinois Press, 2008), 85–86; Balderrama and Rodríguez, *Decade of Betrayal,* 187; and Abraham Hoffman, *Unwanted Mexican Americans in the Great Depression: Repatriation Pressures, 1929–1939* (Tucson: University of Arizona Press, 1976), 37.

119   Letter to San Antonio, Texas Immigration and Naturalization Service District Director from Sumner Welles, the US Under Secretary of State, May 5, 1939, file 55739 / 858, US Immigration Services Files, RG 85, US National Archives and Records Administration, Washington, DC.

120   *El Defensor* (Edinburg, TX), May 22, 1931, p. 2, as cited in Treviño, "Prensa y Patria," 464.

121   Virginia De Anda interview.

122   Virginia De Anda interview.

123   Consuelo De Anda interview.

124   Virginia De Anda interview.

125   Virginia De Anda interview.

126   For a discussion on appropriations of the real estate property of "repatriates," see Balderrama and Rodríguez, *Decade of Betrayal,* 251.

127   Virginia De Anda interview.

128   Joe William Yáñez interview.

129   Guerin-Gonzales, *Mexican Workers and American Dreams,* 101.

130   Other historians have also documented this pattern among relocated families in Mexico. For example, see Balderrama and Rodríguez, *Decade of Betrayal,* 142–145.

131   Consuelo De Anda interview.

132   Joe William Yáñez interview.

133   Virginia De Anda interview.

134   Joe William Yáñez interview.

135 The Mexicanization organizers included Lic. Julio Jiménez Rueda, Prof. Manuel Gallardo, Prof. José María Bonilla, Prof. C. M. Samayoa, Prof. Rubén Vizcarra, Prof. Eugenio Argudín, Prof. Nestor Cuesta, Prof. María de la Luz Garcez, Prof. María Bonilla, Prof. Dona Moreno Elorduy, Lic. José María Gutiérrez, Lic. Jorge Prieto Laurens, and Gabino A. Palma. "Schools for Mexicanization of Immigrants," *El Universal* (Mexico City Spanish-language daily), May 20, 1934, trans. May 21, 1934, by John S. Littell, American Vice Consul from the American Consulate General, Mexico City, Mexico, translation and report prepared for the Departments of the Interior and Labor, file 55875, no. 180, US Department of Labor Files, US National Archives and Records Administration, Washington, DC.

136 "Schools for Mexicanization of Immigrants."

137 Consuelo De Anda interview; Virginia De Anda interview. For more on Mexicanization of banished US-citizen children, see Balderrama and Rodríguez, *Decade of Betrayal*, 243.

138 Consuelo De Anda interview.

139 Joe William Yáñez interview.

140 Virginia De Anda interview.

141 Linda Kerber, *Women of the Republic: Intellect and Ideology in Revolutionary America* (Chapel Hill: University of North Carolina Press, 1980); Sánchez, "'Go After the Women,'" 289.

142 Virginia De Anda interview.

143 Joe William Yáñez, interview conducted in English by author. Digital audio recording, July 16, 2024, Hemet, CA, in author's possession.

144 Virginia De Anda interview.

145 Virginia De Anda interview.

146 Virginia De Anda interview.

147 On women's work and gender norms, see Shawn Malia Kanaiaupuni, "Reframing the Migration Questions: An Analysis of Men, Women, and Gender in Mexico," *Social Forces* 78, no. 4 (2000): 1311–1347; Cecilia Menjívar, "The Intersection of Work and Gender: Central American Immigrant Women and Employment in California," in *Gender and U.S. Immigration: Contemporary Trends,* ed. Pierrette Hondagneu-Sotelo (Berkeley: University of California Press, 2003), 101–126; and Terry A. Repak, *Waiting on Washington: Central American Workers in the Nation's Capital* (Philadelphia: Temple University Press, 1995).

148 Michael C. Meyer and William L. Sherman, *The Course of Mexican History* (New York: Oxford University Press, 1971), 9.

149 Virginia De Anda interview.

150 Consuelo De Anda interview.

151 Kaye Briegel, "Alianza Hispano-Americana and Some Mexican-American Civil Rights Cases in the 1950s," in *An Awakened Minority: The Mexican-Americans,* 2nd ed., ed. Manuel P. Servín (Beverly Hills: Glencoe, 1974), 178; Mario T. García, *Mexican Americans: Leadership, Ideology, and Identity, 1930–1960* (New Haven: Yale University Press, 1989), 43.

152 Catherine S. Ramírez, *The Woman in the Zoot Suit: Gender, Nationalism, and the Cultural Politics of Memory* (Durham: Duke University Press, 2009).

153 Juan Ramon García, *Operation Wetback: The Mass Deportation of Mexican Undocumented Workers in 1954* (Westport: Greenwood Press, 1980); Manuel G. Gonzales, *Mexicanos: A History of Mexicans in the United States,* 2nd ed. (Bloomington: Indiana University Press, 2009), 178–180.

154 Joe William Yáñez interview.

155 Marisa Yáñez, interview conducted in English by author. Digital audio recording, November 27, 2013, Hemet, CA, in author's possession.

156 Marisa Yáñez interview.

3. THE ROBLES FAMILY: TRANSNATIONAL MOTHERHOOD

1 The 1920 Mexican and Mexican American populations are census estimates because they were classified as white in that census, as cited in Natalia Molina, *How Race Is Made in America: Immigration, Citizenship, and the Historical Power of Racial Scripts* (Berkeley: University of California Press, 2014), 75.

2 US Bureau of the Census, *Fifteenth Census of the United States* (Washington: US Government Printing Office, 1931), 27, 80; Wilson T. Longmore and Homer L. Hitt, "A Demographic Analysis of First- and Second-Generation Mexican Population of the United States: 1930," *Southwestern Social Science Quarterly* 24, no. 2 (1943): 140.

3 Molina, *How Race Is Made,* 80.

4 Statement of Rep. William Traeger, *Relating to Naturalization and Citizenship Status of Children Whose Mothers Are Citizens of the United States, and Relating to the Removal of Certain Inequalities in Matters of Nationality,* in Hearings before the United States House Committee on Immigration and Naturalization, Subcommittee on HR 3673 and HR 77, Cong. Rec., 73rd Cong., 1st sess. (Mar. 28, Apr. 10, 1933): 41.

5 Statement of Rep. Charles Kramer, *Relating to Naturalization and Citizenship Status of Children Whose Mothers Are Citizens of the United States, and Relating to the Removal of Certain Inequalities in Matters of Nationality,* in Hearings before the United States House Committee on Immigration and Naturalization, Subcommittee on HR 3673 and HR 77, Cong. Rec., 73rd Cong., 1st sess. (Mar. 28, Apr. 10, 1933): 25–26.

6 Mae M. Ngai, *Impossible Subjects: Illegal Aliens and the Making of Modern America* (Princeton: Princeton University Press, 2004), 173–177.

7 Joseph A. Facci, "The Problem of the Mexican-Americans," report included in a "Rehabilitation for Mexican Farm Laborers" memo to Lauren I. Hoowes Jr. and R. W. Hollenberg, November 18, 1939, box 16, Carey McWilliams Papers (Collection 1243), UCLA Library Special Collections, Charles E. Young Research Library, University of California, Los Angeles.

8 Statement of Rep. William Traeger, *Relating to Naturalization and Citizenship Status of Children,* 41.

9 Roger W. Babson, *Washington and the Depression: Including the Career of W. N. Doak* (New York: Harper, 1932), 92–93; Irving Bernstein, *The Lean Years: A History of the American Worker, 1920–1933* (Boston: Houghton Mifflin, 1969), 334.

10 Babson, *Washington and the Depression,* 93; Francisco E. Balderrama and Raymond Rodríguez, *Decade of Betrayal: Mexican Repatriation in the 1930s,* rev. ed. (Albuquerque: University of New Mexico Press, 2006), 75; Bernstein, *Lean Years,* 335.

11 US President to the Speaker of the House, Transmitting a Supplemental Estimate of Appropriation for the Bureau of Immigration, January 9, 1931, 71st Cong., 3rd sess. H. Doc. 715.

12 Babson, *Washington and the Depression,* 93.

13 Telegram from C[harles]. P. Visel to Colonel Arthur Woods, January 6, 1931, box 62, bundle 7, George P. Clements Papers (Collection 118), UCLA Library Special Collections, Charles E. Young Research Library, University of California, Los Angeles.

14 Telegram from [Colonel Arthur] Woods to [Charles P.] Visel, January 6, 1931, box 62, bundle 7, George P. Clements Papers (Collection 118), UCLA Library Special Collections, Charles E. Young Research Library, University of California, Los Angeles.

15 [Colonel Arthur] Woods to [Charles P.] Visel, January 8, 1931, George P. Clements Papers (Collection 118), UCLA Library Special Collections, Charles E. Young Research Library, University of California, Los Angeles.

16 Telegram from [Charles P.] Visel to [William N.] Doak, January 11, 1931, and Doak to Visel, January 12, 1931, George P. Clements Papers (Collection 118), UCLA Library Special Collections, Charles E. Young Research Library, University of California, Los Angeles.

17 Telegram and attached memorandum from [Charles P.] Visel to [Colonel Arthur] Woods, January 23, 1931, President's Emergency Committee for Employment (PECE) papers, box 620, RG 73, Records of the President's Organization on Unemployment Relief, US National Archives and Records Administration, College Park, MD.

18 Abraham Hoffman, *Unwanted Mexican Americans in the Great Depression: Repatriation Pressures, 1929–1939* (Tucson: University of Arizona Press, 1974), 53.

19 Hoffman, *Unwanted Mexican Americans,* 53.

20 Hoffman, *Unwanted Mexican Americans,* 56.

21 James L. Houghteling to Edward W. Cahill, February 16, 1938, box 14, RG 58, US National Archives and Records Administration, College Park, MD.

22 Erika Lee, *America for Americans: A History of Xenophobia in the United States* (New York: Basic Books, 2019), 148.

23 Balderrama and Rodríguez, *Decade of Betrayal,* 70–71.

24 George L. Coleman, "Mexican Border Conditions Report," addressed to the Commissioner General of Immigration and Naturalization and referred to [Daniel W.] MacCormack, September 16, 1933, file 55877 / 443, RG 85, US National Archives and Records Administration, Washington, DC.

25 Herbert Hoover, *The Memoirs of Herbert Hoover: The Great Depression, 1929–1941,* vol. 3 (New York: Macmillan, 1952), 47–48.

26 [Charles P.] Visel to [William] Watkins, March 16, 1931, President's Emergency Committee for Employment (PECE) papers, box 620, RG 73, Records of the President's Organization on Unemployment Relief, US National Archives and Records Administration, College Park, MD.

27 "US Department of Labor, Immigration and Naturalization Service," June 30, 1930, to June 30, 1939, RG 85, Records of the Immigration and Naturalization Service, 10a–39, as cited in Balderrama and Rodríguez, *Decade of Betrayal,* 67n15.

28 The *Los Angeles Times,* one of the major newspapers regularly reporting on the removal of ethnic Mexicans at the time, demanded an investigation of Los Angeles Immigration Director Walter Carr for his unacceptable methods. An investigation by the Los Angeles County Bar Association generated a report entitled "Lawless Enforcement of the Law," in which the removal tactics

were classified as human rights violations. Balderrama and Rodríguez, *Decade of Betrayal*, 70.

29 General Consul of México, "Informe Especial," no. 71, January 27, 1932, 7.

30 Rex Thomson, interview by Christine Valenciana, August 4, 1976, Mexican American Community History Project, Center for Oral and Public History at California State University, Fullerton.

31 Rex Thomson interview.

32 Rex Thomson interview.

33 "President Ortiz Rubio," *Evening Star* (Washington, DC), September 2, 1932, A–8.

34 Verónica Castillo-Muñoz, *The Other California: Land, Identity, and Politics on the Mexican Borderlands* (Oakland: University of California Press, 2017), 62–63, 82–83.

35 "Funds for Repatriated Approved," *Evening Star* (Washington, DC), January 20, 1933, A–10.

36 "Mexico to Give Land to Jobless," *Brownsville Herald* (Brownsville, TX), June 2, 1932, 10.

37 Castillo-Muñoz, *Other California;* Lynn Stephen, *Viva Zapata! Generation, Gender, and Historical Consciousness in the Reception of Ejido Reform in Oaxaca,* Transformation of Rural Mexico 6 (La Jolla: Center for US-Mexican Studies, University of California, San Diego, 1994); Heather Fowler-Salamini and Mary Kay Vaughan, eds., *Women of the Mexican Countryside, 1850–1990: Creating Spaces, Shaping Transitions* (Tucson: University of Arizona Press, 1994).

38 Castillo-Muñoz, *Other California*, 41.

39 Communication from Dr. Manuel Gamio to Sr. Juan N. Espinosa regarding his application to repatriate from Arizona, March 18, 1938, box 925, record 549.5 / 19, Fondo Lázaro Cárdenas, Archivos Presidenciales, Archivo General de la Nación, Mexico City.

40 Communication from Dr. Manuel Gamio to Sr. Juan N. Espinosa.

41 Communication to Office of the Mexican President from Manuel Rodríguez regarding repatriation assistance from Texas, box 925, record 549.5 / 34, March 20, 1940, Fondo Lázaro Cárdenas, Archivos Presidenciales, Archivo General de la Nación, Mexico City; Communication from Pedro E. Gonzáles regarding repatriation project, May 19, 1939, box 563, record 503.11 / 3, Fondo Lázaro Cárdenas, Archivos Presidenciales, Archivo General de la Nación, Mexico City.

42 Communication to Office of the Mexican President from Flores y Ropon regarding repatriation assistance from Arizona, November 3, 1938, box 925, record 549.5 / 19, Fondo Lázaro Cárdenas, Archivos Presidenciales, Archivo General de la Nación, Mexico City; Communication to Office of the Mexican President from Villareal Silva regarding repatriation assistance from Wisconsin, September 13, 1938, box 924, record 549.5 / 5, Fondo Lázaro Cárdenas, Archivos Presidenciales, Archivo General de la Nación, Mexico City.

43 Communication to Office of the Mexican President from José Cruz Chávez regarding repatriation assistance from Arizona, October 1, 1939, box 925, record 549.5 / 19, Fondo Lázaro Cárdenas, Archivos Presidenciales, Archivo General de la Nación, Mexico City.

44 "Acuerdo: Ferrocarriles Nacionales de México y vías Anexas," August 4, 1938, President of the Republic, box 622, record 513.7 / 27, Fondo Lázaro Cárdenas, Archivos Presidenciales, Archivo General de la Nación, Mexico City.

45 Fernando Saúl Alanís Enciso, *They Should Stay There: The Story of Mexican Migration and Repatriation During the Great Depression* (Chapel Hill: University of North Carolina Press, 2017), 101–103.

46 Memorandum for Edward J. Shaughnessy, US Deputy Commissioner of Immigration and Naturalization regarding April 14, 1939, Department of State conference on Mexican immigration, May 4, 1939, RG 85, file 55739 / 858, "Repatriation of Mexican Nationals," US National Archives and Records Administration, Washington, DC.

47 For more on these conditions among repatriated and banished people, see Alanís Enciso, *They Should Stay There;* Hoffman, *Unwanted Mexican Americans;* and Balderrama and Rodríguez, *Decade of Betrayal.*

48 Balderrama and Rodríguez, *Decade of Betrayal,* 143.

49 "Declared Returning Mexicans Starving," *Bismarck Tribune* (Bismarck, ND), March 18, 1931.

50 Marrion Terriquez to President Roosevelt, November 1, 1933, box 1247, RG 59, US National Archives and Records Administration, College Park, MD.

51 "Regarding the Repatriation of the Family of Mr. Samuel Andrade," January 22, 1935, box 924, record 549.5 / 19, Fondo Lázaro Cárdenas, Archivos Presidenciales, Archivo General de la Nación, Mexico City.

52 Communication to President Cárdenas Regarding Repatriate Samuel Andrade, September 23, 1935, box 924, record 549.5 / 5, Fondo Lázaro Cárdenas, Archivos Presidenciales, Archivo General de la Nación, Mexico City.

53 Communication to President Cárdenas Regarding Repatriate Samuel Andrade.

54 Communication to President Cárdenas Regarding Repatriate Samuel Andrade.

55 Secretary of State to American Consular Officer in Charge, Torreón, Coahuila, Mexico, September 23, 1938, box 1246, RG 59, US National Archives and Records Administration, College Park, MD; Romeo Guzmán, "'I Want to Return to My Country': Ethnic Mexicans Request the Right to Return During the Great Depression," *Journal of American Ethnic History* 44, no. 2 (2025): 100–124.

56 Enrique Vega, interview by Christine Valenciana (interview no. 1295), September 3, 1972, Mexican American Community History Project, Center for Oral and Public History at California State University, Fullerton.

57 Enrique Vega interview.

58 Enrique Vega interview.

59 Emilia Castañeda de Valenciana, interview by Christine Valenciana (interview no. 700), September 8, 1971, Mexican American Community History Project, Center for Oral and Public History at California State University, Fullerton.

60 Archivos Económicos, H03099–H03115, Estadísticas de Migración, Departamento de Migración de México, Secretaría de Gobernación, Biblioteca Miguel Lerdo de Tejeda, Mexico City; Hoffman, *Unwanted Mexican Americans,* 174.

61 José Isabel "Chabelo" Villegas, interview conducted in English by author. Digital audio recording, August 28, 2011, Pasadena, CA, in author's possession.

62 Guillermina Hinojos, interview conducted in Spanish and translated to English by author. Digital audio recording, February 12, 2012, Pasadena, CA, in author's possession.

63 Camille Guerin-Gonzales, *Mexican Workers and American Dreams: Immigration, Repatriation, and California Farm Labor, 1900–1939* (New Brunswick: Rutgers University Press, 1996), 78.

64 Clyde Campbell to INS commissioner, May 20, 1939, box 455, RG 58, US National Archives and Records Administration, College Park, MD.

65 Committee Report on "The Mexican Problem," p. 1, Cleofas Calleros Papers (MS 231), C.L. Sonnichsen Special Collections Department, University of Texas at El Paso Library.

66 Committee Report on "The Mexican Problem," p. 1.

67 Guillermina Hinojos interview.

68 On the poverty and hunger that many repatriated and banished people experienced, see Balderrama and Rodríguez, *Decade of Betrayal,* 142–144.

69 Sara Marie Robles, interview conducted in Spanish and translated to English by author. Digital audio recording, January 22, 2012, Pasadena, CA, in author's possession.

70 Sara Marie Robles interview.

71 Sara Marie Robles interview.

72 Sara Marie Robles interview.

73 Sara Marie Robles interview.

74 Stephen R. Niblo, *Mexico in the 1940s: Modernity, Politics, and Corruption* (Wilmington: Rowman and Littlefield, 1999), 363.

75 Miroslava Chávez-García, *Migrant Longing: Letter Writing Across the U.S.–Mexico Borderlands* (Chapel Hill: University of North Carolina Press, 2018), 9.

76 Sara Marie Robles interview.

77 For the practices and legacies of coverture in Mexico, see Julia María Schiavone Camacho, *Chinese Mexicans: Transpacific Migration and the Search for a Homeland, 1910–1960* (Chapel Hill: University of North Carolina Press, 2012), 106–107.

78 For selected sources on social capital and immigration, see Leisy Abrego, *Sacrificing Families: Navigating Laws, Labor, and Love Across Borders* (Stanford: Stanford University Press, 2014); Gabriela F. Arredondo, *Mexican Chicago: Race, Identity, and Nation, 1916–39* (Chicago: University of Illinois Press, 2008); Pierrette Hondagneu-Sotelo and Ernestine Avila, "'I'm Here, but I'm There': The Meanings of Latina Transnational Motherhood," *Gender and Society* 11, no. 5 (1997): 548–571; Vicki L. Ruiz, *From Out of the Shadows: Mexican Women in Twentieth-Century America* (New York: Oxford University Press, 2008); and Saskia Sassen, "Strategic Instantiations of Gendering in the Global Economy," in *Gender and U.S. Immigration: Contemporary Trends,* ed. Pierrette Hondagneu-Sotelo (Berkeley: University of California Press, 2003), 43–60.

79 Marla A. Ramírez, "The Making of Mexican Illegality: Immigration Exclusions Based on Race, Class Status, and Gender," *Journal of New Political Science* 40, no. 2 (2018): 317–335; Marla A. Ramírez, "Gendered Banishment: Rewriting Mexican Repatriation Through a Transgenerational Oral History Methodology," *Latino Studies* 20, no. 3 (2022): 306–333.

80 For a discussion on women's autonomy during emigration, see Ruiz, *From Out of the Shadows;* and Elaine Bauer and Paul Thompson, "'She's Al-

ways the Person with a Very Global Vision': The Gender Dynamics of Migration, Narrative Interpretation and the Case of Jamaican Transnational Families," *Gender & History* 16, no. 2 (2004): 334–375.

81 For more on this topic, see Guerin-Gonzales, *Mexican Workers and American Dreams.*

82 Sara Marie Robles interview.

83 Sara Marie Robles interview.

84 Immigration and Nationality Act of 1965, Pub. L. no. 89–236, 79 Stat. 911 (1965). For more on the Immigration and Nationality Act of 1965 (also known as the Hart-Celler Act), see Ana Raquel Minian, *Undocumented Lives: The Untold Story of Mexican Migration* (Cambridge: Harvard University Press, 2018), 48; Molina, *How Race Is Made,* 140; and Ngai, *Impossible Subjects,* 227.

85 Minian, *Undocumented Lives,* 49; Molina, *How Race Is Made,* 140; Ngai, *Impossible Subjects,* 227–228.

86 Lynn Stephen, *Transborder Lives: Indigenous Oaxacans in Mexico, California, and Oregon* (Durham: Duke University Press, 2007), 5, 264.

87 For more on transborder communities, see Yu Tokunaga, *Transborder Los Angeles: An Unknown Transpacific History of Japanese-Mexican Relations* (Oakland: University of California Press, 2022), 49.

88 On this topic, see Abrego, *Sacrificing Families;* Deborah A. Boehm, *Intimate Migrations: Gender, Family, and Illegality Among Transnational Mexicans* (New York: New York University Press, 2012); Deborah A. Boehm, "'For My Children:' Constructing Family and Navigating the State in the US-Mexico Transnation," *Anthropological Quarterly* 81, no. 4 (2008): 795–797; Hondagneu-Sotelo and Avila, "'I'm Here, but I'm There'"; Pierrette Hondagneu-Sotelo, *Doméstica: Immigrant Workers Cleaning and Caring in the Shadows of Affluence* (Berkeley: University of California Press, 2001); Ana Elizabeth Rosas, *Abrazando el Espíritu: Bracero Families Confront the US-Mexico Border* (Berkeley: University of California Press, 2014); and Patricia Zavella, *I'm Neither Here nor There: Mexicans' Quotidian Struggles with Migration and Poverty* (Durham: Duke University Press, 2011).

89 Sara Marie Robles interview.

90 Sara Marie Robles interview; State of California Department of Industrial Relations, "History of California's Minimum Wage," https://www .dir.ca.gov/iwc/minimumwagehistory.htm. At that time, in 1965, the California minimum wage was $1.30 an hour, but she was paid by the piece, which resulted in a much lower hourly rate.

91 Sara Marie Robles interview.

92   Alanís Enciso, *They Should Stay There,* 184; Guerin-Gonzales, *Mexican Workers and American Dreams,* 67; Mireya Loza, *Defiant Braceros: How Migrant Workers Fought for Racial, Sexual, and Political Freedom* (Chapel Hill: University of North Carolina Press, 2016), 119–127; Minian, *Undocumented Lives,* 69–70.

93   George P. Clements, M.D., "Mexican Immigration and Its Bearing on California's Agriculture," October 2, 1929, Collection 13, Ronald W. Lopez Papers, Chicano Studies Research Institute, University of California, Los Angeles.

94   James Strom Thurmond in US Senate, 94th Congress, *Hearings Before the Subcommittee on Immigration and Naturalization of the Committee on the Judiciary, United States Senate, Ninety-Fourth Congress, Second Session on S. 3074 to Amend the Immigration and Nationality Act and for Other Purposes* (Washington, DC: US Government Printing Office, 1976), 21, as cited in Minian, *Undocumented Lives,* 69.

95   Statement of AFL-CIO in US Senate, *Immigration 1976: Hearings Before the Subcommittee on Immigration and Naturalization of the Committee of the Judiciary,* 94th Cong., 2nd sess., US Senate, 144.

96   Sara Marie Robles interview.

97   Cecilia Menjívar, "The Intersection of Work and Gender: Central American Immigrant Women and Employment in California," in *Gender and U.S. Immigration: Contemporary Trends,* ed. Pierrette Hondagneu-Sotelo (Berkeley: University of California Press, 2003), 101–126.

98   Abrego, *Sacrificing Families,* 12.

99   Luz María Gordillo, *Mexican Women and the Other Side of Immigration: Engendering Transnational Ties* (Austin: University of Texas Press, 2010), 137; Edna A. Viruell-Fuentes, "'My Heart Is Always There': The Transnational Practice of First-Generation Mexican Immigrant and Second-Generation Mexican American Women," *Identities: Global Studies in Power and Culture* 13, no. 3 (July–September 2006): 335–362.

100   Hondagneu-Sotelo and Avila, "'I'm Here, but I'm There,'" 552.

101   For a discussion on strategies that immigrant men used to claim the social status denied to them in their host country, see Luin Goldring, "Gender, Status, and the State in Transnational Spaces: The Gendering of Political Participation and Mexican Hometown Associations," in *Gender and U.S. Immigration,* ed. Pierrette Hondagneu-Sotelo (Berkeley: University of California Press, 2003), 341–358.

102   Sara Marie Robles interview.

103 Boehm, "'For My Children,'" 781.

104 Boehm, "'For My Children,'" 778–779.

105 Boehm, "'For My Children,'" 779. This is common in transnational families but also among non-transnational working-class families who cannot afford daycare and thus rely on extended family structures and friends for childcare.

106 Hondagneu-Sotelo and Avila, "'I'm Here, but I'm There,'" 548.

107 Marjorie Faulstich Orellana, Barrie Thorne, Anna Chee, and Wan Shun Eva Lam, "Transnational Childhoods: The Participation of Children in Processes of Family Migration," *Social Problems* 48, no. 4 (November 2001): 573.

108 Sara Marie Robles interview.

109 Guillermina Hinojos interview.

110 Bonnie Thornton Dill, "Our Mother's Grief: Racial Ethnic Women and the Maintenance of Families," *Journal of Family History* 13, no. 1 (1988): 415–431.

111 Orellana et al., "Transnational Childhoods," 578.

112 Orellana et al., "Transnational Childhoods," 578.

113 For more on economic and emotional labor among transnational children, see Abrego, *Sacrificing Families;* Boehm, "'For My Children'"; Hondagneu-Sotelo and Avila, "'I'm Here, but I'm There'"; and Orellana et al., "Transnational Childhoods."

114 Guillermina Hinojos interview.

115 Orellana et al., "Transnational Childhoods," 582.

116 José Isabel "Chabelo" Villegas interview.

117 Some childhood labor occurs in most farm families, and it is very common among transnational Mexican families.

118 Sara Marie Robles interview.

119 On this topic, see Cristina M. Alcalde, "Violence Across Borders: Familism, Hegemonic Masculinity, and Self-Sacrificing Femininity in the Lives of Mexican and Peruvian Migrants," *Latino Studies* 8 no. 1 (2010): 48–68; and Abrego, *Sacrificing Families,* 112.

120 Alessandro Portelli, *The Order Has Been Carried Out: History, Memory, and Meaning of a Nazi Massacre in Rome* (New York: Palgrave Macmillan, 2003), 15.

121 Sara Veronica Hinojos, interview conducted in English by author. Digital audio recording, January 31, 2013, Goleta, CA, in author's possession.

122 Sara Veronica Hinojos interview.

123 For more on the relationship between photographs and memory in the examination of history, see Alexander Freund and Alistair Thomson, *Oral History and Photography* (New York: Palgrave Macmillan, 2011); Phillip Gourevitch and Errol Morris, *The Ballad of Abu Ghraib* (New York: Penguin, 2009); and Jennifer Tucker, "Entwined Practices: Engagements with Photography in Historical Inquiry," *History and Theory* 48, no. 4 (2009): 1–8.

124 The family calls Sara Marie "Nana," another Spanish word for grandma. Sara Veronica Hinojos interview.

125 Freund and Thomson, *Oral History and Photography*, 13, 16.

126 Sara Veronica Hinojos interview.

4. THE ESPINOZA FAMILY: IMPERMANENT LEGALITY

1 Espinoza is Ramona's married name and Garcia is her maiden name, but at her request I use Espinoza here because it is the surname she goes by now. Ramona's daughter and her grandson, whose oral history interviews I also use here, share the same last name. For consistency, I have used the surname Espinoza when referring to Ramona and her family before and after her marriage.

2 Ramona Espinoza, interview conducted in Spanish and translated to English by author. Digital audio recording, December 4, 2017, Anaheim, CA, in author's possession.

3 Ramona Espinoza interview.

4 In 1924, Congress created the US Border Patrol as part of the Immigration Service. Bureau of Immigration officers are mentioned when discussing laws or events from 1924 to 1932; thereafter, references are in relation to the United States Immigration and Naturalization Service (INS) officers. For more on this history, see Kelly Lytle Hernández, *Migra! A History of the U.S. Border Patrol* (Berkeley: University of California Press, 2010), 64.

5 Héctor Aguilar Camín and Lorenzo Meyer, *A la Sombra de la Revolución Mexicana* (Mexico City: Cal y Arena Press, 1995); Verónica Castillo-Muñoz, *The Other California: Land, Identity, and Politics on the Mexican Borderlands* (Berkeley: University of California Press, 2017); Mary Kay Vaughan, *Cultural Politics in the Revolution: Teachers, Peasants, and Schools in Mexico, 1930–1940* (Tucson: University of Arizona Press, 1997).

6 Dr. Horacio E. López to Francisco I. Madero, October 1, 1911, Ensenada, Baja California, in *Documentos históricos de la revolución mexicana, Actividades*

políticas y revolucionarias de los hermanos Flores Magón, vol. 10, ed. Isidro Fabela and Josefina E. de Fabela (México City: Editorial Jus, 1966), 361.

7 María Guadalupe Espinoza is referred to here as Guadalupe because it is her preferred name.

8 General Consul of Mexico, "Informe especial sobre las condiciones de los mexicanos en el Distrito Consular de San Bernardino" (Special report on the Mexican conditions in Consular District of San Bernardino), January 6, 1932, p. 6, Archivo de documentos de Secretaría de Relaciones Exteriores (ASRE), Archivo Histórico Genaro Estrada, Mexico City.

9 General Consul of Mexico, "Informe especial."

10 George J. Sánchez, *Becoming Mexican American: Ethnicity, Culture and Identity in Chicano Los Angeles, 1900–1945* (New York: Oxford University Press, 1993), 212; Cybelle Fox, *Three Worlds of Relief: Race, Immigration, and the American Welfare State from the Progressive Era to the New Deal* (Princeton: Princeton University Press, 2012), 53–55.

11 Camille Guerin-Gonzales, *Mexican Workers and American Dreams: Immigration, Repatriation, and California Farm Labor, 1900–1939* (New Brunswick: Rutgers University Press, 1996), 83.

12 Guerin-Gonzales, *Mexican Workers and American Dreams,* 96–97; Gabriela F. Arredondo, *Mexican Chicago: Race, Identity, and Nation 1916–39* (Chicago: University of Illinois Press, 2008), 95.

13 Guerin-Gonzales, *Mexican Workers and American Dreams,* 84.

14 Francisco E. Balderrama and Raymond Rodríguez, *Decade of Betrayal: Mexican Repatriation in the 1930s,* rev. ed. (Albuquerque: University of New Mexico Press, 2006), 95.

15 Cleofas Calleros, "Minutes of the [Texas] State Committee on Mexican Problems," June 26, 1934, box 14, folder 5, Cleofas Calleros Papers, C. L. Sonnichsen Special Collections Department, University of Texas at El Paso Library.

16 Calleros, "Minutes of the [Texas] State Committee on Mexican Problems."

17 "Potato Growers Plan Shipping This Week," *Brownsville Herald* (Brownsville, TX), March 16, 1930, 4.

18 "Mexicans Return to their Home Land," *Coolidge Examiner* (Coolidge, AZ), June 26, 1931.

19 "Mexicans Return to their Home Land."

20 Ramona Espinoza interview.

21 Ramona Espinoza interview.

22 María Guadalupe Espinoza, interview conducted in English by author. Digital audio recording, December 4, 2017, Anaheim, CA, in author's possession.

23 Rex Thomson, interview by Christine Valenciana, August 4, 1976, Mexican American Community History Project, Center for Oral and Public History at California State University, Fullerton.

24 Ramona Espinoza interview.

25 María Guadalupe Espinoza interview.

26 Martha Gardner, *The Qualities of a Citizen: Women, Immigration, and Citizenship, 1870–1965* (Princeton: Princeton University Press, 2005), 157; Elena R. Gutiérrez, *Fertile Matters: The Politics of Mexican-Origin Women's Reproduction* (Austin: University of Texas Press, 2008), 73–74; Vicki L. Ruiz, *From Out of the Shadows: Mexican Women in Twentieth-Century America* (New York: Oxford University Press, 2008), 11.

27 Gutiérrez, *Fertile Matters*, 20, 43–44; Natalie Lira, *Laboratories of Deficiency: Sterilization and Confinement in California, 1900–1950s* (Berkeley: University of California Press, 2022), 77; Natalia Molina, "Constructing Mexicans as Deportable Immigrants: Race, Disease, and the Meaning of 'Public Charge,'" *Identities: Global Studies in Culture and Power* 17, no. 6 (2010): 641–666; Natalia Molina, *Fit to Be Citizens? Public Health and Race in Los Angeles, 1879–1939* (Berkeley: University of California Press, 2006), 136–138; Natalia Molina, *How Race Is Made in America: Immigration, Citizenship, and the Historical Power of Racial Scripts* (Berkeley: University of California Press, 2014), 92–93, 144.

28 Marian Schibsby, "Deportation on the Ground of Being a Public Charge," *Interpreter Releases* 7, no. 42 (December 11, 1930), Records of the American Council for Nationalities Services, Immigration History Research Center, University of Minnesota, Minneapolis; *Research Collections in American Immigration,* ed. Rudolph Vecoli (Frederick: University Publications of America, 1989); Gardner, *Qualities of a Citizen,* 181; William Van Vleck, *The Administrative Control of Aliens: A Study in Administrative Law and Procedure* (New York: Commonwealth Fund, 1932), 126–127, 135–137.

29 Ramona Espinoza interview.

30 Ramona Espinoza interview.

31 Ramona Espinoza interview.

32 Roberto Chao Romero, *The Chinese in Mexico, 1882–1940* (Tucson: University of Arizona Press, 2010), 55.

33 On the impact of the Page Act of 1875 on the immigration of Chinese women and men, see Andrew Gyory, *Closing the Gate: Race, Politics, and the Chinese Exclusion Act* (Chapel Hill: University of North Carolina Press, 1998), 71, 138; Bill Ong Hing, *Making and Remaking Asian America Through Immigration Policy, 1850–1990* (Stanford: Stanford University Press, 1993), 23–24, 36; George Anthony Peffer, "Forbidden Families: Emigration Experiences of Chinese Women Under the Page Law, 1875–1882," *Journal of American Ethnic History* 6, no. 1 (1986): 32; and Anna Pegler-Gordon, *In Sight of America: Photography and the Development of U.S. Immigration Policy* (Berkeley: University of California Press, 2009), 82, 176, 233. On the history of Chinese settlement in Mexico, see Romero, *Chinese in Mexico*; Julian Lim, *Porous Borders: Multiracial Migrations and the Law in the U.S.-Mexico Borderlands* (Chapel Hill: University of North Carolina Press, 2017); Grace Peña Delgado, *Making the Chinese Mexican: Global Migration, Localism, and Exclusion in the U.S.-Mexico Borderlands* (Stanford: Stanford University Press, 2012); and Julia María Schiavone Camacho, *Chinese Mexicans: Transpacific Migration and the Search for a Homeland, 1910–1960* (Chapel Hill: University of North Carolina Press, 2012).

34 On the history of Chinese removals from Mexico, see Castillo-Muñoz, *Other California*; Romero, *Chinese in Mexico;* Lim, *Porous Borders;* Peña Delgado, *Making the Chinese Mexican;* Camacho, *Chinese Mexicans;* Benny J. Andrés Jr., "Invisible Borders: Repatriation and Colonization of Mexican Migrant Workers Along the California Borderlands During the 1930s," *California History* 88, no. 4 (2011): 5–21, 63–65.

35 Divisional Director R. J. Norene to Seattle District Commissioner Marie A. Proctor, "Repatriation of Mexican Nationals," US Department of Labor, September 29, 1938, file 55957 / 456, box 456, RG 85, Records of the Immigration and Naturalization Service, US National Archives and Records Administration, Washington, DC.

36 María Guadalupe Espinoza interview.

37 Ramona Espinoza interview.

38 "Border Patrol Says Alien Influx Due," *Brownsville Herald* (Brownsville, TX), March 7, 1935.

39 "Border Patrol Says Alien Influx Due."

40 George L. Coleman, "Mexican Border Conditions Report," addressed to the Commissioner General of Immigration and Naturalization and referred to [Daniel W.] MacCormack, September 16, 1933, file 55877 / 443, RG 85, US National Archives and Records Administration, Washington, DC.

41   Gardner, *Qualities of a Citizen;* Molina, "Constructing Mexicans"; Marla A. Ramírez, "The Making of Mexican Illegality: Immigration Exclusions Based on Race, Class Status, and Gender," *Journal of New Political Science* 40, no. 2 (2018): 317–335.

42   Ramona Espinoza interview; María Guadalupe Espinoza interview.

43   Ramona Espinoza interview.

44   On the destitution of displaced ethnic Mexicans, see Fernando Saúl Alanís Enciso, *Voces de la repatriación: La sociedad mexicana y la repatriación de mexicanos de Estados Unidos, 1930–1933* (Zamora: El Colegio de Michoacán, 2015); Arredondo, *Mexican Chicago;* Balderrama and Rodríguez, *Decade of Betrayal;* and Marla A. Ramírez, "Gendered Banishment: Rewriting Mexican Repatriation Through a Transgenerational Oral History Methodology," *Latino Studies* 20, no. 3 (2022): 306–333.

45   For more on Mexican President Lázaro Cárdenas's colonization project, see Camacho, *Chinese Mexicans,* 127; Mercedes Carreras de Velasco, *Los mexicanos que devolvió la crisis, 1929–1932* (Tlatelolco, Mexico City: Secretaría de Relaciones Exteriores, 1974), 56; and Castillo-Muñoz, *Other California,* 4–5.

46   Emiliano Zapata, "Plan de Ayala," in *Documentos Inéditos sobre Emiliano Zapata y el Cuartel General: Seleccionados del Archivo de Genovevo de la O, que Conserva el Archivo General de la Nación* (Mexico City: Archivo General de la Nación, 1979); Castillo-Muñoz, *Other California;* Christopher R. Boyer, *Becoming Campesinos: Politics, Identity, and Agrarian Struggle in Postrevolutionary Michoacán, 1920–1935* (Stanford: Stanford University Press, 2003); Gilbert M. Joseph and Daniel Nugent, eds., *Everyday Forms of State Formation: Revolution and the Negotiations of Rule in Modern Mexico* (Durham: Duke University Press, 1994); Kelly Lytle Hernández, *Bad Mexicans: Race, Empire, and Revolution in the Borderlands* (New York: W.W. Norton, 2022).

47   Alanís Enciso, *Voces de la repatriación,* 172; Carreras de Velasco, *Los Mexicanos que devolvió la crisis,* 85.

48   Fernando Saúl Alanís Enciso, "La colonización de Baja California con mexicanos provenientes de Estados Unidos (1935–1939)," *Frontera Norte* 13, no. 26 (2001): 141–163; Arturo Anguiano, *El Estado y la Política Obrera del Cardenismo* (Mexico City: Ediciones Era, 1975); Marjorie Becker, *Setting the Virgin on Fire: Lázaro Cárdenas, Michoacán Peasants, and the Redemption of the Mexican Revolution* (Berkeley: University of California Press, 1995); Nora Hamilton, *The Limits of State Autonomy: Post-Revolutionary Mexico* (Princeton: Princeton University Press, 1982).

49 "35 Mexicans Leave for New Colony: Americans in Charge of Repatriates Moving into Lower California," *Evening Star* (Washington, DC), October 24, 1932.

50 Alanís Enciso, *Voces de la repatriación*, 153–155; Carreras de Velasco, *Los Mexicanos que devolvió la crisis*, 92–93.

51 Alfredo Levy to Luis Borrego Hinojosa (president of the accounts examinations committee of the National Committee of Repatriation), July 1, 1934, Mexico, DF, record 244.1 / 15, Fondo Abelardo L. Rodríguez, Archivos Presidenciales, Archivo General de la Nación, Mexico City; Alfredo Levy (vice-president of the National Committee of Repatriation) to Jesús Manuel García, June 3, 1933, Mexico, DF, record 244 / 11, Fondo Abelardo L. Rodríguez, Archivos Presidenciales, Archivo General de la Nación, Mexico City. Some of the most influential works on repatriation that discuss the National Committee of Repatriation and its "campaña del medio millón" are Alanís Enciso, *Voces de la repatriación*, 152–169; Balderrama and Rodríguez, *Decade of Betrayal*, 175–179; Carreras de Velasco, *Los mexicanos que devolvió la crisis*, 92–97; Abraham Hoffman, *Unwanted Mexican Americans in the Great Depression: Repatriation Pressures, 1929–1939* (Tucson: University of Arizona Press, 1974), 137–140; and Sánchez, *Becoming Mexican American*, 219–220.

52 Alanís Enciso, *Voces de la repatriación*, 155; Balderrama and Rodríguez, *Decade of Betrayal*, 176; Carreras de Velasco, *Los mexicanos que devolvió la crisis*, 95; Hoffman, *Unwanted Mexican Americans*, 137.

53 *El Nacional Revolucionario* (Mexico City), December 19, 1932.

54 Alanís Enciso, *Voces de la repatriación*, 155–156; Carreras de Velasco, *Los Mexicanos que devolvió la crisis*, 96–97.

55 The original deadline to collect the funds, January 31, 1933, was extended to July 1934, when the overall fundraising goal of half a million pesos was not reached. Alanís Enciso, *Voces de la repatriación*, 168.

56 The rejection of banished Mexican American women and children eventually also affected expelled Mexican men, in part due to the fight for limited resources in Mexico. See Manuel Gamio, *Mexican Immigration to the United States* (Chicago: University of Chicago Press, 1930), 146.

57 Constitución Política de los Estados Unidos Mexicanos, CPEUM [Political Constitution of the United Mexican States], Diario Oficial de la Federación [DOF], 05-02-1917, últimas reformas DOF 22-03-2024, art. 27 (Mexico), http://constitucion1917.gob.mx/es/Constitucion1917/Constitucion_1917_Facsimilar.

58 For the gender inequality of land redistribution in Mexico and other parts in Latin America, see Castillo-Muñoz, *Other California;* Lynn Stephen, "Viva Zapata! Generation, Gender, and Historical Consciousness in the Reception of Ejido Reform in Oaxaca," Center for U.S.-Mexican Studies, University of California, San Diego, 1994, https://ideas.repec.org/p/cdl/usmexi/qt4rf64696.html; Heather Fowler-Salamini and Mary Kay Vaughan, eds., *Women of the Mexican Countryside, 1850–1990: Creating Spaces, Shaping Transitions* (Tucson: University of Arizona Press, 1994).

59 Benny J. Andrés Jr., *Power and Control in the Imperial Valley: Nature, Agribusiness, and Workers on the California Borderland, 1900–1940* (College Station: Texas A&M University Press, 2015), 153–155.

60 María Guadalupe Espinoza interview.

61 Gabriela Recio, "Drugs and Alcohol: US Prohibition and the Origins of the Drug Trade in Mexico, 1910–1930," *Journal of Latin American Studies* 34, no. 1 (2002): 28–29; José Ramón Mauleón Gómez, "Políticas Nacionales y Agricultura en la Frontera: Estudio Comparativo de Baja California y País Vasco," *Estudios Fronterizos* 4, nos. 10–11 (1986): 97–128.

62 Both Mexico and the United States were invested in Baja California. Mexico needed to populate the area to govern it and used displaced ethnic Mexicans for this purpose. US investors saw Baja California as an economic development opportunity and invested in mining, railroads, and agribusiness in four states: Baja California, Chihuahua, Coahuila, and Sonora. See John Mason Hart, *Empire and Revolution: The Americans in Mexico Since the Civil War* (Berkeley: University of California Press, 2002), 75–78.

63 Andrés, *Power and Control,* 93–97; Castillo-Muñoz, *Other California,* 11.

64 Ramona Espinoza interview.

65 María Guadalupe Espinoza interview.

66 Ramona Espinoza interview.

67 Ramona Espinoza interview.

68 Ramona Espinoza interview.

69 For more about the economic and emotional labor of migrant children, see Leisy Abrego, *Sacrificing Families: Navigating Laws, Labor, and Love Across Borders* (Stanford: Stanford University Press, 2014); Deborah A. Boehm, "'For My Children': Constructing Family and Navigating the State in the US-Mexico Transnation," *Anthropological Quarterly* 81, no. 4 (2008); Pierrette Hondagneu-Sotelo and Ernestine Avila, "'I'm Here, but I'm There': The Meaning of Latina Transnational Motherhood," *Gender & Society* 11, no. 5

(1997); and Marjorie Faulstich Orellana, Barrie Thorne, Anna Chee, and Wan Shun Eva Lam, "Transnational Childhoods: The Participation of Children in Processes of Family Migration," *Social Problems* 48, no. 4 (November 2001): 572–591.

70 "U.S. Deporting 11,500 Monthly: Doak Devises New Method of Attack," *Daily Worker* (New York, NY), April 17, 1931; "Declared Returning Mexicans Starving," *Bismarck Tribune* (Bismarck, ND), March 18, 1931.

71 Ramona Espinoza interview.

72 María Guadalupe Espinoza interview.

73 Balderrama and Rodríguez, *Decade of Betrayal,* 244.

74 Ramona Espinoza interview.

75 Ramona Espinoza interview.

76 Castillo-Muñoz, *Other California,* 31; Robert H. Duncan, "The Chinese and the Economic Development of Northern Baja California, 1889–1929," *Hispanic American Historical Review* 74, no. 4 (1994): 617–618; Romero, *Chinese in Mexico,* 55.

77 Castillo-Muñoz, *Other California,* 39.

78 Ramona Espinoza interview.

79 Immigration Act of February 5, 1917, ch. 29, 39 Stat. 874; Immigration Act of May 25, 1924, ch. 190, 43 Stat. 153; War Time Passport Act of May 22, 1918, ch. 81, 40 Stat. 559. For an account of the increased border policing that began during World War I, see Lytle Hernández, *Migra!,* 33–34; S. Deborah Kang, *The INS on the Line: Making Immigration Law on the US-Mexico Border, 1917–1954* (New York: Oxford University Press, 2017), 24–25; and Craig Robertson, *The Passport in America: The History of a Document* (New York: Oxford University Press, 2010), 162–163.

80 Kang, *INS on the Line,* 24–25.

81 Ramona Espinoza interview.

82 Andrés, *Power and Control,* 74–75.

83 CRLC drafted sales contracts with a twenty-year payment period and a clause that reserved land control for the company until local farmers paid in full. For more on this, see Dorothy Pierson Kerig, "Yankee Enclave: The Colorado River Land Company and Mexican Agrarian Reform in Baja California, 1902–1944" (PhD diss., University of California, Irvine, 1988), 365–367; George Luna-Peña, "'Little More than Desert Wasteland': Race, Development, and Settler Colonialism in the Mexicali Valley," *Critical Ethnic Studies* 1, no. 2 (Fall 2015): 94; Oscar Sánchez Ramírez, "Development of the Structure of Agriculture in the Mexicali Valley in the Early Twentieth Century," in

Imperial-Mexicali Valleys: Development and the Environment of the U.S.-Mexican Border Region, ed. Kimberly Collins, Paul Ganster, Cheryl Mason, Eduardo Sánchez López, and Margarito Quintero-Núñez (San Diego: San Diego State University Press, 2004), 35.

84 Ramona Espinoza interview.

85 Castillo-Muñoz, *Other California,* 41.

86 Ramona Espinoza interview.

87 Ramona Espinoza interview.

88 Ramona Espinoza interview.

89 Ruiz, *From Out of the Shadows,* 61, 63–65.

90 María Guadalupe Espinoza interview.

91 Ramona Espinoza interview.

92 Lori A. Flores, *Grounds for Dreaming: Mexican Americans, Mexican Immigrants, and the California Farmworker Movement* (New Haven: Yale University Press, 2016), 19–20; Lytle Hernández, *Migra!,* 89.

93 Rick Baldoz, *The Third Asiatic Invasion: Empire and Migration in Filipino America* (New York: New York University Press, 2011), 9; Dawn Bohulano Mabalon, *Little Manila Is in the Heart: The Making of the Filipina/o American Community in Stockton, California* (Durham: Duke University Press, 2013), 60–61; Flores, *Grounds for Dreaming,* 21–22; Mae M. Ngai, *Impossible Subjects: Illegal Aliens and the Making of Modern America* (Princeton: Princeton University Press, 2004), 103.

94 Immigration Act of 1917, Pub. L. no. 64–301, 39 Stat. 874 (1917); Alvin Hoi-Chun Hung, "Deconstructing the Decolonizing Plot of the Tydings-McDuffie Act: A Review of America's International Relations in Asia in the Early Twentieth Century," *University of Pennsylvania Asian Law Review* 19, no. 1 (2023): 158.

95 Some Filipinos immigrated to the continental United States as college students, while others were recruited as laborers. But Filipino students who needed a summer income also worked in canneries. See Chris Friday, *Organizing Asian American Labor: The Pacific Coast Canned-Salmon Industry, 1870–1942* (Philadelphia: Temple University Press, 1994), 125–127; Yen Le Espiritu, *Filipino American Lives* (Philadelphia: Temple University Press, 1995), 12–13.

96 Philippine Independence Act (Tydings-McDuffie Act) of Mar. 24, 1934, Pub. L. no. 73–127, 48 Stat. 456; the Filipino Repatriation Act of July 10, 1935, Pub. L. no. 74–271, 49 Stat. 478.

97 Filipino Repatriation Act of July 10, 1935, Pub. L. no. 74–271, 49 Stat. 478; Casiano Pagdilao Coloma, "A Study of the Filipino Repatriation Movement" (master's thesis, University of Southern California, 1939), 56–57; Carey McWilliams, "Exit the Filipino," *Nation*, September 4, 1935; Mabalon, *Little Manila*, 144–146; Ngai, *Impossible Subjects*, 120–121.

98 Philippines Independence Act of July 10, 1935 (49 Stat. 478); "Filipinos' Status Problem for U.S.: Joint Committee of Experts Studying Commercial Relations," *Sunday Star* (Washington, DC), May 16, 1937.

99 Excerpts from Report of June 1939, Carey McWilliams Papers (Collection 1243), UCLA Library Special Collections, Charles E. Young Research Library, University of California, Los Angeles.

100 Excerpts from Report of June 1939.

101 Excerpts from Report of June 1939.

102 Mabalon, *Little Manila*, 93–96.

103 Mabalon, *Little Manila*, 241.

104 "Labor Shortage Menaces County Asparagus Crop," *Stockton Daily Evening Record*, February 26, 1942; "Asparagus Crop Faces Labor Shortage Threat: Decrease in Filipino Workers, Probable Removal of Japanese, Main Factors," *Stockton Daily Evening Record*, March 5, 1942; Friday, *Organizing Asian American Labor*, 149–192; Mabalon, *Little Manila*, 241–242; Ngai, *Impossible Subjects*, 125.

105 Representative Alfred J. Elliott of California, speaking during special order on the Dust Bowl "migrant problem," 86 Cong. Rec. 2676 (1940) (statement of Rep. Elliott); Migratory Labor Statistics, March 11, 1940, box 14, Carey McWilliams Papers (Collection 1243), UCLA Library Special Collections, Charles E. Young Research Library, University of California, Los Angeles; US House of Representatives, *Interstate Migration: Hearings Before the Select Committee to Investigate the Interstate Migration of Destitute Citizens*, 76th Cong., 3rd sess. (Washington, DC: US Government Printing Office, 1940), 21.

106 Representative Alfred J. Elliott of California, 86 Cong. Rec. 2676 (1940). For a study of the Dust Bowl migration to California that peaked between 1935 and 1939, see James Gregory, *American Exodus: The Dust Bowl Migration and Okie Culture in California* (Oxford, UK: Oxford University Press, 1989), 28–29, 72; Flores, *Grounds for Dreaming*, 28–34; Manuel G. Gonzales, *Mexicanos: A History of Mexicans in the United States*, 2nd ed. (Bloomington: Indiana University Press, 2009), 150–151; Devra Weber, *Dark Sweat, White Gold: California*

Farm Workers, Cotton, and the New Deal (Berkeley: University of California Press, 1996), 164–167.

107 David Montejano, *Anglos and Mexicans in the Making of Texas, 1836–1986* (Austin: University of Texas Press, 1987), 177; Weber, *Dark Sweat, White Gold,* 37.

108 Montejano, *Anglos and Mexicans,* 37–38; Ngai, *Impossible Subjects,* 135–137; Fox, *Three Worlds of Relief,* 4–6; Weber, *Dark Sweat, White Gold,* 37–40.

109 "Severe Labor Shortage Threatens Agriculture in Imperial Valley Fields: Grower-Shipper Agents Look for Boost in Wages While Scarcity Develops in Migrant Ranks: Mexicans Unavailable," *Imperial Valley Press* (El Centro, CA), September 23, 1941.

110 "Severe Labor Shortage."

111 "Severe Labor Shortage"; "Relief Commission Ruling Brings on Acute Shortage of Agricultural Labor," *Imperial Valley Press* (El Centro, CA), May 22, 1939.

112 Petitions, 77th Cong., 1st sess., 87 Cong. Rec. 7713 (1941).

113 Representative Samuel Dickstein of New York, speaking on the need for the Committee on Immigration and Naturalization to investigate the organized importation of Mexican labor and other "undesirable" immigrants, 86 Cong. Rec. 2815 (1940).

114 Flores, *Grounds for Dreaming,* 19; Guerin-Gonzales, *Mexican Workers and American Dreams,* 33–34; Mario T. García, *Desert Immigrants: The Mexicans of El Paso* (New Haven: Yale University Press, 1982), 35.

115 Richard Laban Adams and T. R. Kelly, *A Study of Farm Labor in California* (Berkeley: University of California Press, 1918), 17–21, 57–58; N. Ray Gilmore and Gladys W. Gilmore, "The Bracero in California," *Pacific Historical Review* 32, no. 3 (August 1963): 268.

116 George P. Clements, Manager of the Agricultural Department of Los Angeles Chamber of Commerce, talk before the annual conference of "Friends of the Mexicans" at Pomona College, November 13, 1926, box 4, Carey McWilliams Papers (Collection 1243), UCLA Library Special Collections, Charles E. Young Research Library, University of California, Los Angeles.

117 Ramona Espinoza interview.

118 In 1918, during World War I, Congress authorized the president to restrict immigration and amended and approved the same presidential power in 1941 during World War II. Act of May 22, 1918, 40 Stat. 559 (1918); Act of

June 21, 1941, Pub. L. no. 114, ch. 210, 55 Stat. 252 (1941); Presidential Proclamation No. 2523, 55 Stat. 1696 (Nov. 14, 1941).

119 Presidential Proclamation no. 2523, 55 Stat. 1696 §§ 1–2 (Nov. 14, 1941).

120 Pegler-Gordon, *In Sight of America*, 188–189; John Torpey, *Invention of the Passport: Surveillance, Citizenship and the State* (Cambridge: Cambridge University Press, 2000), 111–112.

121 Ramona Espinoza interview.

122 The US consulate was in Mexicali from 1918 to 1973 before moving to its current location in Tijuana, Baja California, Mexico.

123 Pegler-Gordon, *In Sight of America*, 206n61.

124 Ramona Espinoza interview.

125 Matt Garcia, *A World of Its Own: Race, Labor, and Citrus in the Making of Greater Los Angeles, 1900–1970* (Chapel Hill: University of North Carolina Press, 2001), 158–165; Mireya Loza, *Defiant Braceros: How Migrant Workers Fought for Racial, Sexual, and Political Freedom* (Chapel Hill: University of North Carolina Press, 2016), 97–100; Vicki L. Ruiz, *Cannery Women, Cannery Lives: Mexican Women, Unionization, and the California Food Processing Industry, 1930–1950* (Albuquerque: University of New Mexico Press, 1987), 74–77.

126 Ruiz, *Cannery Women, Cannery Lives*, 25, 28.

127 Ramona Espinoza interview.

128 Maribel Marin, "Export Vegetable Production in Mexicali Valley: A Case of Unequal Development Along the Mexican-U.S. Border" (master's thesis, Massachusetts Institute of Technology, 1989), 24.

129 Munson W. Dowd, "Imperial Valley Looks to the Future," *Engineering and Science Monthly* 4, no. 11 (November 1946): 1–8.

130 The destitution, hunger, and child labor of banished Mexican Americans have been well documented. See Balderrama and Rodríguez, *Decade of Betrayal;* Guerin-Gonzales, *Mexican Workers and American Dreams;* Hoffman, *Unwanted Mexican Americans;* Alanís Enciso, *Voces de la repatriación;* and Carreras de Velasco, *Los Mexicanos que devolvió la crisis.*

131 María Guadalupe Espinoza interview.

132 María Guadalupe Espinoza interview.

133 Ramona Espinoza interview.

134 María Guadalupe Espinoza interview.

135 Arturo Espinoza, interview conducted in English. Digital audio recording, November 21, 2018, San Diego, CA, in author's possession.

136 Ramona Espinoza interview.

5. THE APOLOGY ACT AND REDRESS RECOMMENDATIONS

1 Barton Myers, "Sherman's Field Order No. 15," *New Georgia Encyclopedia,* https://www.georgiaencyclopedia.org/articles/history-archaeology/shermans-field-order-no-15/.

2 For more details on reparations for formerly enslaved people and their descendants, see Adjoa A. Aiyetoro, "Formulating Reparations Litigation Through the Eyes of the Movement," *NYU Annual Survey of American Law* 58, no. 457 (2003): 457–474; and Roy L. Brooks, "Part 6: Slavery," in *When Sorry Isn't Enough* 1999, ed. Roy L. Brooks (New York: New York University Press, 1999), 309–390.

3 Aiyetoro, "Formulating Reparations"; Brooks, "Part 6."

4 On this topic, see Francisco E. Balderrama and Raymond Rodríguez, *Decade of Betrayal: Mexican Repatriation in the 1930s,* rev. ed. (Albuquerque: University of New Mexico Press, 2006), 299–318; Emma Coleman Jordan, "The Non-Monetary Value of Reparation Rhetoric," *African American Law & Policy Report* 6, no. 1 (2004): 23; Eric L. Ray, "Mexican Repatriation and the Possibility for a Federal Cause of Action: A Comparative Analysis on Reparations," *University of Miami Inter-American Law Review* 37, no. 1 (Fall 2005): 171–196; Christine Valenciana, "Unconstitutional Deportation of Mexican Americans During the 1930s: A Family History & Oral History," *Multicultural Education* 13, no. 3 (2006): 4–9.

5 Jordan, "Non-Monetary Value," 23.

6 Ramona Espinoza, interview conducted in Spanish and translated to English by author. Digital audio recording, December 4, 2017, Anaheim, CA, in author's possession.

7 Ramona Espinoza interview.

8 Ramona Espinoza interview.

9 María Guadalupe Espinoza's comment, Ramona Espinoza interview.

10 María Guadalupe Espinoza, interview conducted in English by author. Digital audio recording, December 4, 2017, Anaheim, CA, in author's possession.

11 Sara Marie Robles, interview conducted in Spanish and translated to English by author. Digital audio recording, January 22, 2012, Pasadena, CA, in author's possession.

12 Sara Veronica Hinojos, interview conducted in English by author. Digital audio recording, January 31, 2013, Goleta, CA, in author's possession.

13 José Isabel "Chabelo" Villegas, interview conducted in English by author. Digital audio recording, August 28, 2011, Pasadena, CA, in author's possession.

14 On the topic of immigrant transnational families, see Leisy Abrego, *Sacrificing Families: Navigating Laws, Labor, and Love Across Borders* (Stanford: Stanford University Press, 2014); Deborah A. Boehm, *Intimate Migrations: Gender, Family, and Illegality Among Transnational Mexicans* (New York: New York University Press, 2012); Pierrette Hondagneu-Sotelo and Ernestine Avila, "'I'm Here, but I'm There': The Meanings of Latina Transnational Motherhood," *Gender and Society* 11, no. 5 (1997): 548–571; Patricia Zavella, *I'm Neither Here nor There: Mexicans' Quotidian Struggles with Migration and Poverty* (Durham: Duke University Press, 2011).

15 Sara Veronica Hinojos interview.

16 Sara Veronica Hinojos interview.

17 For a more detailed discussion on the trauma and dehumanization that result from the lack of acknowledgment of loss or a tragic event, see Yvette G. Flores, *Chicana and Chicano Mental Health: Alma, Mente, y Corazón* (Tucson: University of Arizona Press, 2013), 45–48.

18 Kirk Savage, *Standing Soldiers, Kneeling Slaves: Race, War, and Monument in Nineteenth-Century America*, 2nd ed. (Princeton: Princeton University Press, 2018), 4, 70.

19 María Guadalupe Espinoza interview. On the value of reparations through revised academic curriculum, see Jordan, "Non-Monetary Value," 24–25.

20 Joe Yáñez, interview conducted in English by author. Digital audio recording, May 20, 2012, Santa Ana, CA, in author's possession.

21 Marisa Yáñez, interview conducted in English by author. Digital audio recording, November 27, 2013, Hemet, CA, in author's possession.

22 Public Act 96–0629 (2010), codified at 105 Ill. Comp. Stat. 5 / 27-21.

23 Cal. Assemb. Bill 146 (Garcia), 2015–2016 Reg. Sess. (Cal. 2015).

24 Jesús Molina, in Molina family group interview, conducted in Spanish and translated to English by author. Video recording, July 14, 2012, Rosemead, CA, in author's possession.

25 Carmela Molina, in Molina family group interview.

26 Recent immigration debates and bills include the "likely to become public charge" and "good moral character" clauses. Some examples include the 1986 Immigration Reform and Control Act (IRCA), 2012 Deferred Action for Childhood Arrivals (DACA), and 2014 Deferred Action for Parental Accountability (DAPA).

27 Virginia (Yáñez) De Anda, interview conducted in Spanish and translated to English by author. Digital audio recording, March 3, 2012, Hemet, CA, in author's possession.

28 Consuelo De Anda, interview conducted in Spanish and translated to English by author. Digital audio recording, March 3, 2012, Hemet, CA, in author's possession.

29 Virginia (Yáñez) De Anda interview.

30 Senator Dunn learned about the mass removals after his field representative and California State University, Fullerton alum, Bernie Enriquez, introduced him to the book *Decade of Betrayal* by Balderrama and Rodríguez. Valerie Orleans, "1930s Mexican Deportation," CSUF News, March 17, 2005, http://calstate.fullerton.edu/news/2005/valenciana.html.

31 Gregg Jones, "Apology Sought for Latino 'Repatriation' Drive in '30s," *Los Angeles Times*, July 15, 2003; Edward Sifuentes, "Bills Would Address 'Wrongful Deportations' in 1930s," *San Diego Union-Tribune*, September 8, 2004; Balderrama and Rodríguez, *Decade of Betrayal,* 338–340.

32 "Apology Act for the 1930s Mexican Repatriation Program," Cal. Sen. B. 670, 2005–2006 Reg. Sess., ch. 8.5 (Cal. Stat. 2005).

33 Ari Bloomekatz, "Los Angeles County Superiors Apologize for Deportations," *Los Angeles Times*, February 21, 2012, AA4; "LA County Officials Issue Formal Apology for 1930s Repatriation of More Than 1 Million Citizens to Mexico," *CBS News Los Angeles*, February 21, 2012.

34 Monica Muñoz Martinez, *The Injustice Never Leaves You: Anti-Mexican Violence in Texas* (Cambridge: Harvard University Press, 2018), 273–274.

35 The co-sponsors were motivated to bring back attention to this topic after Becker met with high-school student Tamara Gisiger. After writing a research paper on the history of Mexican repatriation, Gisiger urged for broader awareness about this history, specially under the renewed threats of mass deportations under President Donald Trump's second term. Angie Orellana Hernandez, "A High School Student's Paper on the Mexican Repatriation Could Lead to a New Statue in L.A.," *Los Angeles Times*, August 14, 2024.

36 Cal. Sen. Bill 537 (Becker), 2023–2024 Reg. Sess. (Cal. 2024).

37 Virginia (Yáñez) De Anda interview.

38 Cal. Sen. Bill 37 (Dunn), 2003–2004 Reg. Sess. (Cal. 2004). For more on ethnic Mexicans' mass imprisonment during the interwar period, see Kelly Lytle Hernández, *City of Inmates: Conquest, Rebellion, and the Rise of Human Caging in Los Angeles, 1771–1965* (Chapel Hill: University of North Carolina Press, 2017), esp. chap. 5; Allison Powers, *Arbitrating Empire: United States Expansion and the Transformation of International Law* (New York: Oxford University Press, 2024), 173–176.

39 Cal. Sen. Bill 37 (Dunn).

40 Cal. Sen. Bill 933 (Dunn), 2003–2004 Reg. Sess. (Cal. 2003).

41 Gregg Jones, "Reparations Sought for '30s Expulsion Program: Campaign Begins on Behalf of 1-Million-Plus People Forced to Leave the U.S. for Mexico," *Los Angeles Times*, July 16, 2003.

42 The California State Assembly voted 69 (in favor) versus 1 (against), and the California State Senate voted 28 (in favor) versus 8 (against). Cal. Sen. Bill 933 (Dunn), enrolled on September 12, 2003, vetoed by Gov. Gray Davis on October 12, 2003.

43 Francisco Balderrama, "Deportations During the Great Depression," in *Latinas in the United States: A Historical Encyclopedia,* ed. Vicki L. Ruiz and Virginia Sánchez Korrol (Bloomington: Indiana University Press, 2006), 211.

44 Cal. Sen. Bill 933 (Dunn).

45 Cal. Assemb. Bill 2913 (Firebaugh), 2001–2002 Reg. Sess., ch. 1070 (Cal. Stat. 2002). Other California legislation that extended the statute of limitations includes SB 1245 (1999), which granted an eleven-year window for World War II's slave-labor survivors; AB 1915 (2000), which created a ten-year window for Armenian genocide survivors to file lawsuits; and AB 1758 (2002), which granted an eight-year window for victims of Nazi oppression to take legal action to recover stolen artwork during the Holocaust era. For more details about these topics, see Cal. Sen. Bill 1245 (Hayden), 1999–2000 Reg. Sess., ch. 216 (Cal. Stat. 1999); Cal. Assemb. Bill 1915 (Poochigian), 1999–2000 Reg. Sess., ch. 543 (Cal. Stat. 2000); Cal. Assemb. Bill 1758 (Nakano), 2001–2002 Reg. Sess., ch. 332 (Cal. Stat. 2002); and Cal. Assemb. Bill 2913 (Firebaugh), 2001–2002 Reg. Sess., ch. 1070 (Cal. Stat. 2002).

46 Gov. Gray Davis, Veto Message to SB 933, in 2 J. Sen. State of Cal. 2647–48 (October 12, 2003).

47 Gov. Gray Davis, Veto Message to SB 933. For commentary on the Cypress Freeway collapse, see Daniel M. Weintraub, "Quake Road Rebuilding Put at $1.5 Billion Highways: Caltrans Warns Local Governments They May Have to Fend for Themselves. Plan Outlined to Compensate Nimitz Freeway victims," *Los Angeles Times*, November 2, 1989.

48 Gov. Gray Davis, Veto Message to SB 933.

49 Cal. Sen. Bill 427 (Dunn), 2003–2004 Reg. Sess. (Cal. 2003).

50 Gov. Arnold Schwarzenegger, Veto Message to Cal. Sen. Bill 427, in 4 J. Sen. State of Cal. 5597 (September 29, 2004).

51 Gov. Arnold Schwarzenegger, Veto Message to Cal. Sen. Bill 427.

52 Cal. Sen. Bill 645 (Dunn), 2005–2006 Reg. Sess. (Cal. 2005).

53 Gov. Arnold Schwarzenegger, Veto Message to Cal. Sen. Bill 645, in J. Sen. State of Cal. 2832 (Oct. 11, 2005).

54 For additional information on reparations efforts by the state of Michigan, see Balderrama and Rodríguez, *Decade of Betrayal,* 316–317.

55 Public Act 96–0629 (2010), codified at 105 Ill. Comp. Stat. 5/27-21.

56 Commission on Mexican-American Removal During 1929–1941 Act, H.R. 5161, 109th Cong. (2006); Commission on the Removal of Mexican-Americans to Mexico Act, H.R. 6314, 114th Cong. (2016); Commission on the Removal of Mexican-Americans to Mexico Act, H.R. 1412, 115th Cong. (2017).

57 Cal. Sen. J. Res. 21 (Dunn), 2003–2004 Reg. Sess. (Cal. 2004).

58 Cal. Sen. J. Res. 21 (Dunn).

59 Representatives Luis V. Gutierrez, Howard Berman, Mike Honda, Emanuel Cleaver, Doris Matsui, John Lewis, Barbara Lee, and Zoe Lofgren co-sponsored HR 5161.

60 Commission on Mexican-American Removal During 1929–1941 Act, H.R. 5161, 109th Cong. (2006).

61 Commission on Mexican-American Removal During 1929–1941 Act.

62 Valenciana, "Unconstitutional Deportation," 4.

63 Valenciana, "Unconstitutional Deportation," 7.

64 California Federation of Teachers, "Resolution 34.04: Unknown History: Deportation of Mexican Americans," 2004 CFT Resolutions, p. 44, https://www.cft.org/sites/main/files/file-attachments/2004_cft_res.pdf ?1547666072.

65 California Federation of Teachers, "Resolution 34.04."

66 For specific details on the membership and voting procedures of the California Federation of Teachers, see California Federation of Teachers, "Policies, Positions and Resolutions," https://www.cft.org/resolutions-and -policy.

67 Araceli Cruz, "Mexican Repatriation During the Great Depression, Explained," *Teen Vogue*, August 30, 2017; Lani Cupchoy, "The Fifth-Graders Who Put Mexican Repatriation Back into History Books," *Yes! Magazine*, August 4, 2016.

68 Cal. Assemb. Bill 146 (Garcia).

69 Cal. Assemb. Bill 146 (Garcia).

70 Gilbert Paul Carrasco, "Latinos in the U.S.: Invitation and Exile," in *Immigrants Out!,* ed. Juan F. Perea (New York: New York University Press, 1997), 194.

71 Carey McWilliams, "Getting Rid of the Mexican," *American Mercury* 28 (March 1933), 86.

72 María Guadalupe Espinoza interview.

73 *United States v. Kubrick,* 444 US 111, 117 (1979).

EPILOGUE

1 Filipino Repatriation Act of July 10, 1935, Pub. L. no. 74–271, 49 Stat. 478. Filipino repatriation is further examined in Chapter 4.

2 Dawn Bohulano Mabalon, *Little Manila Is in the Heart: The Making of the Filipina/o American Community in Stockton, California* (Durham: Duke University Press, 2013), 143–148; Mae M. Ngai, *Impossible Subjects: Illegal Aliens and the Making of Modern America* (Princeton: Princeton University Press, 2004), 120–126.

3 George P. Clements to Honorable Isaac Jones, April 26, 1929, Collection 13, Ronald W. Lopez Papers, Chicano Studies Research Institute, University of California, Los Angeles.

4 George P. Clements to Honorable Isaac Jones, April 26, 1929.

5 George P. Clements, "Mexican Immigration and Its Bearing on California's Agricultural Report," Collection 13, Ronald W. Lopez Papers, Chicano Studies Research Institute, University of California, Los Angeles.

6 For the conditions and demographics in Mexican barrios, see Mario T. García, *Desert Immigrants: The Immigrants of El Paso, 1880–1920* (New Haven: Yale University Press, 1981); Albert Camarillo, *Chicanos in a Changing Society: From Mexican Pueblos to American Barrios in Santa Barbara and Southern California, 1848–1930* (Cambridge: Harvard University Press, 1979).

7 Clements, "Mexican Immigration."

8 Files IV-341-13, IV-550-9, Archivo de documentos de Secretaría de Relaciones Exteriores, Archivo Histórico Genaro Estrada, Mexico City, as cited in Julia María Shiavone Camacho, *Chinese Mexicans: Transpacific Migration and the Search for a Homeland, 1910–1960* (Chapel Hill: University of North Carolina Press, 2012), 105.

9 Camacho, *Chinese Mexicans*, 17, 181n24.

10 Lisa Marie Cacho, *Social Death: Racialized Rightlessness and the Criminalization of the Unprotected* (New York: New York University Press, 2012), 4.

11 Jeffrey S. Passel and Jens Manuel Krogstad, "What We Know About Unauthorized Immigrants Living in the U.S.," Pew Research Center, Washington, DC, July 22, 2024.

12 Matthew Lisiecki and Gerard Apruzzese, "Proposed 2024 Mass Deportation Program Would Socially and Economically Devastate American Families," Center for Migration Studies, New York, October 9, 2024; Jeffrey S. Passel and D'Vera Cohn, "A Portrait of Unauthorized Immigrants

in the United States: Demographic and Family Characteristics," Pew Hispanic Center, Washington, DC, April 14, 2009.

13 Immigration and Nationality Act § 245(a), 8 U.S.C. § 1255(a) (2018).

14 Lisiecki and Apruzzese, "Proposed 2024 Mass Deportation Program."

15 Immigration and Nationality Act § 245(a), 8 U.S.C. § 1255(a) (2018).

16 Matthew Lisiecki, "CMS Finds Parole-in-Place Will Benefit 455,000 US Families and Improve the US Economy: Most Living in California and Texas," Center for Migration Studies, New York, July 5, 2024.

17 Lisiecki, "CMS Finds Parole-in-Place."

18 Tierney Sneed, "Federal Judge Strikes Down Biden Immigration Policy Shielding Select Undocumented Spouses of US Citizens from Deportation," *CNN Politics,* November 7, 2024; "Where Do We Go from Here? An Update on Keeping Families Together Parole in Place Process," *Immigration Legal Resource Center,* November 13, 2024.

19 Cecilia Vega, "Trump's Mass Deportation Plan for Undocumented Immigrants Could Cost Billions a Year," *60 Minutes,* CBS News, October 27, 2024.

20 Ngai, *Impossible Subjects,* 3–5, 56–58.

21 "A Snapshot of Trump's First Month: Making America Safe Again," US Department of Homeland Security, February 20, 2025.

22 Carey L. Biron, "Amid Trump Deportation Threats, U.S. Communities Prepare," *Thomson Reuters Foundation*, March 12, 2025.

23 Press release, "DHS Announces Nationwide and International Ad Campaign Warning Illegal Aliens to Self-Deport and Stay Out," *US Department of Homeland Security,* February 17, 2025.

24 Press release, "DHS Launches CBP Home App with Self-Deport Reporting Feature," *US Department of Homeland Security,* March 10, 2025; "Warning—Domestic" video advertisement, *US Department of Homeland Security,* n.d., Media Library, Making America Safe Again Collection.

25 Press release, "DHS Launches CBP Home App."

26 Press release, "DHS Launches CBP Home App."

27 Bernd Debusmann Jr., "US Unveils New App for 'Self-Deportations,'" *BBC News*, April 6, 2025.

28 See Chapter 5 for more on this subject.

ACKNOWLEDGMENTS

This book would not have been possible without the participation of the banished mixed-status families who contributed their personal histories and private collections. The De Anda, Espinoza, Robles, and Rodríguez families generously agreed to share their transgenerational banishment memories and private records with me so that I could share them with you. Over the years I have had numerous meetings with members of three generations of each family. Arturo Espinoza, María Guadalupe Espinoza, Ramona Espinoza, Consuelo De Anda, Virginia De Anda, Guillermina Hinojos, Sara Veronica Hinojos, Jesús Molina, Refugio Molina, Sara Marie Robles, Carmela Ruano, José Isabel "Chabelo" Villegas, Joe William Yáñez, Marisa Yáñez, and Pablo "Paul" Yáñez all met with me multiple times for recorded oral history interviews, to share their family's private collections, and to answer my questions. They also offered clarifications by phone, e-mail, and in-person as I revised this book. Guadalupe and Ramona Espinoza, Guillermina Hinojos, Carmela Ruano, Chabelo Villegas, and Joe and Paul Yáñez also met with me on various occasions to share additional documents they had found in their private records. When this book entered production, they welcomed me back into their homes so that I could scan high-resolution copies of their precious family images, which they had initially shared as lower-quality electronic copies. I am eternally thankful for their generosity.

The history of Mexican immigration law became a topic of interest early in my life. My family emigrated from Zamora, Michoacán, Mexico to east Los Angeles, California, United States when I was eleven years old; we then moved to north Long Beach where I was raised. It was my personal experience that first drove me to understand US immigration law to help my family navigate our long and complex immigration adjustment cases. My interest in the effects that immigration and naturalization law can have on mixed-status families like mine would, many years later, develop into one of my academic research interests. My investigation of the history of racialized illegality and the gendered limitations of US citizenship in relation to mass removals have benefited from the generosity of the numerous mentors, friends, family members, archivists, librarians, colleagues, and funding organizations that supported this book project at different stages during its development. The views expressed here, and any mistakes are, of course, still my responsibility.

I have benefited from brilliant and dedicated mentors at different stages of my career. At the University of California, Santa Barbara (UCSB), Miroslava Chávez-García and Dolores Inés Casillas believed in this project from its inception. This book is stronger thanks to their guidance, inspiration, and invaluable feedback on multiple drafts of each chapter and other articles, all of which guided my writing in immeasurable ways. Miros's insightful questions pushed me to find crucial archival sources and allowed me to expand my migration analysis through a transnational lens. I am thankful for her support in helping me situate the history of banishment within the larger history of US-Mexico migrations and mass removals. I am a historian thanks to Miros. Inés guided my analysis of ethnic Mexicans' quotidian life in the United States. Her willingness to listen to my writing struggles—as well as her motivational texts, conversations, and hugs—made the writing process bearable even in my most vulnerable days.

Laury Oaks and Laura Gómez also deserve special thanks for helping me frame my gender and legal analyses, respectively. Laury pushed me to examine gendered migrations in nuanced ways by linking the micro and macro experiences of gender. Laura Gómez motivated me to engage with legal scholars through the Law and Society Association and provided insightful feedback on my legal examination of the processes under which banishment took place. I am also deeply thankful for having met and worked with Horacio N. Roque Ramírez. Horacio introduced me to the field and methodology of oral history. His dedication to the work of documenting the unrecorded histories of everyday people who are living archives inspired and guided my methodological approaches. I could not have written this book without Horacio's mentorship and scholarship. I imagine he is somewhere in the universe still listening to the voices of everyday history makers as his legacy lives on. *¡Horacio, presente!* Many of the early ideas for this book were workshopped in seminars led by Gerardo Aldana, Eileen Boris, Dolores Inés Casillas, Teresa Figueroa, Mario T. García, Laury Oaks, Carolyn Pinedo-Turnovsky, William Robinson, Horacio N. Roque Ramírez, Chela Sandoval, and Zaragosa Vargas. Writing can be a lonely process. I am thankful for colleagues who became friends at various institutions where I drafted different iterations of this book. They provided company and accountability in various writing groups, offered words of encouragement when I needed them most, and shared numerous laughs over delicious food during much-needed breaks. I am deeply grateful to Eddy Francisco Álvarez, Janett Barragán Miranda, William Calvo-Quirós, Thomas Carrasco, Nicholas Centino, Sebastián Ferrada, Melissa Flores, Sara Veronica Hinojos, Adrianna Santos, Natalia Villanueva Nieves, and Adanari Zarate who helped workshop my ideas and gifted me with their company during revitalizing breaks throughout my time at UCSB. I am also thankful to the members of the 2016 faculty cohort at San Francisco State University (SFSU), including Olivia Albiero, Elif Balin, Fatima Zahrae Chrifi Alaoui, Lara Cushing, Mark Davis, Kat DeGuzman, Valerie Francisco-Menchavez, Melissa Guzman-Garcia, Rachel Gross, Ron Hayduk, Cesar "Ché" Rodriguez, Celine Perreñas Shimizu, Autumn Thoyre, and Dilara Yarbrough. They shared welcoming writing spaces and energizing weekend gatherings that sustained me during long writing and research periods.

Postdoctoral fellowships provided writing time and crucial feedback to revise and expand this book. The 2015–2016 Chancellor's Postdoctoral Fellowship in the Department of Latina/Latino Studies at the University of Illinois at Urbana-Champaign (UIUC) allowed me to rethink my framework, host a book manuscript workshop, and begin the first full revision of this book. I am extremely thankful to Natalia Molina, Adrian Burgos, and Leisy Ábrego, who read the entire manuscript and offered insightful comments during a daylong workshop. My follow-up conversations with Natalia on her feedback helped me untangle my arguments. At UIUC, I also benefited from feedback offered during one-on-one conversations and in a productive discussion after my fellowship's research presentation. I offer my gratitude to Julie Dowling, Jonathan Xavier Inda, Natalie Lira, Mireya Loza, Isabel Molina-Guzmán, Gilberto Rosas, Sandra Ruiz, and Edna A. Viruell-Fuentes. I also benefited tremendously from conversations with Mireya Loza at UIUC about her own writing process as she completed her first book.

The 2018–2019 Mahindra Humanities Center's Postdoctoral Fellowship at Harvard gave me the resources and time I needed to collect additional archival research in Mexico, conduct the oral history interviews with the Espinoza family that made Chapter 4 possible, and revise the full manuscript. I am particularly thankful to Gabriela Soto Laveaga for her thoughtful comments during my research presentation for the "Migration and the Humanities" Mellon Foundation Seminar at Harvard, which was based on this book, and for her additional guidance during our one-on-one meetings. I am also grateful to Janett Barragán Miranda, Alice Baumgartner, Homi Bhabha, Steven Biel, Yareli Castro Sevilla, Samuel Dolbee, Sonia Gomez, Roberto G. Gonzales, Jesse Howell, Zhou Hau Liew, Yim King (Kathy) Mak for their helpful suggestions on new additions to this book during my time at Harvard.

I am tremendously thankful for my community at the University of Wisconsin-Madison (UW-M) for their invaluable support of my research, writing, teaching, mentoring, professional development, and community-engaged research projects. They also shared their company in invigorating gatherings that offered respite from long writing stretches. *Mil gracias* to Verenize Arceo, Andrea-Teresa "Tess" Arenas, Simon Balto, Mou Banerjee, Brandon Bloch, August Brereton, Ashley Brown, Kacie Lucchini Butcher, Emily Callaci, Giuliana Chamedes, Kathryn Ciancia, Dustin Cohan, Joshua Doyle-Raso, Edna Ely-Ledesma, Khaled Esseissah, Paige Glotzer, Pablo Gómez, Ana Fernández, April Haynes, Elizabeth Hennessy, Francine Hirsch, Florence Hsia, Patrick Iber, Steve Kantrowitz, Devin Kennedy, Charles Kim, Monica Kim, Judd Kinzley, Michael Martoccio, Benjamin Márquez, Sara McKinnon, Jorell Meléndez-Badillo, Rubén Medina, Almita Miranda, Alfonso Morales, Brand Nakashima, Mariana Pacheco, Allison Powers Useche, Julia Prado, Jennifer Ratner-Rosenhagen, Bree Ann Romero, Sarah Rios, Diego Román, Aurora Santiago Ortiz, Carolina Sarmiento, Karl Shoemaker, Revel Sims, Sasha Maria Suarez, Sarah Thal, Matt Villeneuve, Kate Vieira, Gloria Whiting, Daniel Williford, and Louise Young. I could not have completed this book without my UW-M faculty mentors, Cindy I-Fen Cheng, Theresa Delgadillo, and Armando Ibarra—they have been my guiding stars. I am in eternal gratitude for their support, guidance, feedback, and multiple conversations that not only made this book stronger but also helped me become a better educator, writer, and historian. My deepest thanks to Cindy, who read and commented on the full manuscript, then met with me multiple times to outline a revision plan. I also extend my thanks to dedicated administrators, including Leslie Abadie, Carol Cizauskas, Davis Fugate, Peter Haney, Iain McLoughlin, and Yasi Rezai, who offered their expertise to help me navigate funding sources. My utmost gratitude to past and current chairs of the Department of History at UW-M, including Laird Boswell, Anne Hansen, Neil Kodesh, and Leonora Neville for granting financial support to advance the completion of this book. You all make Madison, Wisconsin, an amazing place to live and work.

My most sincere gratitude to Kathleen McDermott, who guided my framing of this project from my book proposal to the initial manuscript submission. I am forever thankful to Kathleen for believing in my book and acquiring it for Harvard University Press. When Kathleen retired in 2023, I was fortunate to begin working with Emily Silk, who is a dedicated editor and deeply committed to the craft. I am extremely grateful to Emily, who guided my book from the initial submission to publication with unmatched dedication and care. Emily provided close feedback on different chapters of the book, found the peer reviewers who helped strengthen my arguments, included my input in the production of the cover design, worked with the marketing team on different drafts of the descriptive copy, and guided me through every step of the production process. I would not have been able to navigate the review and production processes without Emily's guidance and support. Staff at Harvard University Press also provided incredible assistance on the different components of the book. I am forever thankful to Julie Carlson for her careful review and constructive copy edits, Sana Mohtadi for her dedicated assistance with the art program, designer Joan Wong for powerfully capturing the themes of this book in the cover design, production editor Mary Ribesky for her support in bringing this book into print, and Stephanie Vyce for her legal guidance with permissions. Many thanks also to other staff who worked behind the scenes to bring this book to press.

Numerous colleagues at various institutions have selflessly contributed to my professional development. My sincere thanks to Steven Alvarez, Nancy Bercaw, Christopher Bettinger, Genevieve Carpio, Teresa Carrillo, Christopher Carrington, Verónica Castillo-Muñoz, Andreana Clay, Matt Garcia, Terri Gomez, Aída Hurtado, Gaye Theresa Johnson, Allen LeBlanc, Rosina Lozano, Alexis Martinez, Katynka Martinez, John Mckiernan-González, Rita Meléndez, Ana Raquel Minian, Natalia Molina, Lorena Oropeza, John S. Park, Monica Perales, Stephen Pitti, Jessica Pliley, Elvira Pulitano, Catherine S. Ramirez, George J. Sánchez, Alicia Schmidt Camacho, Denise Segura, Marc Stein, Amy Sueyoshi, Howard Winant, Grace Yeh, and Elliot Young. Vicki L. Ruiz deserves special thanks for always making herself available to discuss big career questions with me over lunch meetings in Pasadena, California, and during coffee breaks at national conferences. Vicki has trained numerous historians, and I am so fortunate that she graciously made time to meet with me when I needed her guidance and for always reminding me to find my writing muse.

I am also thankful to the librarians and archivists who assisted me during my data collection at local, national, and international archives. To the librarians and archivists at the University of California, Los Angeles Special Collections; Archivo Histórico Genaro Estrada; Departamento de Migración de México, Secretaría de Gobernación; Biblioteca Miguel Lerdo de Tejada; Archivos Presidenciales, Archivo General de la Nación; Center for Oral and Public History at California State University, Fullerton; The Huntington Library; University of Texas at El Paso; Los Angeles Central Public Library; Bancroft Library; California State Railroad Museum Library; Immigration History Research Center, University of Minnesota, Twin Cities; National Archives and Records Administration, Immigration and Naturalization Services Historical Reference Library; Chicano Studies Research Institute, University of California, Los Angeles; and Los Angeles City archives, thank you for your researching savvy, assistance, and patience with my multiple questions. Special thanks are due to Francisco Balderrama and Raymond Rodríguez, who generously granted access to their personal copies of repatriation archival documents collected from the Archivo General de la Nación en México when I was a graduate student and unable to leave the country because my immigration adjustment case was still pending (and continued pending for a total of more than thirteen years). Late professor Raymond Rodríguez and his wife opened their home office to me so that I could search through the collected archival documents, *mil gracias!* Once I had adjusted my legal status in 2018, I was able to finally travel to Mexico and conduct my own archival research for this book.

One of the joys of teaching is the opportunity to foster mentoring relationships with students, some of whom worked with me as research assistants. *Un millón de gracias* to Kimberly Gama, Erika Jáuregui, Nataly Martinez, Juan Tejeda, and Saharai Salas for their work as undergraduate research assistants at SFSU. They were vital to creating an organizational system for thousands of primary sources. My utmost thanks to undergraduate assistants Zevdah Drizin and Lezly Vejar, and graduate project assistants Sonia Olmos, Julia Prado, and Cynthia Villatoro, who worked with me at UW-M. They sifted through a large online newspaper database and assisted with transcribing oral history interviews. Both undergraduate and graduate student assistants were vital to the completion of this book.

This project was also possible thanks to different generous funding sources. I am extremely thankful for the multiple research grants provided by the Chicano Studies Institute (CSI) at the University of California, Santa Barbara (UCSB). CSI provided seven grants from 2008 to 2015 to assist with my archival data collection, oral history transcriptions, summertime off to write, and financial support to attend national conferences to workshop early chapter drafts. The University of California Center for New Racial Studies Research Grant allowed me to visit local and national archives to collect primary sources. The National Science Foundation provided summer research support. I am also thankful to the Ford Multidisciplinary Graduate Student Fellowship, which allowed me receive feedback on an early version of Chapter 1 during my participation in the American Association of Hispanics in Higher Education (AAHHE) annual meeting. SFSU awarded Development for Research and Creativity funds that assisted with archival research trips. At UW-M, the Office of the Vice Chancellor for Research with funding from the Wisconsin Alumni Research Foundation granted generous research funds that allowed me to revise the full manuscript, conduct additional archival research, travel to California and Mexico to conduct follow-up meetings with oral history narrators, and hire students to assist with my research. Additionally, two fellowships provided time to revise and finish this book, the 2021–2022 Nellie McKay Fellowship and the spring 2024 Race, Ethnicity, and Indigeneity Faculty Fellowship at the Institute for Research in the Humanities. I am thankful to Steven Nadler, Katie Apsey, and the fellows at the Institute for Research in the Humanities for their feedback during my research talk based on this book. I also benefited from a second manuscript workshop through the first-book seminar funded by the Mellon Foundation and the Center for the Humanities at UW-M. I am thankful to Russ Castronovo for his support and insightful recommendations on the seminar organizing process. My deepest gratitude to Monica Perales, Cindy I-Fen Cheng, and Matt Garcia for providing insightful suggestions on the full manuscript, which allowed me to revise this book for submission to Harvard University Press. I am also extremely thankful to Anitra Grisales and Lawrence Lan for reading and commenting on multiple drafts of the full manuscript.

Outreach programs gave me invaluable support at different stages in my career. The Building Future Faculty Program at North Carolina State University provided professional development during the early stages in my career. Special thanks to Martha Crowley, Kim Ebert, Marcia Gumpertz,

Nora Haenn, Blair Kelley, Garry and Dawn Morgan, and Jonathan Ocko. The UC Diversity Initiative for Graduate Study in the Social Sciences (UC DIGSSS) at the University of California, Santa Barbara, also provided tremendous support in my early academic training for professional development. *Muchísimas gracias* Inés Casillas for referring me to the Advance Oral History Summer Institute at the Regional Oral History Office at the Bancroft Library at the University of California, Berkeley, which was key to grounding my oral history methodology. I am thankful to all the faculty, staff, and colleagues who participated in this summer institute, but Robin Li deserves special mention for her mentorship during the institute. The UCLA Law Fellows Program also helped develop the legal analysis for my book. My most sincere thanks to Devon W. Carbado, Laura Gómez, Tony Tolbert, Leo Trujillo-Cox, and to the 2012 Law Fellows for their support.

The Ronald E. McNair Scholars Programs at Claremont Graduate University (CGU) and at UCLA are why I applied to doctoral programs in the first place. As a McNair Scholar, I learned about my academic options— opportunities I had no idea about since my parents only have a sixth-grade education and I was the first one in my family to complete BA, MA, and PhD degrees. Thanks to La'Tonya Rease Miles, the 2006 UCLA McNair Scholars Program Director, for believing that I could contribute to academia and for helping me become a McNair Scholar despite the obstacles as an immigrant applicant. I am thankful to the McNair Scholars Program at Claremont Graduate University (CGU) for admitting me as a scholar and changing my life. I also have immense gratitude for the 2007 CGU McNair director, Leon Wood Jr., Assistant Director Heidi Coronado, the staff, and professors who worked with CGU McNair, including Bettina Casad, Gilda Ochoa, Robin L. Owens, and William Pérez. They inspired me to become a professor. La'Tonya, Leon, and Heidi used to always say, "we are changing the world one Dr. at the time." Thank you for changing my world and helping me to earn the PhD that would lead to the publication of this book. I am also grateful to my McNair cohort—including Cynthia Alcantar, Ana Cisneros Alvarez, Monique Cadle, Elizabeth Cobacho, Linell Edwards, Jasmine Heim, Vanessa Monterosa, Diana Rehfeldt, Christopher S. Reina, Miguel Rodriguez, and Mariana Zamboni—which became an important support system.

My family deserves special recognition for their unconditional love, support, and encouragement. My grandmothers Soledad Moreno and Guadalupe Oregel, as well as my grandfather Benito Ramírez, instilled in me a passion for oral history. I grew up listening to their stories about migration and family adventures, and their late-night scary stories (*historias de miedo*). My parents, María de Lourdes and Leonardo Javier Ramírez, always encouraged me academically with their signature saying: "Echale ganas al estudio, mija." My parents sacrificed everything they had and even left their own families behind to immigrate to the United States so that my four sisters and I could have the opportunities they could only dream about. *Les debo tanto a mi mamá y papá, muchísimas gracias por todo.* My sisters Karina, Araceli, Citlalli, and María made my years growing up a true adventure and still make sure to make me laugh when I need it most, which helped immensely during the writing process. They made time to talk and laugh with me on the phone during my walking breaks. My sisters and parents also had long conversations filled with laughter, danced, and shared delicious meals with me during my archival research visits to California. The person who has been my pillar of strength through my highest and lowest while I researched, drafted, and revised this book is my life partner and husband, José. He has moved around the country with me so that I could advance my career. José also often took over the non-wage labor at home so that I could concentrate on my writing. He took me on walking, biking, running, and dancing breaks between long hours of writing, delivered warm food to my campus office, university libraries, and coffee shops so that I could write without interruption, spent long days with me finding his own work to do as a way to motivate me to stay focused, and went on most of my archival research trips with me. He helped me photograph primary sources and kept me company while I organized and analyzed the collected data. He has seen me present different versions of this book dozens of times and always cheers me on as if it was the first time. José knows me as a person and an academic more than anyone else. I am *eternamente agradecida* for his love and support that helped me complete this book. The past twenty-five years by his side have been a beautiful adventure. *Te amo y te amaré por siempre, mi amor.*

CREDITS

Map 1 Data source: Natural Earth Data (basemap and locator map) and conabio. gob.mx (Mexico cities); map projections: NAD 1983 (2011) UTM Zone 13N_1 (central map) and North America Albers Equal Area Conic (locator map); map created by NT Nawshin, UW Cartography Lab.

Map 2 Data source: Natural Earth Data (basemap and locator map) and conabio. gob.mx (Mexico cities); map projections: NAD 1983 (2011) UTM Zone 13N_1 (central map) and North America Albers Equal Area Conic (locator map); map created by NT Nawshin, UW Cartography Lab.

Figure I.1 "Mexicans returning home by train," *Herald Examiner* Collection, Los Angeles Public Library Digital Photo Collection, January 12, 1932.

Figure I.2 "Mexicans returning home by train," *Herald Examiner* Collection, Los Angeles Public Library Digital Photo Collection, March 8, 1932.

Table I.1 Repatriated Alien Records, May 1939 to October 1940, US Department of Labor, Immigration and Naturalization Service, National Archives and Records Administration, Washington, DC.

Figure 1.1 Courtesy of Jesús Molina.

Figure 1.3 Courtesy of Jesús Molina.

Figure 1.4 Courtesy of Jesús Molina.

Figure 1.5 Courtesy of Jesús Molina.

Figure 1.6	Courtesy of Jesús Molina.

Figure 2.1	Courtesy of Joe William Yáñez.

Figure 2.4	Courtesy of Joe William Yáñez.

Figure 2.5	Reproduced from the California Commission of Immigration and Housing's Second Annual Report, 1916.

Figure 2.6	Photograph by author.

Figure 2.7	Photograph by author.

Figure 3.1	Courtesy of Guillermina Hinojos.

Figure 3.2	Courtesy of Guillermina Hinojos.

Figure 3.4	Courtesy of Guillermina Hinojos.

Figure 3.5a	Courtesy of Guillermina Hinojos.

Figure 3.5b	Courtesy of Guillermina Hinojos.

Figure 3.6	Courtesy of Guillermina Hinojos.

Figure 4.1	Photograph by author.

Figure 4.3a	Courtesy of María Guadalupe Espinoza.

Figure 4.3b	Courtesy of María Guadalupe Espinoza.

Figure 4.4a	Courtesy of María Guadalupe Espinoza.

Figure 4.4b	Courtesy of María Guadalupe Espinoza.

Figure 4.5	Courtesy of María Guadalupe Espinoza.

Figure 4.6a	Courtesy of María Guadalupe Espinoza.

Figure 4.6b	Courtesy of María Guadalupe Espinoza.

Figure 4.7a	Courtesy of María Guadalupe Espinoza.

Figure 4.7b Courtesy of María Guadalupe Espinoza.

Figure 4.8 Photograph by author.

Figure 5.1 Photograph by author.

Figure 5.2a Courtesy of Joe William Yáñez.

Figure 5.2b Cindy Carcamo, "Faces of Immigration: 83 years after her removal to Mexico," *Orange County Register,* February 28, 2012.

INDEX